"*Sons of the Arghandab* by Joseph J. Fontenot is a must-read. This compelling work is written from the perspective of young leaders with the wisdom and maturity of more senior and seasoned combat veterans. The narrative vividly portrays the experiences of front-line soldiers from a field artillery battalion who were trained and transformed into a dismounted infantry unit, facing the formidable challenges of a harsh environment against a relentless and determined enemy. Readers will gain profound insights into the depths of courage soldiers demonstrate and what they are willing to do for their country, what they are willing to endure for their unit, and what they are willing to sacrifice for one another. We will also be reminded that the war doesn't end on the battlefield and that some of the most difficult fights are fought after the war. I am proud of this unit and these soldiers, not because they were my soldiers, but because they did what was asked of them—they won the fight, and they loved each other. 'Fight Where You're Told and Win Where you Fight' STRIKE! Well done Top Guns!"

—Scott C. Schroeder, 2/101st Strike CSM 2007–10,
101st Airborne Division CSM 2010–12

"For 10 months, I traversed the Arghandab River Valley, where I came face-to-face with evil on multiple occasions, watching as nearly half of my platoon was either killed or injured. When our time (82nd Airborne) came to an end, it was the men of the 101st who were next in line. We knew they weren't ready. No amount of training could ever prepare anyone for the hell that lurked in what we had come to call the 'Devil's Playground.' To make matters worse, they were an artillery unit tasked with an infantry mission, thrust into hostile terrain that demanded more than just firepower—it required relentless will and unyielding courage.

We did our best to impart every lesson we had learned, warning them of the brutal realities ahead, hoping to spare them the hardships we had endured. But in the end, they faced similar fates, forced to navigate the same dangers we had confronted. Even with the odds stacked against them, they pushed forward, carrying on the mission we had started. With unparalleled determination, they took the foothold we had seized and completed the task of securing the entire Arghandab River Valley. Their grit, their tenacity, and their sacrifice showcase the unbreakable spirit of the American soldier. This is their story."

—Dale J. Knollinger, 2-C-2, 508th PIR, 82nd ABN, 2007–11

"Another amazing volume in the story of the American warriors who fought through the daily nightmare of the Arghandab River Valley in Afghanistan. Joseph Fontenot's *Sons of the Arghandab* is a brutal portrayal of the year-long deployment of the soldiers of 1-320th Field Artillery Regiment. His detailed descriptions of the chaos and carnage of the battlefield transport the reader directly into the valley where every step could cost you a limb or your life. The bitter losses and hard-fought victories are beautifully woven together with the crises of courage and frustrating leadership challenges that so many Operation *Enduring Freedom* (OEF) veterans can readily relate to. The perseverance, tenacity, and adaptability of the men and leaders is as inspiring as it is astounding. *Sons of the Arghandab* is an exceptional testament to those who fought there; both those that made the ultimate sacrifice and those who will bear their wounds, seen and unseen, for the rest of their days."

—SSG (Ret.) Dan Baker, *Tracer Burnout Podcast* co-host

"Capturing military history in digestible form is often left to those who can reflect through an eternal lens. Joseph Fontenot's account of bearing witness to lethal agony is akin to Fehrenbach's *This Kind of War*; an author sane enough to share an insane story. This is an 'always remember' tale, spun by a skilled Warrior Poet whose words stem from an inkwell of dirt and blood collected from a common understanding: we protect each other. Joseph vividly describes an environment of true uncertainty in extremis, of startling explosions, frantic redistribution of ammo under fire, and the graceful warmth of memories that follow in the troublesome wake of catastrophic events. These experiences are scarring, and Joseph captures the internalized reality of a Guardian's return with his shield rather than on it. Fontenot's narrative about life beyond the Forward Operating Base highlights the enduring truth that another patrol always awaits. This perspective is invaluable for veterans to fully reintegrate with an American society still reconciling its role in the Global War on Terror. The Top Guns from this tour of duty are emblematic of a generation that redefined counterinsurgency while in contact. As they close in on their twilight years, Fontenot eloquently maps out what it took and continues to take to live. *Sons of the Arghandab* presents what seems like a divine source of the purpose, an echoing reminder of the reason why—a brother's eternal love is worth treasuring."

—Tarpon S. Wiseman, Colonel, US Army (Ret.), Former 1-320th FAR Executive Officer and Commander (Top Gun 5 and 6), Distinguished and Honorary Member of the 502nd Infantry Regiment

SONS OF THE ARGHANDAB

Top Guns in the Devil's Playground

JOSEPH J. FONTENOT

Pennsylvania & Yorkshire

Published in the United States of America and Great Britain in 2025 by
CASEMATE PUBLISHERS
1950 Lawrence Road, Havertown, PA 19083, USA
and
47 Church Street, Barnsley, S70 2AS, UK

Copyright © 2025 Joseph J. Fontenot

Hardcover Edition: ISBN 978-1-63624-520-1
Digital Edition: ISBN 978-1-63624-521-8

A CIP record for this book is available from the British Library

All rights reserved. No part of this book may be reproduced or transmitted in any form or by any means, electronic or mechanical including photocopying, recording or by any information storage and retrieval system, without permission from the publisher in writing.

Printed and bound in the United Kingdom by CPI Group (UK) Ltd, Croydon, CR0 4YY
Typeset in India by DiTech Publishing Services

For a complete list of Casemate titles, please contact:

CASEMATE PUBLISHERS (US)
Telephone (610) 853-9131
Fax (610) 853-9146
Email: casemate@casematepublishers.com
www.casematepublishers.com

CASEMATE PUBLISHERS (UK)
Telephone (0)1226 734350
Email: casemate@casemateuk.com
www.casemateuk.com

The views expressed in this publication are those of the author and do not necessarily reflect the official policy or position of the Department of Defense or the US government. The public release clearance of this publication by the Department of Defense does not imply Department of Defense endorsement or factual accuracy of the material.

All images from author's collection unless otherwise credited.

The Publisher's authorised representative in the EU for product safety is Authorised Rep Compliance Ltd., Ground Floor, 71 Lower Baggot Street, Dublin D02 P593, Ireland.
www.arccompliance.com

Contents

Foreword by Emma Wright   vii
Acknowledgments   xii

1	The Death of Innocence	1
2	The RIP	9
3	Into the Devil's Playground	19
4	The Alamo (COP Nolen)	35
5	Luck Always Runs Out	41
6	Battle for Bakersfield (COP Stout)	51
7	The Boys of Babur (COP Babur)	67
8	The Longest Day	81
9	Hard Right Over the Easy Wrong	97
10	Welcome to the Havoc	109
11	Ant Trails to the Man at the First Canal	125
12	Cigarette Embers, MICLICs, and Tarok Kolache	133
13	The Men Hidden Beneath the Rocks	145
14	Strong Point Stansbery	153
15	Strong Point Weaver	163
16	Infrared Chem Lights and IEDs	169
17	Living in the Grape Furrows Watching the Leaves Turn	179
18	Graveyards Filled with Broken Dreams	187
19	The Final Mission	199
20	Eulogies, Uniforms, and Sad Stories	209

The reality of war is that no one goes home unscathed.

Foreword

If you were to ask me whether I thought myself qualified to be writing these words, I'd have likely told you "No." With the general idea of a book foreword being an introduction to the subject to follow, one might expect to see a fellow scholar or subject-matter expert who could weigh in based on their vast or direct experience rather than, say, myself. My name is Emma Wright, and I would not call myself an expert in anything, let alone war. I am, however, someone who has had the pleasure and privilege of getting to know and call a friend the author of this book, Joseph Fontenot. The only reason we know the other is the Arghandab (River Valley) events during the summer of 2010.

For Joseph, a squad leader or section chief, the Arghandab claimed and maimed too many of his fellow soldiers, stole his youth, and decimated his peace. From me, the Arghandab was to take my first husband, 1st Lieutenant Todd W. Weaver, the father of our infant daughter, on September 9, 2010. While I can never fully comprehend the chaos of war, its cruel consequences have certainly touched my life. Perhaps it's understandable that, as a Gold Star Spouse, I find meaningful and lifelong connections to many of my late husband's battle buddies, such as Joseph. They will always be there for me; they always are, as I am always there for them. We carry an invisible pain, allowing this reciprocal understanding of our shared losses. In what can often feel like an abyss of pain, there is a purpose in its existence. We all went on that deployment. Physically, no, but every heart holding one of those soldiers dear was right there with them in every other way: hoping, praying, maybe bargaining with their God, … and always wishing them every good thought they had for their safe return. Unbeknown to me at the time, saying "goodbye" and watching my husband leave for that fateful deployment was the first of many difficult things I was to face.

I was already blessed to have built a fiercely supportive friendship with a small group of Army wives, one of whose husbands left alongside Todd that morning. Together, Kelly and I walked back to our cars as we tried to convince each other that we could get through this time. We indulged in light retail therapy to distract our minds before ending our day with dinner at The Cheesecake Factory. The mood was not one of celebration but a marking of the start of what was to be a shared chapter of our lives. None of us would face this next year alone if we had each other. We had trained for this day. Going into this deployment, my trepidation hovered a bit higher than the rest of our group, although I tried to hide it. Todd and I were dating during his first deployment to Iraq in 2004–05, where he had experienced a close call. I was already familiar with the panic of not knowing whether he was okay. Perhaps being a mother to a nine-month-old was the perfect remedy for that anxiety, as caring for her kept me well distracted from my worries. Todd and I kept in contact at every opportunity through email, letters, and Skype calls. I sent videos of her reaching important milestones, like learning to walk. We even celebrated her first birthday over Skype!

Twenty-three days later, the entirety of my world collapsed. On September 9, just before dawn, my doorbell rang, and there were the notification officer and a chaplain before me. I remember my automatic response was to hope he was just injured. As the officer began to speak the script that every military spouse fears to hear the most … I knew. Even now, everything after that moment is still blurry. I remember getting the baby because she was crying. I remember calling my parents, Todd's parents, and Kelly, who then alerted the rest of the friend group, who immediately all came to be with me. I recall my Family Readiness Group leader coming over or calling; I'm unsure which, but she was there to support me however she could. I remember being on the phone often while the girls fielded calls, completing paperwork for the Army, and discussing the next steps. Nothing felt real. The Casualty Affairs Officer was explaining how I would be flying to Dover Air Force Base to receive Todd's body. I'll never forget that I was looking down at my hands with the bright blue nail polish on. Todd was never a fan of brightly colored nails. I immediately started to repaint them with a more appropriate, neutral shade.

I only remember bits and pieces of that first and second year without him. My Army wives, friends, family, Todd's friends, my CAOs, the Army's Survivor Outreach Services program, various charitable organizations, and his many battle buddies held me up entirely. A whirlwind of decisions for my life seemed to happen all at once. Much time was spent with friends and family as we celebrated events, memorials, and dedications in Todd's honor. I moved back to my hometown and into the condo Todd and I had once shared. I stayed in touch with my Army wives, taking trips here and there to see them. On one such visit, Amy, Kirby, and I were able to be with Kelly to help support her in delivering her precious baby girl, as her husband was still deployed. Watching her gracefully bring new life into this world was a cathartic and healing moment for all of us. However, it was hard not to be reminded of some problematic thoughts. In some of my last correspondence with Todd, we had been talking about me transitioning the baby from nursing to be able to try for baby #2 when he came home for his R&R. That day never came for me. That was hard.

Looking back now, I recognize how blessed I was in the early days of my grief journey. For that is not always how it goes. At no time did I feel abandoned by the Army; even all these years later, I am still included in Fort Campbell's Survivor Outreach Services emails regarding their monthly support groups for Gold Star Families. Then, finally, there was the return of both Todd's units, 2-502 ID and 1-320 FAR, as well as the husbands of all my friends! Having them all at home felt like I could breathe again. The heavy weight of worry I carried for them all was lifted! Of course, it could not be helped that their homecomings served as a stark reminder of what the Arghandab River Valley had taken from us, robbed us of the life we had only just begun. Talking with those who served alongside my husband helped bring peace to my mind. While challenging, they gave me a better understanding of how my late husband's death came to be. Reliving and retelling the events leading up to and after his last step, detonating that IED, must have been as traumatic for them to get through as it was to hear. I was grateful for their willingness to provide me with some much-needed closure. I was able to listen to many of Todd's battle buddies describe their own experiences, some leading to devastating injuries. I was naturally able to empathize with how they were feeling about their loss. I could hear their hearts and offer comfort and support in all instances. I did my best to suppress any feelings of "Well, at least you came home." Knowing everyone's version of personal tragedy differs helped me not to judge or compare our pain. If the loss of one's ability to do what they loved due to an injury were to be the worst thing they could imagine, they would most likely mourn that loss with an equivalence to that of any other. It was a privilege to be there for them, as they had been for Todd.

What I didn't know then was how my grief journey was about to change. Going back to 2008, we saw the era of blogging. I was newly married and settling into life in Georgia as Todd started Ranger School when I found out I was pregnant. I hopped on the trend; with a small audience of family and friends, I updated on my pregnancy's progression and Todd's news. Over the next several months, I continued to share milestone moments, such as his graduation from Ranger School and the birth of our daughter. After his passing, I continued with it, but what I needed to write had changed. On those nights when insomnia reigned and the thoughts in my mind had nowhere else to go, I found comfort in processing them on my blog. Six months had passed when I felt the urge to share what I attributed to having given me a renewed sense of strength in the face of my "new normal." Todd had written letters to his daughter and me should he perish. I discovered the letters on the laptop when they were returned with his personal effects. His words had given me such peace that I thought sharing them with my friends and family might also bring them peace. I see now my naivety in having made that choice. A few months later, I came across a crudely rewritten version of my words, letters and all, sold to a popular gossip site. From there, "Our Story," as I'd gotten used to calling it, took on a life of its own as it continued to spread through various platforms; it metamorphosed into something I no longer recognized as my own. Having had a sheltered upbringing, I was admittedly ignorant as to the cruelty that exists just for the sake of existing online, leaving me unprepared for how to handle much of the response that followed.

When my heart was ready to open to love again, I was blessed; it found me exactly who I needed. I told a friend that if I had decided to start dating again, they would have had to know Todd or serve in the military. In my mind, that would be the only kind of person who would be able to handle coming into my life. I had no intention of ever not keeping Todd's memory alive, for I had a daughter I had promised to teach all about her "Dada." To me, that would be the kind of person who would understand. It wasn't my first time meeting Alex; he had also lost Todd. They had known each other while in ROTC at The College of William & Mary. He was a rescue swimmer in the US Coast Guard then, and he was deployed in the Middle East when we started exchanging messages. While deployed, Alex was involved in a terrible accident that almost blinded him in one eye; he was then transported to Walter Reed Medical Center for several surgeries. I was there for him as he navigated the healing process and, upsettingly, the medical discharge that followed. He was there for us as we all navigated new beginnings. He was respectful in every way for the loss we had endured, always supporting our needs and honoring Todd's ultimate sacrifice. When he proposed, I happily accepted. He recovered from his injury and joined the Navy. He adopted our daughter, and we later celebrated a courthouse wedding with a small ceremony. Not long after, we headed to his first duty station, Guam.

It was March 2013 when we arrived, and one of the first things I did was to look for my Gold Star Family community. That wasn't easy, for it was several months before we found them. Our son had been born by the time we met in person! Unfortunately, I discovered the vast disparities these families faced regarding support compared to the States. Even after finding my community, I realized there weren't the same support networks in place, as it was a smaller community. They had been so used to supporting themselves that they knew nothing different. I had come from areas where I was well supported and could participate in various care groups should I want to. Bearing witness to this community, having never known of such things, broke my heart. Having fewer opportunities to access organizations for military grief and healing impacted me over time. I saw "Our Story" do laps through online platforms with little regard for accuracy. Don't get me wrong; beautiful things came from sharing that entry. People from all over who were reading and watching versions of his story were impacted positively, leaving kind words of support in the comment threads that, yes, I read. While many may point out the consensus not to read the comments, I must wonder why that is the answer. Instead, perhaps do not comment on the experiences of others had you not been there. Over time, there was a shift in how our story was being used. Comments became increasingly judgmental depending on how long that creator decided to stretch and manipulate the video. My blog was no longer a healthy outlet as the more I wrote only served to fuel the creation of content for others. Todd's ultimate sacrifice was being sensationalized, dramatized, politicized, and monetized, and I blamed myself. I carried guilt and shame for not knowing how predatory the internet was, embarrassed even. I was hurt by those so-called "authors" who had taken my life's worst nightmare and sold it to gossip sites, who then published that content without verifying. The tactics of manipulating their viewers into consuming their content by exploiting his sacrifice while pushing multiple sponsored advertisements were disturbing. I was struggling with more than just the loss itself. I was struggling to forgive myself for what I felt I had done to my late husband's legacy.

This may not make much sense to others, but it took several years of letting these feelings consume me before I could healthily process them. By then, it had been 13 years since Todd had passed, 11 of which had been spent in Guam. It wasn't until my physical health had noticeably declined that I was willing to acknowledge how differently I could (or maybe should) have tackled my pain. With the help of a therapist, I could change my perspective and outlook on my experiences. Next to losing my first husband, learning to love who I am and make peace with myself has been the hardest thing I've done thus far. I learned how to ask for help when I needed it. I've learned a lifetime of lessons, a journey that began among field artillerymen in the pomegranate orchards and grape furrows of the Arghandab River Valley of Afghanistan.

Emma Wright
October 2024

Acknowledgments

This book is dedicated to every soldier who's ever walked in "the Valley of Death," known as the Arghandab River Valley. None of us can say we left unscathed and without scars. Some carry visible scars from the battlegrounds of yesteryear, while others carry invisible scars that still haunt them. I am eternally grateful to each of you who contributed to the completion of our story. Many thanks to the guys of Two Charlie, especially Bragg, Knollinger, and Lachance. To our Gold Star Family members, including Mrs. Moon, for allowing me to continue to tell Chris's story, and Mrs. Emma Wright, for answering my message and empowering me to tell Todd's story. Without your permission, I don't know that I would have been able to do it justice. Mrs. Christy Durham for encouraging me while I was swimming in a well of darkness, and Mrs. Carolyn King for sharing more of Brandon's story. To the "Sons of the Arghandab" that directly contributed to this story: Naquin, Pantaleo, "Smoke" Tatro, Wilke, Robertson, Zavala, Pedro Torres, "Doc" Stegehuis, "Doc" Dozeman, Richards, Deatherage, Mazariegos, Parker, Casey, CSM Tivao, LTC Smithson, "Smoke" (Ret.), Manley, MAJ (Ret.) Kinsel, CW3 (Ret.) Lyon and many others, thank you for helping me paint our picture correctly. This was always intended to be "Our Story," not mine. There were so many angles to our deployment and the events that transpired that, without your help, I never could've done any of your experiences justice. Your shared stories have connected us in a way that words alone could never express. To my extended family, Mike Daniels and Milo Matz, thank you for being the brothers I never had. To Tyler Loveridge my adopted son, we walked every step together until the end. I'll miss you. To my Mom and Dad, Brayden, Tommy Viator, and Scott James Leger Jr., I love all of you. To Stephanie Powers, the shining star in my sky of darkness in the ARV, you were the only person I spoke to when all seemed lost in the orchards. I've always told you that, now everyone reading this book knows as well. So, thank you for being there for me even when you weren't physically there. Last but not least, "99-24" when hell's currents tried to pull me under, heaven's gates allowed you to come in to save me. Thank you for being the fantastic sounding board and support I needed in my time of need.

CHAPTER I

The Death of Innocence

> The first casualty of war is innocence. Don't be so eager to find this out. I assure you, war is ugly.
>
> SL BUCKLEY (1986)

As dusk approached in the Fort Campbell sky, soldiers of the 1st Battalion, 320th Field Artillery Regiment "Top Guns" and 2nd Brigade Combat Team "Strike" readied themselves to board a plane bound for the Afghan province of Kandahar. President Obama had issued an order for an additional 30,000 American troops to be sent to Afghanistan in support of the ongoing counterinsurgency effort. The brigade commander, Colonel Kandarian, informed the Strike Brigade that while their division, the 101st Airborne Division, would be the "tip of the spear," the brigade would be the tip of the tip of that spear. It was June 9, 2010, 2nd Lieutenant Pantaleo's birthday. Pantaleo would turn 23 years old, and, at that age he would be taking on an unfathomable responsibility: he would be leading about twenty-three men into battle for the first time, and he would be holding their lives in his hands. A multitude of One Bravo's (Bravo Battery, 1st Battalion, 320th Field Artillery) men was about to enter a dangerous area in Afghanistan that had already taken the lives of numerous experienced soldiers; additionally, this sector was known to be typically patrolled by infantrymen rather than artillerymen. Pantaleo felt uneasy as he boarded the plane. He became increasingly stressed as he researched the Arghandab and the upcoming mission. It was an uncontrollable area where he and his men would be patrolling, but he tried to be a leader of soldiers and stay calm under pressure. Pantaleo and One Bravo were notified via short notice that they would travel to the Arghandab River Valley (ARV) in Afghanistan to conduct an infantry mission. They didn't have to look far to learn that, during the Global War on Terror, the Arghandab was renowned for being one of the bloodiest and most hostile battlegrounds for American troops.

Ironically, One Bravo's deployment would put them in direct combat with a faceless adversary using only infantry tactics rather than utilizing their howitzers as a support element for the foot soldiers. To the dismay of the senior noncommissioned officers, their howitzers would be prohibited from leaving Kandahar and remain folded throughout the deployment. Ultimately, the Top Guns' soldiers would become known as "Provisional Infantrymen." It wouldn't usually be a big deal because this wasn't the 101st's first short-notice alert about a deployment; however, Pantaleo and Sergeant First Class Tatro's platoon had been training and certifying on artillery support and were well known for their skill with M119A2 howitzers rather than infantry tactics.

The ARV is renowned for its luxuriant vegetation, which includes pomegranate orchards and grape furrows. In addition to being the birthplace of numerous Taliban commanders, including Mullah Omar and Akhtar Mohammad Mansour, it is also well known for being a key crossing point for weapons entering Kandahar from Pakistan, one of the Top Guns' primary targets. The Taliban traces its origins to the Arghandab. When the Russian tanks started to bog down among the pomegranate trees during the Soviet-Afghan War (1979–89), they knew they had to launch a brutal ground offensive from the north. They then attempted to attack Jelawur and Chaharqolbeh Ye'Olya. It was at this point that a group of underprivileged religious students, known as "Talib" in Pashto, started carrying firearms to aid the Mujahideen in their fight. This proved to be a strategic turning point in the battle. The Talib and Mujahideen fighters maintained their position and refused to cede the territory to the Russians. The Taliban gained notoriety during this brutal and terrible conflict, which the locals referred to as "The Battle of the Arghandab." However, very little information about it can be found in publications.

The platoon under the leadership of Pantaleo and Tatro, sometimes known as "Smoke Tatro," had training in infantry tactics at the Joint Readiness Training Center (JRTC) in Louisiana. Cannon artillery was known for producing much smoke during the Revolutionary War. This smoke would obscure a large section of the battlefield where the cannons were positioned. A bystander once pointed out that the platoon sergeant would still be directing his guns after the smoke cleared. This leader was dubbed "Smoke." The field artillery gunnery sergeant's duty was to ensure the cannons were "laid correctly and safely." This earned the gunnery sergeant the cherished nickname "Gunny." While at JRTC, the platoon focused its training on patrolling and key leader engagements. The platoon was led by experienced section chiefs, Staff Sergeants Fontenot and Peltier, who had patrolled Iraq; however, the terrain and the nature of patrolling in Iraq and Afghanistan were likely to differ significantly.

Along with other "Top Guns" Battalion members, the Bravo Battery "Bulls" were leaving with a platoon of nervous soldiers for their next rendezvous with destiny. Their plane made a brief stop in Kyrgyzstan before reaching Afghanistan. Their experience in Kyrgyzstan did not accurately predict their future experiences in Afghanistan. The men had access to two alcoholic beverages throughout their stay, a well-furnished gym with a basketball court and an internet cafe, and well-lit tent structures for sleeping in. The roads were primarily paved, and the streets had good lighting, just like most streets in America. Nevertheless, they were only in Kyrgyzstan for a little more than a day, which might have been advantageous because it prevented them from adopting the idea that this would be their new reality. As they descended towards Kandahar on June 11, 2010, they came across a group of Taliban fighters who were waiting to fire at arriving aircraft in the hopes of hitting one by chance with rocket-propelled grenades (RPG) and small weapons fire.

Inside the aircraft, the soldiers were crammed together like sardines, their gear resting on the tops of their legs and between their feet. Many leaders attempted to sleep as they flew in, but some, like Pantaleo, couldn't rest. One red light illuminated the soldiers inside the gloomy plane. The pilot warned the soldiers over the intercom to hold on since they were about to make a combat landing. As the plane descended, it sounded like popcorn was popping inside the fuselage. It was Fontenot's 35th birthday, and he was thinking, "If this is how it ends, at least I'll go out with a BANG!" "We're getting ready to land at Kandahar Airfield," the pilot said over the intercom once more as they felt the pressure drain from the cabin. The aircraft made a sharp dive shortly after the announcement was made. The men grabbed onto their equipment as it began to float in midair; the sound of the wings flexing gave them the impression that the fuselage might separate from the wings. In what seemed like seconds, they had landed. They were now officially in Kandahar. Their deployment clock was officially set to start.

Fontenot thought, "The heat from these engines isn't half as bad as this violent sun."

The air smelled of human excrement, years of body odor, and the putrid smell of decaying bones and flesh. So far, the initial introduction to the new men's area was far from invigorating; nevertheless, it accurately represented the ARV.

Being deployed with Bravo Battery from 2007 to 2009 during Operation *Iraqi Freedom*, Fontenot; and a few other "Bulls," including Stout, Casey, Howard, Creighton, and others, had grown close. Staff Sergeant Bigelow was one of the noncommissioned officers (NCO) who moved forward on the advanced party. Once they reached their lodgings, Bigelow pulled Fontenot aside:

"What's up, Bigs?" Fontenot asked.

"Brother, this is not Iraq. We've already had several casualties."

"That bad, huh?"

"Yeah, man, remember Hunter, our PAO from Iraq?"

"Yeah, man, I remember him."

"An IED killed him."

Staff Sergeant Hunter, the Strike Brigade's public affairs NCO, could travel freely across the area of operation. As a result, he got to know everyone well throughout his Iraq deployment. Hunter and Private First Class (PFC) Park were killed on June 18, 2010, when an improvised explosive device (IED) struck their patrol. It didn't take long for the battalion members to realize this battle would not be like their mission in Iraq. An RPG had struck Brigade Command Sergeant Major Smith's convoy on June 13, just a week before Hunter hit the IED. When the RPG struck and destroyed the MATV (mine-resistant, ambush-protected (MRAP) all-terrain vehicle) carrying Smith, shrapnel flew throughout the vehicle, injuring his lower leg and necessitating a medical evacuation When Bravo Battery arrived at Kandahar Airfield (KAF) in the late evening, they were scheduled to attend a "ramp ceremony" for Hunter and Park. A ramp ceremony honors soldiers who have died in combat and is staged at an airfield close to the area (the ramp) where an aircraft is waiting. The crew then escorts the soldier's remains home. The overwhelming weight of what was happening started to sink in for everyone as the Strike Brigade soldiers marched up to the ceremony to pay their respects. Hearing "Taps" being played and seeing coffins covered in American flags was a shocking experience for many of the young soldiers. It was another reminder that they were far from home.

Everyone's patience was starting to wear thin as the weeks passed. Leaders needed help to keep the soldiers engaged. Most soldiers were occupying their time either visiting the boardwalk or attempting to get in touch with loved ones. Since the boardwalk offered an escape from reality, some of the soldiers seized the chance to snap photos with one another. PFC Santoro, PFC Little, and Captain Cabebe were among those who did so. There were TGI Fridays, ice-cream shops, jewelry stores, and other comforts of home on the boardwalk. For several soldiers, it was easy to realize they were far from home. The air was heavy with the rotten smell of "Poo Pond," and the heat seemed to intensify any residual cloud. There wasn't much to be done in the early morning but by 6:00 am, the temperature had risen to above 90° Fahrenheit and was quickly approaching 100. Getting accustomed to being among Afghan peers was challenging because of the known fact that some of them were former Taliban fighters who were now contractors. Two soldiers were heard talking to each other in the KAF chow hall.

"How do we know these guys aren't just going to turn their backs on us?" said one. "Who's to say they don't still have allegiance to the Taliban, and they aren't telling them where our communication towers, chow halls, and sleeping quarters are for them to attack?"

"I have no clue, man," said the other.

Bravo Battery's relocation to Forward Operating Base (FOB) Jelawur had finally come. The men were loaded onto the Chinooks and Black Hawks. For the first time, Fontenot, Beaudrie, Peltier, Creighton, Tatro, Pantaleo, and their brothers were witnessing the Tetris-like game the pomegranate orchards and grape furrows in the Arghandab seemed to play. They were flying across the mountaintops from Kandahar. They watched as the rudimentary city buildings of Kandahar appeared to vanish behind the mountains, replaced by flooded orchards and rows of greenery. The river snaked like a hungry serpent ready to devour the men of the 101st; however, it provided ample freedom for enemy fighters to move from the south side of the river into the IED-littered fields of the orchards and vineyards.

The leadership was shown to tents upon arrival at FOB Jelawur, and instructions were given on the dos and don'ts of the FOB. The men of Bravo Battery were instructed to appoint a sergeant of the guard and place soldiers inside guard towers as soon as they had all their equipment accounted for and their tents assigned. Specialist Parker was in a watch tower not long after landing. Despite the tower's several thousand meters of separation from the grape furrows and pomegranate orchards, the troops were frequently in contact with the enemy. From the perspective of a fanboy, it was simple to get caught in the Hollywood visuals in war films with Kiowa helicopters flying low and doing gun runs. But it became more difficult to ignore that the men of the 82nd Airborne Division and soon-to-be 101st had their lives changed when the earth shook, and smoke filled the air explosion after explosion. It was becoming increasingly clear that death was becoming more likely as the soldiers observed from a distance. The "Devil's Playground's" killing fields were calling, and the Top Guns were on speed dial. The battalion command team moved Alpha and Bravo Batteries to their new locations as Captain Ward, the commander of Bravo, and First Sergeant Banister obtained additional information. The area of operation became clear: Bravo Battery was going to Combat Outpost (COP) Tynes, and Alpha Battery was going to COP Nolen. The latter was south of the battalion's new home, Terra Nova, along Route Red Dog. COP Nolen was a former school with exterior walls of tall mud blocks and internal mud huts used as sleeping quarters and operational areas.

Outside of the COP was a nightmare: to the south and southwest of the compound were pomegranate orchards; to the east was an exposed location, and shortly after, the men entered fields of grass that led them to mud-wall structures in farmlands. COP Tynes was east of Terra Nova on Route Red Dog and was positioned at the corner of Mariners and Red Dog. Because additional compounds backed up to the complex, which exposed the entire property and made an enemy attack possible, the compound was in a terrible strategic location. The enemy's vehicle-borne IEDs posed a substantial threat to the small COP. It was a strategic death trap because it had only one point of entry and no point of escape. It was an old girls' school with nothing but mud walls, like COP Nolen. New MATVs and MRAPs were delivered to the batteries to replace outdated Humvees. Compared to the Humvee used in the Iraq War, these vehicles provided improved protection for the troops. The new vehicles' designs protected soldiers within the cabin by angling the blast from an IED outward, so much of its force missed the hull and instead damaged it at an angle. Usually, an explosion in an older vehicle would kill the crew; since it would go straight into the cab, but with this new design, it would usually destroy the engine first. Staff Sergeant McCorkhill, a seasoned section chief with three deployments under his belt, and Sergeant Casey were conducting a perimeter patrol around FOB Jelawur to get used to the suspension and capabilities of their new vehicle when they had an unfortunate accident;

their MATV rolled into an irrigation canal running along the perimeter of FOB Jelawur. In a sense, it demonstrated to leadership the vehicle's capacity to protect the soldiers inside its walls. If Casey had been inside the gunner hatch, he would have been spared any serious injuries.

When the day's excitement subsided, it was time for the battery leadership and the first soldiers to depart for COP Tynes. It was decided that section chiefs, now referred to as squad leaders and platoon leadership, would set out to start providing relief in place. The leaders loaded their equipment and prepared to move to COP Tynes. The unsettling noise of gunfire and explosions in the background warned them of the sinister and unwelcoming environment that awaited Bravo Battery. It was clear to everyone that they wouldn't be greeted with open arms. Anything that would have suggested they would be sipping chai tea and telling stories with elders about how fantastic their future in the Arghandab would be was quickly wiped away. The leaders got their first look at the Afghan settlement and its inhabitants as the MRAP navigated the rugged terrain of Route Red Dog, which passed through the center of Jelawur.

Rocks pelted the outside of the vehicle, and Specialist Parker in the gunner hatch was shocked at how much the Americans were despised by the villagers they were meant to assist. Fontenot could hear the constant vandalism as it occurred. He, Peltier, and Bartoszek observed how the locals in the village regarded the Americans as they passed by.

Parker said, "Smoke, you can almost feel the hate simply by looking at their eyes."

"Smoke" Tatro replied, "Well, if another one of these little motherfuckers hits my window with one of the boulders, we're gonna stop this convoy, and I'm gonna settle them down."

Regardless of how enraged he was, it left little doubt that his platoon was about to face a mountain of struggle. The Arghandab had quickly lost its innocence, and the reality of the situation was now at the forefront of their minds. They were hated, and that thought would be the fuel that would propel them to accomplish the unthinkable challenges they had yet to encounter.

The Top Guns were now born into the world of the "Dab," where you can check out but never leave.

CHAPTER 2

The RIP

> A man does what he must, despite personal consequences, despite obstacles and dangers and pressures, and that is the basis of all human morality.
>
> WINSTON CHURCHILL

The Top Guns had officially arrived at their new residences to commence their relief in place. The battery soldiers had begun acclimating at a snail's pace with their counterparts at Combat Outpost (COP) Tynes and had not made a favorable impression. In the military, first impressions are usually game-changers; in this case, they may be life-changing. The soldiers from Two Charlie of the 82nd Airborne Division were initially given a more relaxed deployment than they had encountered in the Arghandab.

They were initially attached to the Canadian Army and had seen little action. The paratroopers were not supposed to support another force, such as the Canadians. They are the 82nd paratroopers; they were created to be on the front line, not provide security for others. Not long before being moved from Panjwai to the Arghandab, their convoy was returning to their COP when it detonated a catastrophic improvised explosive device (IED), killing Private First Class Tynes and Sergeant Nolen, both of whom were crucial and impactful soldiers in Two Charlie. Their deployment took a nasty, violent turn that day, which continued when they were sent to their new home in the Arghandab River Valley (ARV). The men of Two Charlie would be replacing a Stryker company, which had suffered numerous fatalities in recent months, including one disastrous IED that killed six soldiers. Following Two Charlie's arrival in the ARV, they had the opportunity to watch as the sleeping monster appeared to come alive. When they arrived at COP Tynes, they were given nothing more than the bare mud-wall-structured compounds they had taken over from the previous unit; fortunately, they were able to erect shelters and sleeping quarters because the fighting season had not started yet. When the guys from One Bravo arrived at COP Tynes, it didn't appear to be much, but what the men from Two Charlie had achieved was monumental.

Beginning in March 2010, Two Charlie watched as the fighting season blossomed. The fields changed from a bleak, aggressive, and gloomy brown to a vivid, brilliant, and colorful green. The shift gave cover and concealment for enemy fighters to attack Two Charlie in the orchards, allowing the Taliban to litter the farms with IEDs in locations where soldiers had previously traveled freely. Two Charlie lost several friends and brothers in recent months. They witnessed as locals became victims and were killed by the same IEDs their combat companions had fallen to; children were turned into a blood mist, and locals and villagers withdrew in terror.

Sergeant Knollinger, one of Two Charlie's team leaders, and several soldiers volunteered to assist the 101st Field Artillery soldiers with fundamental infantry techniques they knew would pay dividends in their new area of responsibility. Two Charlie's first impression of the artillerymen was that they were larger and bulkier than the average infantry soldier, almost like heavyweight fighters in a middleweight battle. They lacked some of the skills required to survive in such a hostile environment as the Arghandab, and it was quite possible that some of them would die. It was like watching your younger brother get into a battle and realizing he wasn't prepared or couldn't fathom the lengths his opponent was willing to go to in order to defeat him. First Sergeant Banister of the "Bulls" was a faithful first sergeant among the soldiers. His soldiers admired him and his desire to build influential leaders. As the battery's first sergeant, he valued the chance to lead his men before Afghanistan, but he was troubled by the prospect of not bringing all his soldiers home. Banister was a forward observer by trade but as a first sergeant, he now led a field artillery battery. He was usually optimistic and tried his hardest to make the best of a difficult circumstance, yet harsh love is often required, especially in a place like the ARV. Looking at your soldiers and identifying their flaws might help them improve and even save their lives in combat. The officers and noncommissioned officers (NCO) who had boarded COP Tynes in this initial wave were not making the best of impressions, but it was time to lace up their boots and head out into the sector.

The first patrol, led by Two Charlie, moved to the north side of Route Red Dog and north of Druia, the village located directly east of Bravo Battery's new home. Typically, its population was between 100 and 200 villagers. During harvest, also known as fighting season, that number could easily triple. It was clear that, while the artillerymen had the opportunity to train in infantry tactics, they were less skilled than the battle-hardened soldiers of

Two Charlie. Throughout the patrol, the men of Two Charlie continued to remind the leaders of the 101st to watch their spacing. As the patrol moved across the north side of Druia, Staff Sergeant Fontenot identified that the artillery soldiers were going to need to work on patrolling, specifically on their spacing; they would be moving in modified wedges in this environment often, which would provide them with maximum dispersion, but their current movement appeared disorganized and susceptible to enemy attack. The terrain, which fluctuated on uneven, disconnected fields and irrigation trenches, was so heavily compressed that the 101st leadership appeared to struggle while navigating through it. After moving a few meters, they repeatedly would have to make their way from one trench into an open space. They kept doing this until they ultimately came to a group of grape furrows where they could set up an overwatch. The movement, or patrol, covered about a thousand meters to where we moved, it wasn't a far distance. They could tell villagers from Druia, and Babur were observing them as they passed behind a few compounds. The grape furrows north of Route Red Dog were an acceptable introduction for the leaders from the 101st; however, these furrows weren't nearly as bad as the suffering that awaited them in the furrows south of the canals.

"As you can see, once you reach a certain point, the land ends, and the fields begin. Once the fields begin, all hell breaks loose," said Sergeant Bragg.

"What kind of issues have y'all had?" asked Fontenot.

"You see the holes in the mud walls? Those are murder holes; the Taliban will shoot at you from the holes in the walls, so you'll need to be careful of that. Stay off the raised paths; if it's a path, don't walk on it; walk anywhere else but a path because it will have an IED if it's a path."

"I'll remember that. Thanks."

As the patrol approached the end of Druia and the waddy, between Druia and Babur, everyone paused for an extended period to take up an overwatch position. This would provide the men and leaders of the 101st with their first view of their new responsibilities. The new guys looked at the Arghandab with a sense of innocence, which the soldiers from Two Charlie identified. Unaware of the violence and cruelty lying in wait beyond the fields of grapevines and pomegranate orchards and the harsh conditions entangled in their surroundings, the leadership gazed over the colorful orchards across the canals, admiring the beauty.

As the patrol returned to COP Tynes, the troops of Two Charlie recounted heartbreaking incidents that would haunt them for the rest of their lives. Memories of dismembered friends who lived, as well as memories of those whose blood stained the soil in such a way, they would be a permanent part of this tortured land forever. Each man from Two Charlie spoke with almost a quiver in his voice when it came time to patrol the area. Upon returning to Tynes, there was a sense of reprieve, of one more patrol completed. Some soldiers removed their gear and retreated to nothing more than wearing their pink Crocs, with Army physical fitness shorts and a tan T-shirt; others weren't as fortunate as it was their turn to assume tower guard. The men from Two Charlie had constructed a pool from plastic and plywood; it was their saving grace after patrolling in 116° Fahrenheit heat.

Bravo Battery was perplexed as to what standard to follow. They felt as if they had just walked into the Wild, Wild West, and uniform standards were out the window despite the men having to be ready to roll at a second's notice. The oldest member of the platoon and self-described gym rat back home at Fort Campbell, Fontenot was in good physical condition. When the leadership arrived at Tynes, he went to the makeshift gym the 82nd soldiers had constructed to see what he had to work with. It was clear that, while he was strong, endurance would be a necessary enemy in this environment because strength alone would not help him to survive the deployment. Knollinger, Staff Sergeant Rosa, and a few other men were working out in the gym; it provided a private setting to talk openly about the Arghandab. Additionally, since they would be out of sight from other people, the Two Charlie men could speak freely without any concerns they might have about rank.

Fontenot asked, "Do y'all mind telling me what happened to your platoon sergeant?"

"Well, the Third Squad was on patrol in Babur, and the First Squad was headed to secure the new battalion sergeant major at COP Nolen," Knollinger began. "While we were on patrol, we heard the blast. Shortly after, we heard over the radio that First Squad hit an IED on Route Phillies. We began running from Babur to Route Phillies to try and help, but that's a long haul, especially in the kit, when it's 116 degrees. The First Squad was on a mounted patrol when the MATV [mine-resistant, ambush-protected all-terrain vehicle] hit the IED, causing it to do a flip. While in the air, the door was blown open, and Santos came partially out, and the truck crushed him. Sergeant Bragg and Sergeant Maher worked on getting the other guys out until QRF [quick-reaction force] got there, but by the time Third Squad made it from Babur, it was too late; there was nothing we could do."

Fontenot replied, "Thanks. I'm sorry to hear about your platoon sergeant. Smoke Tatro is our platoon sergeant. Those guys mean so much to us."

As a platoon sergeant, Tatro was getting close to retirement and had a considerably more composed manner than Fontenot. He was, in a sense, the calm before the storm. Tatro was also a paratrooper from the 82nd, but an infantryman he was not! Being an artilleryman was his passion, and he was reluctant to go on patrol. He entrusted this to Fontenot and resolved to be available at any time to help with the QRF if Peltier, Pantaleo, or Fontenot needed him. Tatro and "Smoke" Krabbenhoft, Three Bravo's platoon sergeants were still at Forward Operating Base Jelawur with the remainder of the battery; however, so for now, 2nd Lieutenant Pantaleo and Staff Sergeants Fontenot and Peltier were leading the way for One Bravo, and Staff Sergeant Bartoszek and 1st Lieutenant Mark were in charge of Three Bravo. Bartoszek and Fontenot had known each other since they were privates and always had a friendly rivalry. They competed at every level for rank, soldier, and NCO-of-the-month boards, and eventually, they were promoted around the same time. Along with being stationed in South Korea, they were deployed to Iraq together, but this time, they would be operating independently inside their respective platoons, carrying a lot more responsibility. They were going to be patrolling in places where the enemy held a newfound hate for Americans. Three Bravo was accompanied by an infantry squad attached to the battery and had Staff Sergeant Anderson an infantry squad leader and Sergeant Huber, who would also be helping the men in the 3rd Platoon throughout the deployment. Anderson was an engaging personality to whom the men from Bravo had been recently introduced, and despite being new to the battery, his fiery personality and desire to make himself well-known within the men of Two Charlie had become apparent.

It was now July 6, 2010, and getting to the height of the fighting season. A typical day in the Arghandab was generally about 116° Fahrenheit at Tynes and probably 10 more in the orchards and furrows. Bravo's commander, Captain Ward, mentioned wanting to push a patrol into the village of Babur; the men of Two Charlie knew the inherent risks of this patrol, but they figured it was an opportunity for the soldiers of the 101st to get into a firefight and get their first introduction to real life in the ARV. In understanding the high level of uncertainty that accompanied the patrol and the considerable size of the element going out, Knollinger spoke with First Sergeant Banister and asked him to provide his best men for the patrol. Despite knowing the 101st had nothing but their leadership on the ground, after looking over some of the gear the men were going to carry, Knollinger had doubts about whether this was the best they had to offer. Regardless, it was time to execute the patrol. Due to the excessively high tempo, Two Charlie had kept over the past few months, they wanted to give the guys a mental break. It was determined that Two Charlie's medic, "Doc" Taylor, would sit the patrol out and allow the One Bravo medic,

"Doc" Stegehuis, an opportunity to be on the patrol alone. Stegehuis was a young man from the Detroit metro area who hadn't had much chance outside Advanced Individual Training and the Joint Readiness Training Center to refine his skills. Still, he had performed well before coming to Afghanistan, so he had the confidence of his leaders. Some of the leaders accompanying Two Charlie would be from Three Bravo—Mark, Bartoszek, and Anderson—and One Bravo—Pantaleo, Fontenot, Peltier, and Doc Stegehuis—along with Banister from the headquarters element; the leaders would be separated among the squads that would be crossing the waddy between Druia and Babur. Due to the excessive uncertainty that accompanied the patrol, it was determined the sniper from the 82nd, Specialist Moon, would also be on the patrol. Christopher Moon was 20 years old and from Tucson, Arizona. He had given up a full college scholarship to join the Army. Before this patrol, Moon spoke with his mom, Marsha, over a satellite phone. He had climbed on top of COP Tynes to ensure he didn't lose reception; as he spoke to his mom, she could sense a melancholy tone. It was something unusual not there previously. Moon would generally ask his mom to pray for the men of Two Charlie; however, this time, he asked her to pray for him. Maybe it was because he knew each step in the "Devil's Playground" was a risk. As the patrol reached the ruins at the end of Druia, the leaders from the 82nd huddled together to try to determine who would go where; ultimately, it was decided the heavy weapon section, along with the M240 machine gun, would head south towards the first canal. It was also determined Moon and his spotter, Sergeant Rush, would go with them. At the same time, Knollinger and Staff Sergeant Farnsworth would cross the open area. The way it was broken down for the 101st men would separate Fontenot, Pantaleo, and Peltier, with Knollinger and Farnsworth crossing the open area. At the same time, Bartoszek, Mark, Anderson, Doc Stegehuis, and Banister would go south of the first canal with the heavy weapon section. It wasn't long before the Afghan interpreter intercepted communications that said the Taliban was watching the movement of the men.

As the two squads split and the heavy weapon section went south, Sergeant Rush identified that the men of the 101st were bunching up in their spacing; he addressed the spacing and had everyone spread out to approximately ten meters between each soldier. Moon had instructed Doc Stegehuis to stay back. Shortly after the men began their movement, Moon, cradling his sniper rifle, looked back at Rush; he then looked north toward the rest of the men, and the next thing everyone heard was a thunderous BOOM. Any time an IED goes off, the next few minutes are chaos, and this was no different: dust, debris, and shrapnel flying through the air, the toxic smell of homemade explosives, the sulfurous smell of burning flesh, screams all around, all while leaders are trying to get accountability over radios, while not knowing who the victim is that is suffering under the umbrella of all this chaos.

"IED, IED, IED!"

Knollinger got on the radio to check on his men, and so did the other Two Charlie leaders, until the cries of "MEDIC!" were heard from Rush. The IED had hit Moon; at the time, no one knew if it was a pressure-plate IED or otherwise. All they knew was he was down. Another critical component troops must consider is secondary IEDs and complex ambushes when assisting. While several of the Two Charlie men rushed over to help Moon, others took charge of those receiving small-arms fire from Babur and the orchards and set in a security force that would ultimately protect Moon and those attempting to help him. At first glance, Moon's apparent wounds were amputations of both his legs: the right one above the knee, ending in severed muscle and flesh; the left ending just below the knee, exposing his bone. His right wrist and hand had a hole exposing his ligaments and bone, as well as a missing thumb. His left arm was less damaged comparatively but was burned and lacerated over a large area. Certain sensations from these moments are undeniable: the sounds, the sights, the smells of burning flesh and oxidized blood combined with the Afghan dust. Ultimately, it is chaos. Many of the soldiers were helping pack Moon's wounds, so Doc Stegehuis took a second to prepare for the next step, as it was likely Moon was also suffering from internal injuries. Tensions were at fever pitch.

Knollinger yelled, "Doc, fucking apply morphine!"

Doc's auto-injector found a spot in the side of Moon's exposed hip. He was concerned the morphine might cause Moon's breathing to stop, but it was clear his pain was too much, and to not apply the medication seemed heartless. The next step was to try to establish an intravenous (IV) port, which Moon would need in the foreseeable future. His veins were almost unnoticeable, but as Doc pressed the needle into his arm, the men treating Moon began to take small-arms fire from enemy combatants somewhere close by. Doc covered his patient, trying to shield him as helicopters conducted gun runs overhead. They needed to move Moon immediately to prevent any further casualties. As a nine-line medevac was being called up, the men gathered inside the tactical operations center at COP Tynes and attempted to listen closely, not knowing if it was someone from the 82nd or the 101st who had been hit. The men gathered up a QRF element, knowing they would need to support those on the ground. Bragg, Rosa, and others were instantly ready to act. Rosa was nearly sick as soon as they heard Moon had been hit. All he could think was, "Not again!"

The men quickly loaded up to support the troops in contact. Doc Stegehuis's equipment availability was limited to a portable mesh litter. With the help of several others, they lifted Moon and began to retreat to the safety of the ruins where the other squad of men had initially stayed. During the transport, Moon began to sag and slip towards the litter's rear, prompting the team to try to set him down to reset; his exposed bone had gotten caught on one of the team member's clothing, causing him further anguish. With the assistance of Mark and several of the Two Charlie soldiers, they began to bandage Moon further. The morphine had started to take effect, which caused his wounds to seep more. After retightening the leg tourniquets, Doc noticed the IV had become dislodged. Moon's left arm was mainly intact; luckily, Doc could establish a line. Moon had taken a liter of saline, which brought about the dilemma of whether further fluids would diminish his blood's ability to clot. He needed blood and emergency surgery as soon as possible. The men had finished with their lifesaving interventions, including stopping bleeding, ensuring Moon's airway was open, and establishing an IV. The QRF element had arrived on the ground. They were providing cover for the troops and providing aid; Doc Taylor, Two Charlie's medic, was now on the ground and quickly attempting to help Moon.

Stegehuis said, "I did everything I could to help him."

Taylor was, however, focused on seeing if there was anything further he could do while waiting for the medevac. Typically, the medevac birds want the medic to ride with them; however, Moon had requested Rush go with him. Rush insisted on boarding the helicopter, declaring nothing would prevent him from going with Moon. At that point, all they could do was wait, and wait, and wait, for what seemed like forever for the helicopter to arrive. The time from serious injury to life-saving surgery is known as the "golden hour," which states the casualty has a much better chance of achieving a positive outcome if they are taken into surgery within an hour of being struck. It had felt like an eternity from the time Moon was hit, to applying aid, to finishing up, to loading him, and eventually seeing him fly off towards Kandahar Airfield to receive the medical care he desperately needed. As the Black Hawk eventually lifted into the amber-colored sky's fury, the men's somber mood was palpable.

Moon was a loss Two Charlie didn't want, especially this close to going home, but for now, he was lifted to safety. Despite all the pandemonium that ensues after an IED goes off, one of the things that is often a priority for higher headquarters is whether sensitive items are accounted for. With Moon being a sniper, headquarters wanted to know if his M110 sniper rifle had been recovered.

Understanding that, without the rifle, the men of Two Charlie and the 101st would have to continue looking for it, with hesitation in their voices, they responded that they did not have his sensitive items. Headquarters informed them they were to continue to look for the rifle and would continue to request a situation report (SITREP) periodically. Much to the dismay of the men on the ground, a SITREP was requested every 10 minutes. After several hours of being on the ground and searching through the pomegranate orchards, it was identified that Moon had been hit by a remote-controlled IED (RCIED), and the enemy fighter had likely singled him out due to his tan-colored sniper rifle. After several hours, not much of the rifle had been found besides the buffer spring, a cover for the scope, and the laser mount. However, pieces of Moon were also found, including charred flesh and his kneecap, which were picked up and placed in a body bag. Eventually, as the sun set, the men were given the order to return to COP Tynes. As they returned to Tynes, each man hoped to hear good news. Unfortunately, the only news to come was that Moon was stable. The soldiers from the 82nd and 101st had a warm meal ready for them, but many declined to eat. It was a shock to the system for all the 101st leadership. They were no longer in a training scenario, and death had become all too real. They were now having to endure the harsh reality that even the slightest misstep could result in the death of one of their soldiers. The innocence Two Charlie had seen in their faces merely days before was gone. This gruesome event would forever bond the men of Two Charlie and the 101st. Two Charlie still wasn't done yet, however; plans were being formulated that would rattle the battle-hardened men to their core as they put their soldiers in harm's way in the "Devil's Playground" for one last patrol.

Captain Ward intended to send a patrol into Druia to conduct a critical-leader engagement the following day. The objective was to engage with residents, particularly the village imam, and assess their feelings about the recent Moon incident. An imam is an Islamic spiritual leader who leads daily prayers, teaches people about the Quran, and is highly respected within their communities.

The patrol pushed just east of COP Tynes down Route Red Dog. Two Charlie and Bravo soldiers provided security for the commander so he could speak to locals and the imam. As Ward engaged the imam, not much information was being given. The imam was a typical Afghan-looking gentleman with a long, ragged, dirty white robe, dirty white headdress, and long, shaggy beard. As the Afghan interpreter translated, Rosa and Fontenot couldn't help but notice the exchange between the men wasn't going well. The imam acted as if nothing had happened, and he had no information of any IED going off.

The patrol continued pushing east towards the end of Druia and the waddy, where Moon had been hit the day before. Just as the patrol was getting near the end of Druia, another IED exploded. As dust and debris engulfed the air, everyone was on their radios. This time, the enemy fighters had failed. The RCIED was set up on the Red Dog Bypass about fifty meters south of Route Red Dog, and the patrol was on Route Red Dog, so they missed. Two Charlie and Bravo were lucky. They had escaped yet another attempt from enemy fighters to hit them with an explosive device. They returned to COP Tynes to begin planning their next and final joint patrol. It would again lead them into the orchards, into the "Devil's Playground." Still, this time, it would challenge every soldier's physical and mental character, including the hardened paratroopers on their last patrol.

CHAPTER 3

Into the Devil's Playground

> Regard your soldiers as your children, and they will follow you into the deepest valleys; look upon them as your beloved sons, and they will stand by you even unto death.
>
> SUN TZU

With one final joint mission left to complete, the men from Two Charlie huddled up to attempt to determine who would be going on this last patrol. None of them genuinely wanted to go; however, they also did not want to leave without giving the men from the 101st a proper handoff. As they sat and discussed who would go, those who held the bottle offered a variety of perspectives. The bottle signified that the person who held it had the authority to speak freely without interruption; it allowed each man to voice his concerns without retribution. The mission the leadership from the 101st wanted to execute was going to include approximately 23 men from the 101st, who had been at Combat Outpost (COP) Tynes less than 24 hours, going south of the second canal into the pomegranate orchards and furrows with several men from Two Charlie. The goal would be to occupy a compound identified using aerial imagery, which the soldiers would later call "Building 666." Some of the men expressed that they didn't feel any of Two Charlie's men should be going on this patrol, while others believed the 101st deserved a proper handoff, and if any of the men were going, they would be going as well. The soldiers would later be forced into the orchards in the early morning by decisions made above all their pay grades. Knowing which paths they had previously used, the soldiers of Two Charlie met with 2nd Lieutenant Pantaleo and Staff Sergeant Fontenot from One Bravo inside the tactical operations center (TOC) at COP Tynes to plot the route for the next morning. They expressed it was paramount to follow the planned route. Drifting a few meters off track could have fatal consequences for the mission's success and the soldiers' lives. As an extra security measure to move into the field, the leadership had acquired the services of a Navy dog team that specialized in bomb detection. The dog was a wide-eyed German Shepherd called Dix. The dog team had arrived late in the evening the night before and was briefed on the plan for the next morning. The remaining Bravo Battery personnel arrived at Tynes during the day and were informed they would be leaving for a mission the next day that would be a 36-hour warm base, so pack accordingly. The leadership from One Bravo was the only personnel within the platoon to have experienced the terrain firsthand. As a result, it was nearly impossible for their newly taken-in soldiers to properly realize or prepare for what they were trying to encounter. The new soldiers had no knowledge or experience of the area and couldn't possibly perceive the intensity this mission would hurl at them. As the men began bedding down for the night, some focused on ensuring their weapons were prepared for the next day; some prepared ammunition, water, and food; others took time to write a letter home in case they didn't return. Death had become all too real for the men recently, and it was better to be prepared and leave a legacy gift for your loved ones rather than not be ready for an unforeseen event and leave nothing.

Early the following day, at approximately 3:00 am, the men began lining up for pre-combat checks and inspections. As squad leaders and team leaders were checking their soldiers, it was identified that the communications specialist from the 101st had loaded the wrong fill in the radios. Their start point time would now be delayed. Staff Sergeant Gerhardt was furious at this misstep because this was the first strategic error of the day, and they hadn't left yet. Gerhardt unleashed a tirade-filled verbal barrage, letting his frustrations be known.

"I'm going to kill you, commo man!" he yelled into the darkness.

One of the benefits the men had was they were leaving under the cover of darkness. This advantage would be lost if the communication problem wasn't resolved. As the soldiers finally left COP Tynes, Dix leading barely under cover of darkness, there was tension in the air; the men were practically anticipating not if they would step on a pressure-plate improvised explosive device (IED) but when. As they moved to the outskirts of the town of Jelawur to begin entering the fields, the green glow from their night-vision goggles (NVG) made a trail from the front of the formation to the rear. As the men began awkwardly crossing the first canal, they were losing the cover of darkness. It was decided to protect the NVGs to prevent anyone from losing sensitive items and to conserve their batteries for the upcoming 36-hour warm base. As the men were navigating their route through the orchards, Specialist Miller, a seasoned soldier from One Bravo who had been on multiple Iraq deployments and was a fire-control specialist for the platoon, twisted his ankle while jumping over a mud wall, perhaps because of the intense heat, perhaps because of the pressure, or possibly because his mind was numb. Knollinger, having no sympathy for him and his injury, decided to fuel the fire.

"Do you need me to call the Greyhound bus so they can come and pick you up?"

"Fuck you."

Miller stood up, feeling contempt for the ridicule and refusal to abandon his platoon. Two Charlie wasn't aware the men from One Bravo adopted the namesake "The Bastards," not because it was cute and not because it was vulgar, but because they genuinely felt like the outcasts of their unit most of the time. They went above and beyond to work as hard as they possibly could; they refused to stay down, regardless of whether they were hurt or not, and sometimes they would accept outsiders that were considered throwaways from other areas within the battery because they knew if they could make them feel like part of the family, then that person would genuinely go to war for them.

In another instance, before leaving Forward Operating Base (FOB) Jelawur early in the deployment, there was an incident between Private First Class Dulaney and Specialist Branch. Their issue got entirely out of hand and led to Dulaney threatening Branch. Staff Sergeant Fontenot was told he would be receiving Dulaney into his squad, and the man would be a "leadership challenge" for him. Dulaney was a heavyset young man who struggled to meet the height and weight standards of the Army; he was the exact opposite of what one would imagine a soldier should look like. He wasn't athletic and had trouble passing an Army physical fitness test. However, he was brilliant, possibly one of the brightest individuals in the battery, and preferred anything over athletics; his face was often buried in a book during his downtime. Dulaney went to Fontenot's tent to report in. He had his M4 in one hand and his bolt in another. He handed his bolt to Fontenot.

"Here you go, Chief."

"What the fuck am I supposed to do with this, Dulaney?"

"I was told to give it to you."

"What the fuck good are you to me if you don't have a bolt in your rifle?"

"I imagine I'm not much good to you, Chief."

"I don't care what happened before right now. 'D,' you are starting at zero. I will judge you based on what you do for my section and our platoon from here on out. Here's your bolt. Put it back in your fucking rifle."

That was a turning point for Dulaney; he was no longer an outsider in his eyes; he was now a part of The Bastards, and that meant something special to him. As the men were walking into the orchards, Dulaney was carrying the M240B machine gun, the heaviest and most casualty-producing weapon the platoon had with them; he was also carrying a bag full of ammunition. Never once did he complain; he executed to the best of his ability, crouching under low-hanging pomegranate trees and hopping over walls and grape furrows. Dulaney and Specialist Miller were just two of the members of The Bastards who felt like throwaways that had something to prove.

As the patrol reached its objective, everyone took a short halt and pulled security. A small team led by Dix began clearing the compound. Some of the men who entered the compound with the initial team were Knollinger, Fontenot, Gerhart, Taylor, and Farnsworth.

As the men entered from the west side, they could see the room adjacent to their entry point was not occupied; the room had sheets on the floor that looked like, at some point, someone had been there to pray, but they had no way of knowing how recent it had been. On the eastern flank of the compound were sunflowers and marijuana plants that stood approximately six feet tall. On the northern side of the compound was a row of well-preserved and strategically connected rooms, and just outside the area was a trellis where green grapes grew aplenty. In the split second since the soldiers had begun occupying the compound, and as security positions were being set, the sun had reached a point in the sky where its heat radiated across the fields. The humidity effortlessly choked the soldiers, who were unaccustomed to the conditions, as the heat methodically drained them of any prior hydration efforts. Once inside the compound, the leaders of Two Charlie and One Bravo started recognizing the necessity for enhanced security measures. Men with M240 machine guns were positioned on rooftops, as were those with M249 SAWs (Squad Automatic Weapons). To help secure the compound, the 82nd sniper, Staff Sergeant Farnsworth, climbed on the roof near Specialist Cheatham to reinforce the position facing east. Farnsworth could traverse north or wherever needed at a moment's notice. Cheatham had been through training to understand basic Pashto; during that training, some of the things taught to the soldiers were how to communicate with locals when you wanted to get them to come to you, stay away, or give you information. Cheatham identified three Taliban fighters with weapons at a "T" intersection. He attempted to draw them in, yelling "Delta Raasha," "Come here" in Pashto. However, the men didn't respond.

Cheatham turned to Fontenot.

"I just saw three men at the intersection with weapons, and they took off running in different directions."

"Why didn't you shoot at them?"

"Because they weren't shooting at me."

"If you encounter someone with a weapon, consider them a threat and engage them."

The Afghan interpreter, Mike, picked up traffic over the radio and came running with a look of fear in his eyes. "They know where we are. They are positioning to attack us."

The men from Two Charlie had been in this position before and knew contact was imminent. Only a few seconds later, the troops heard the first shot, which would be the first of many. CRACK, CRACK! Instantly, every 101st gunner on the roof opened fire like every World War II movie they'd seen.

"Stop shooting; it's just harassing fire. At this rate, you'll shoot all your ammunition and have nothing left to fight with. Control your rate of fire, and don't let them bait you into a firefight," Knollinger yelled.

This advice would prove critical as the mission would linger into the later hours of the operation. Anytime ammunition, water, or medical supplies began to dwindle, a potential saving grace in the Arghandab could be a speed bag. A speed bag is dropped from a Black Hawk and intended to aid in emergency resupply efforts for combat operations. Due to the historically hostile nature of the "Devil's Playground," requesting a speed bag from higher headquarters was typically denied. The use of helicopters in the Arghandab, and Afghanistan in general, had become primarily used for deliberate or hasty extractions or for medical evacuations. Requesting air support for things like speed bags had become a last resort. In the past when requests were made for additional support it was often denied due to thick vegetation and the helicopters being unable to utilize jungle penetrators or the fact that helicopters were needed for wounded soldiers.

As the harassing fire continued to ramp up, one of the shots from an enemy fighter nearly hit Farnsworth in the face. It had become apparent that a movement-to-contact patrol was needed sooner rather than later. While the soldiers from the 82nd were discussing the possibility of deploying a patrol, they were unaware the leadership from the 101st was also making plans for the same patrol. It is often said that "many hands make light work," but it is also true that "too many hands in the pot are a bad thing." In this case, the latter was true; with more than one leadership team attempting to formulate a plan, mixed information was bound to go out, and when it did, the leader on the ground would default to whatever had worked in the past. Captain Ward had already sent radio traffic to Pantaleo to spin up a patrol to move into the orchards. Pantaleo was in the process of identifying who he was sending out as the element to conduct the movement-to-contact patrol. Based on Pantaleo's initial guidance from Ward, Fontenot, Cheatham, Cox, and Parker were identified. Staff Sergeants Gerhart and Knollinger then approached Pantaleo regarding getting some of his men to push out a patrol into the orchards. Pantaleo had already identified his personnel and, with new information from Gerhart and Knollinger, adjusted his list by only a few men. Although Gerhart had only been with Two Charlie for a few days, he had previously been with Alpha Company and witnessed Moon's catastrophic injury. Due in part to seeing Moon hit the way he was, Gerhart made a simple request of Knollinger: if he were to get hit and become a double amputee, don't let anyone save him.

By this point, the men had been in the compound for several hours, and the heat was now at a fever pitch. Mike, the 101st Afghan interpreter, came to the leadership with a terrified look.

"Sir, I must tell you something."

"What's up, Mike?" asked Pantaleo.

"I heard the Taliban commander delivering a message to his men on the ICOM. He told them, 'Kill them all, don't let any of them leave alive.'"

The time was now for the men to push out the patrol; further delays could have grave consequences. Pantaleo removed Cheatham from his position on the roof; after being in a gun position for several hours, he would go on patrol with Fontenot to serve as his machine gunner. Replacing him would be Dulaney, who volunteered to go to Cheatham's vacated position. Dulaney moved to this new position after being relieved from his SAW position. Sergeant Cox would assist Cheatham as his assistant gunner. Specialists Parker, Cooper, and Private First Class Castro; would also be going along with several men from Two Charlie, including Gerhart and Lachance. Staff Sergeant Lachance was the forward observer for Two Charlie; he was a pivotal member of the team and well respected for his exceptional ability to remain calm under fire. His ability to walk the Kiowas, Apaches, and Black Hawks onto objectives was unparalleled. The goal was to draw enemy fire, enlist the aid of the Kiowa pilots, and take in the spectacle as they showered steel on every hostile position; Lachance's abilities would be much sought after in the fields. According to the brief Fontenot received from Pantaleo, the patrol was to push out into the orchards about 100–150 meters and attempt to draw fire or observe when enemy fighters shot at the compound. Then, the patrol would flank these fighters with top cover from the machine guns on the roofs. That was the plan anyway.

Upon entering the compound, the men from Two Charlie had the forethought to set in Claymore mines at each entry point; with rounds impacting the doors the patrol would exit, this was already paying dividends. The soldiers knew the exfil needed to be fast and furious. One of the members of the 82nd suggested detonating a Claymore, then throwing a grenade, followed by a quick exit. All agreed, so the men lined up and prepared to exit the compound. Once the Claymore was detonated, the men set out with overhead cover from Sergeant Jackson and his M4. They swiftly turned left into the pomegranate orchards and were gone in seconds.

Taliban chatter was immediately picked up, with enemy combatants asking each other if it was their IED the Americans had set off. As each of the combatants answered it was not their IED; it was just another confirmation to the men inside the compound that the fields directly outside their walls were littered with explosives.

The first movement of the patrol was successful as it moved just east, overlooking the compound. It was an open field surrounded by pomegranate orchards; the grass was overgrown, which provided lots of concealment from the enemy. However, it would do little to entice the enemy into a firefight. There were multiple mud walls and several compounds surrounding Building 666 that could potentially draw out the firefight the patrol was looking for. As they pushed out approximately 300 meters into the open field, some of the soldiers from One Bravo fell behind, and Castro fell far behind. Cooper sprinted back to him. The patrol took cover inside a grape furrow, providing concealment and cover but trapping excessive moisture and raising humidity, suffocating unacclimated soldiers. Due to fatigue and dehydration, most of the soldiers from One Bravo did not position themselves in a security posture.

Gerhart yelled at Fontenot, "Hey man, get your fucking guys in security!"

Although Fontenot felt that, in a way, he was being belittled and wasn't given much of a chance to fix his men on his own, this was no time for an argument or a pissing match, so he just pulled in his team leader, and had them position the men in a 360° security. He set the M240 facing towards the east with Cheatham and Cox to ensure they would have the most casualty-producing weapon in position if anyone trailed the element.

"Excuse me, sir, the ICOM traffic says that the Taliban fighters are going to attack once the helicopters are no longer around," Mike said.

Hearing this, Lachance had *Longknife* fly off station. Unfortunately for them, shortly after that, the chaos that no one expected began.

"Chief, I think I'm going down," Cheatham said.

"Cheatham, come on, man, keep drinking water. I need you, bro, to be in the fight," Fontenot implored.

"Chief, I'm going down."

The next thing Fontenot saw was Cheatham's head bounce off the butt stock of his machine gun as his body succumbed to the heat in what seemed like seconds. Instantly, Fontenot grabbed Cheatham, pulled him to the side, and started loosening his clothing to get him airflow and cool him down.

Gerhart yelled, "Doc, come over here and check on your guy!"

Fontenot said, "Sergeant Cox, jump on the 240."

In what seemed like mere minutes, the chaos of Doc working on Cheatham, Fontenot giving Cheatham his water, and Taliban fighters still shooting at their position, the next unexpected event occurred.

"Chief, I think I'm going down," Cox said.

"What the fuck? No way."

"Yeah, Chief, I'm dizzy. I think I'm going down."

The temperature had now elevated to approximately 116° Fahrenheit and about 125° in the fields. The humidity was extreme; the soldiers from One Bravo had been at COP Tynes for less than 24 hours and now found themselves in the middle of a running gun battle and a fight against the elements. With the situation not improving, they struggled to help Cheatham and Cox. Without warning, there it was again. Another cry for the medic was heard, this time for Cooper, who was well known for being one of the guys who would always keep everyone's morale up. He wasn't the most physically fit soldier in the platoon; however, there was never an instance where his ability to overcome or complete a goal was questioned. Fontenot and Doc hunkered down at the furrow's edge, near where Cheatham lay; as a result, Doc could continue to monitor him.

"Doc, what's everyone's status?" Fontenot asked.

"Chief, Cheatham is in a dangerous position. I'm worried about him. He may have a heat stroke soon. We need to get him out of here. Cox is badly dehydrated, and we need to get him out of here as well. Coop is dehydrated but stable, and I have an IV on him."

"Fine, let's keep an eye on these guys. I think Lachance is getting a medevac en route. I'll confirm with him, but we should be able to get them out soon. Do you think we can get an IV started on Cheatham?"

"I don't know, Chief," Doc said, "his veins are pretty collapsed, but I'll do my best."

They were trying to get an IV started on Cox as well as Cheatham, who was now stripped down to his underwear and barely responsive. With another cry for the medic, Doc was off to Castro, who had also gone down as a heat casualty but wasn't nearly as bad as the others. Castro was being treated for dehydration, and they were doing their best to rehydrate him to see if they could get him back into the fight. Parker was giving up his water to Castro but, in doing so, was now out of water. As bad as the now four heat casualties were, the enemy radio chatter had also picked up.

Mike said, "Sir, Taliban are saying, 'We have them pinned down. We need to attack now!'"

Lachance tried to establish an anticipated arrival time for the medevac by radioing *Longknife*. Fontenot had given Cheatham all his water to sustain him for as long as he could while waiting for the medevac to arrive, and Parker had done the same for Castro. Hearing about the situation in the field, the soldiers at the compound spun up a QRF (quick-reaction force) element, including "Smoke" Tatro. As the men maneuvered through the fields, the Taliban fighters provided resistance. It had become evident the 101st was getting the fight they wanted; however, not only were they getting it, but the men of Two Charlie were getting it as part of their last patrol. To avoid hitting any IEDs, Knollinger and the QRF element chose the shortest path to the soldiers in the field. They detected more enemy radio chatter as they maneuvered to support the original group.

The Taliban commander was heard to say, "There is another element going to meet them; wait until they're together, then we will attack them!"

Upon reaching the grape furrow, the QRF attempted to replenish and relieve as many men as possible, providing them with water to ensure their survival and ability to return to the compound. To ensure the QRF could continue for an extended timeline, the soldiers cross-loaded ammunition.

In a brief conversation between Knollinger and Gerhart, the latter said, "Bro, it's so fucking good to see you. The way the 101 soldiers are going down, we might all be dead."

Unfortunately, Fontenot's fatigue and dehydration had brought him to the point where he was experiencing full-blown heat cramps. He had strained his body like everyone else in the elements, but he had given Cheatham all his water. He risked his life for his soldier but had no idea how to care for himself.

Fortunately, "Smoke" Tatro had come with the QRF and made sure Fontenot had enough water, not much, but enough to pour it on him to lower his body temperature and give him something to drink. Lachance was running low on water and struggling with dehydration at this point.

As the soldiers continued providing medical support to the casualties, they were all in critical condition. The medevac had finally arrived, and casualties were being loaded into the Black Hawk, peppered by enemy fire as Cheatham and Cox were handed over. Taliban fighters took the opportunity to attempt once again to shoot down an American aircraft when the second medevac came for Cooper and Castro. Regardless of the enemy fire, both Black Hawks were successfully lifted into the air, and all casualties were now in the care of the flight medics. As soon as the Black Hawks began to lift off, their downdraft blew down the vegetation around the second canal; this provided an open field of fire for Dulaney to shoot a Taliban fighter near the canal with his M249. Dulaney volunteered to be on QRF to help his brothers out in the field; despite coming from multiple rotations of the gun positions on the rooftops. Gerhart and the men of Two Charlie knew everyone was getting low on ammunition and water. They knew the situation was critical and that everyone needed to return to the compound immediately. Among the soldiers, Knollinger was the strongest, so he took control of the 240 and started shooting from the hip while everyone started to march back to the facility. Taliban fighters continued engaging from an elevated point with no success for hours.

They were engaging the element throughout the movement back. Taliban fighters ramped up their attack on the troops utilizing their machine guns known as PKMs or *Pulemot Kalashnikova Modernizirovannyi* (modernized Kalashnikov machine gun). This turned into a running gun battle, where each man, regardless of dehydration, fatigue, or injury, was willing to sacrifice everything to ensure the man next to him made it back. As each man continued to maneuver across the field, they provided covering fire for each other, attempting to keep the Taliban fighters from accurately engaging them.

They had finally reached a point where they could see the compound; all they needed to do was cross a T-intersection. They found themselves in a field of thick grass, not knowing if IEDs were lurking beneath and with an elevated enemy still engaging them. Additionally, there were two Taliban fighters at the T-intersection they needed to cross. Figuring they would likely sustain casualties while crossing the intersection, the men attempted to figure out precisely what to do. A few from Two Charlie began arguing about how they would maneuver across the T-intersection; this was possibly out of frustration at the 101st or because they saw themselves being so close to going home, and they may have seen it as a losing fight. Knollinger, being heavily experienced in intense engagements, told McDaniels and Jackson from Two Charlie to throw grenades; they grabbed a few grenades and hurled them over the wall, hitting one of the Taliban fighters.

BOOM! BOOM!

"Hurry up, let's fucking get going," McDaniels yelled.

They saw one of the fighters dragging the other's lifeless body into the furrow. Despite continuing to be under fire, the patrol could get cover from the compound's gun positions, entering the structure shortly after. Despite the obstacles they had just faced, the four heat casualties, a determined enemy, and relentless and unforgiving terrain littered with IEDs, they had suffered no casualties from enemy fighters.

Once everyone had finally made it back into the compound and was secure, it became evident the men of Two Charlie were verbally and visually angry with the soldiers from One Bravo.

"Fuck those guys," McDaniels screamed. In his eyes, the 101st had just put the men of Two Charlie in harm's way.

Another soldier was heard saying, "I'm not sure how we made it back alive, to be honest." Gerhart said, "Thank y'all for coming to save our asses."

As he expressed his gratitude, he was interrupted by yells inside the compound.

"What the fuck is that?" a Two Charlie soldier was overheard saying.

Doc Taylor went over to figure out what was happening; Fontenot was experiencing full-body heat cramps, and his back muscles were seizing up.

"Shut the fuck up, man. They can hear you and think that they got the best of you," Taylor said.

At that time, Fontenot did his best not to make another sound. Doc Taylor offered him an IV, but Fontenot told him to save it for casualties who needed them later. He continued drinking water and eating grapes, hoping the sugar would help the cramps subside. Several soldiers from One Bravo, including Doc Stegehuis and Private First Class Junk, were helping to massage the muscles in Fontenot's legs to try to relieve some of the relentless pain he was feeling; nothing was working. Doc Taylor gave him Twizzlers from an MRE (meal, ready to eat). They were able to stop the cramps almost instantly. Everything up to that point had failed; something as simple and seemingly trivial as a pack of Twizzlers in an MRE was able to get him back in the fight. Fontenot wanted to rejoin his men and check everyone's status as soon as possible, but now he was back upright.

Fontenot's attempt to re-acclimate himself with his men and the men from Two Charlie would be short-lived.

Pantaleo called him over. "Fonty, how are you feeling, man?"

"I'm feeling better, sir. I'll keep drinking water and be ready to go shortly."

"Fonty, look, man, there's a Black Hawk inbound to drop off a speed bag with more ammunition, water, and medical supplies. It will pick you, Parker, and Jackson up and take y'all to Terra Nova for further evaluations.

"The fuck they are, sir. If my guys are here, I'm here, sir, you know that."

"Fonty, look, man, you know this isn't a discussion. This is the way it is. This decision is above us. I know you want to stay, and I want you to stay, but we need you for the rest of the deployment."

They would also be inserting replacements to bring fresh legs into the fight. Until now, the Two Bravo men had just been waiting for someone to call them forward. By this point, Fontenot's uniform looked like he had been through a battle, like most of the guys from Two Charlie. The crotch of his pants was now ripped almost down to the knee, there were blood stains from IVs that were started on soldiers in the field, and he was drenched with sweat. Despite his best efforts, it was a losing battle as the command team decided that, due to his section now missing Cheatham, Cox, Cooper, and Castro, they would pull him and Parker out, and Two Bravo would supplement the platoon. As the helicopters arrived to drop off the resupply, the soldiers littered the fields to provide a mad minute of support by fire. Once the Black Hawks were downloaded and ready for the personnel to be extracted, the men from One Bravo began to load into the first helicopter against their better judgment. Four Soldiers from One Bravo went on the first Black Hawk, while two soldiers from Two Charlie loaded on a second. No man from One Bravo wanted to leave; however, that decision had come from higher up. Hence, they did as they were instructed. The two men from Two Charlie had sustained minor injuries that would prevent them from being quick on their feet if needed. As Fontenot looked down on Building 666, he knew if any of his men were to become casualties, he would never forgive himself. Lifting off into the unforgiving sky of the Arghandab, Fontenot and the other men of One Bravo felt helpless as they were pulled away from their platoon.

As the replacements got on the ground, they were directed where to go, as they had no idea where the compound even was. Like the soldiers from One Bravo, Two Bravo had just gotten into the sector, so they saw everything for the first time. As soon as they got on the ground, the men from Two Charlie instructed them to take over the gun positions on the roof and relieve their soldiers. The day had run its course; the tempers were as heated as the sun at its highest point during the day. In the lone shot fired, since the replacements had arrived, Farnsworth had been grazed on his arm, so Doc Taylor had tended to him. Captain Ward was also on the ground and attempting to plan an exit with both the leadership of the 101st and the men of Two Charlie, who had the apparent concern that, due to the amount of time they had been inside the compound and been stagnant, the Taliban fighters might have positioned explosive devices on the exfil routes. The men from Two Charlie suggested to Ward the remaining personnel in the compound be airlifted out. He advised them air assets had been allocated elsewhere, so they would have to leave on foot. Considering all they had been through, Ward decided they would exfil once the sun went down; the men from Two Charlie recommended waiting until the morning so their soldiers could rest. Ultimately, they agreed to wait until morning and move just before the first light.

As the replacements from Two Bravo and the remainder of One Bravo prepared to push back to COP Tynes with Two Charlie, tensions were high. Two Charlie anticipated hitting an IED as they began their movement back. While in theory, the movement back appeared short on a map, it was anything but. During the exfil, the patrol would once again have to navigate successfully through the orchards while somehow managing to avoid IEDs. Once the men reached the canal, they could head east to position themselves directly south of Tynes. Patrolling in the middle of the canal was safer to an extent than being on land because they could avoid the IEDs, but God only knew what dangers lurked inside those canals. Eventually, they began heading north towards Tynes in the second canal.

A replacement said, "The patrol wasn't that bad."

"Shut up," said Lachance, partly angry because they were not adhering to noise discipline and partially because he was just annoyed with the lack of exclamation of leadership.

"I'm simply saying it wasn't that bad, that's all."

"Look, man, you're going to fucking die! As soon as we aren't here to save your ass, you're fucking dead!"

Having realized the harshness of his words and that he, too, was breaking the rule of noise discipline, he decided it wasn't worth the effort and remained quiet for the remainder of the patrol.

The last patrol for the men of Two Charlie in the "Devil's Playground" was officially completed. They had walked away, for the most part, unscathed. The artillerymen had the opportunity to go behind enemy lines and see firsthand what life in the Arghandab would hold for them for the foreseeable future. They sustained heat casualties, but nothing so life-altering that it would be catastrophic and would prevent them from moving forward. The soldiers and leadership from Bravo Battery had learned valuable lessons that would carry them forward throughout the deployment. Lessons that would be lifesaving and help ensure they would be prepared the next time they encountered an enemy attack. Once they settled in back at COP Tynes, several men from Two Charlie, including Gerhart, Lachance, and Knollinger, provided the command team with a back brief known as an after-action review. Most of the topics brought up were relatively simple fixes for the troops.

When First Sergeant Banister and Captain Ward asked Gerhart about some of their observations, Gerhart, not one to hold back, chose to take the gloves off.

He said, "Well, First Sergeant, I'll start with proper hydration. When we were out in the furrows, we noticed some guys had energy drinks in their assault packs. Proper inspections by leaders would prevent that."

"I can agree with that," Banister replied. "They were also getting on the ground and may still have had some of that stuff in their bags."

"Your guys need to work on patrolling," Gerhart continued. "I understand they aren't infantrymen, and y'all were dropped into this mission, and it'll take time, but time isn't something you have. They need to work on spacing, and team leaders need to do better at inspecting equipment to ensure that soldiers have ammunition taken out of ammo cans."

"We didn't get the time we needed to prepare for this fight, as this is not a COIN fight," Banister argued. "We'll keep at it, and I have confidence our Smokes will train them to patrol."

"Lastly, First Sergeant, this isn't a walk in the park, and your men shouldn't treat it as such. If they do, you'll lose a lot of your guys."

"Look, I don't like your condescending attitude," retorted Banister. "I understand that we are not an infantry unit, and I also understand that we will probably take casualties. However, don't count us out. We are a fighting force and won't disappoint anyone."

With that, they concluded their meeting, and the men from Two Charlie knew the fight in the Arghandab was no longer theirs. The artillerymen would now have to embrace the terrain, the heat, and all that accompanies the Arghandab. As they began transitioning all their equipment and signing over the property to the Bulls, the men of Two Charlie felt relieved they were finally done with the fields that had taken so much from them. Just before leaving for the final time, they received a message for Farnsworth on the SIPRNet. He needed to contact First Sergeant Gondek. As Farnsworth went into the TOC for the last time, he called over the satellite phone with those inside the TOC attempting to listen to what was being said. It was apparent the happiness on Farnsworth's face from seconds before was now gone. Having just walked away from a celebration with Two Charlie a moment before made Farnsworth's call even more tragic. He retreated to the southernmost area of COP Tynes to brief the men on the details of his conversation. They were all still joyous because they were getting ready to leave.

Farnsworth said, "Guys, please settle down."

With a tremble in his voice, Farnsworth said, "Guys, Moon didn't make it. He passed away today in Germany of septic shock. Moon's body developed an infection that he could not shake, and he is gone."

It was like life had been pulled from the area in an instant. Shortly after his announcement, the desert heat of the Arghandab was still, and a calming breeze came through it. It was quiet, almost eerie. Christopher Moon could've been among his men at that moment, giving them peace and relief from the chaos. Once again, even as their deployment clock was ending, victory was being pulled away from Two Charlie just as they thought they had finally had a victory. Their mantra had come to be "The Valley Always Wins." Once again, the valley had seemingly proved it right.

It may not have seemed like it at that moment, but Two Charlie had just set in motion something no other unit had accomplished in the history of the Arghandab River Valley. Units were known to come into the valley and continue to patrol on the north side of the first canal and end up with catastrophic IEDs hitting their vehicles, or they would patrol in the orchards and lose the battle due to casualties. The operation conducted with the men from One Bravo may have often been dire to the men of Two Charlie. However, the lessons learned would catapult the Top Guns in future operations. Where the infantry units of the past had continued to fail was that they were unable to seize and hold ground from the Taliban. There were plans from the brigade and battalion command teams that would change the course of the entire deployment for the Top Guns. Nothing in combat comes without a cost. However, having the ability to inflict more casualties on the enemy and taking their killing fields away from them was the victory Two Charlie had long sought. They would never see it firsthand, but that was the gift the men of Bravo Battery and the Top Guns were fighting to give to them.

CHAPTER 4

The Alamo (COP Nolen)

Wars have never hurt anybody except the people who die.

SALVADOR DALI

After arriving at Combat Outpost (COP) Nolen, soldiers of Alpha Battery were getting a firsthand look at what lay ahead for them over the next 12 months. They felt the 82nd Airborne paratroopers had encountered their share of mayhem in the Arghandab and were unwilling to venture outside the wire. As a result, First Sergeant Hartlaub and his counterpart from the 82nd got into a heated disagreement. The 82nd soldiers were preparing to leave, and their first sergeant didn't want to jeopardize his men's lives, so Alpha Battery was informed the 82nd would no longer be patrolling outside of COP Nolen.

Sergeant Wilke was one of the first to arrive at COP Nolen. He was perplexed why the outpost ran straight into the pomegranate orchards. To him, it appeared there was zero standoff between enemy fighters and the outside perimeter. Nonetheless, it was time to get their hands dirty. Alpha Battery's few patrols with the 82nd were insignificant; the men learned little to nothing about their new area of responsibility or what it would be like to combat a faceless enemy. Unlike Bravo Battery, who were lucky enough to have the Two Charlie soldiers accompany them to their sector to explain the area of operation (AO), Alpha would have to discover their AO for themselves. Though every relief in place is different, Bravo had entered their area with Two Charlie, crossed the canals, entered the orchards, and battled alongside the 82nd. Wilke understood that circumstances must have been worse than imagined when one of the 82nd soldiers ingested glass to avoid walking beyond the Hesco barriers again. The soldier was later placed on a medevac and received what he desired when he was transported to Kandahar, but he did not return to Nolen. Alpha Battery recognized from that desperate action that they were entering a world of misery.

The attacks against the Strike men soon started to accumulate. Just north of COP Nolen, enemy fighters ambushed Captain Thomasson, the Alpha Battery commander, and his patrol while navigating the orchards. Thomasson sustained several injuries from small-weapons fire. He moved his element forward despite his wounds, forcing the enemy fighters back into the grape furrows. The enemy was unaware Sergeant Major White, the acting brigade command sergeant major and his personal security detail (PSD) were trying to flank the fighters on the other side. The PSD team flanked the enemy while Thomasson's element continued to engage. The five-man PSD team, however, discovered they were pinned down and in a tight spot. This gave Thomasson more time to defeat the enemy fighters. White could adapt to the situation and refocus his team's fires, so most of their efforts were focused on those engaging his unit. After a short spurt, enemy fighters were forced to break contact as the Alpha element's superior firepower proved too much. Thomasson's element kept repelling them from Route Phillies back into the orchards. It was later identified that Route Phillies had become a hotbed for pressure-plate improvised explosive devices (IED), which had quickly become the preferred method of engagement for the Taliban. Putting explosives on expected paths American forces would either patrol or drive on allowed enemy fighters plenty of time to place the devices and flee without coming into direct contact. The following day, on June 29, 2010, Staff Sergeant Mosley, a soldier assigned to Alpha Battery from 3rd Battalion, 44 Psychological Operations, was also part of a patrol that encountered the same enemy fighters who had fought the Bravo Soldiers at Building 666. The battalion command team swiftly saw the necessity to stop the bleeding on Nolen's eastern flank. At this point, Bravo Battery, and now Alpha Battery, encountered fighters daily. Most of the fighting occurred near Khosrow Solfa, just south of the intersection of Route Highlife and the second canal crossing on Route Mariners. When Alpha was attacked, Mosley received multiple wounds after the patrol was hit by a rocket-propelled grenade (RPG).

The Fourth of July, Independence Day, is one of the most widely observed holidays in the United States, which far too many Americans take for granted. As Staff Sergeant Zavala arrived at COP Nolen for the first time, he thought about how ironic it was that he arrived on July 4. Americans frequently celebrate their independence without thinking about the lyrics of their national anthem and the impact they have had on military heroes over time—"And the rockets' red glare, the bombs bursting in air." When arriving at COP Nolen, it appeared to be a Fourth of July debacle. Zavala had seen his Alpha Battery brothers in close-quarters contact; the pomegranate orchards gave the Americans in the Arghandab minimal, if any, margin for error. Soldiers couldn't leave COP Nolen for even 50 meters without encountering hostile combatants.

The soldiers inside the COP Nolen towers were also exposed. The towers had little or no netting to help disguise the occupants, leaving them exposed most of the time. Sandbags were used to fortify the front of the towers, shielding them from potential frontal attacks, but ultimately, they were targets in the open.

On Route Phillies, one of the first convoys to leave COP Nolen was destroyed by a raging inferno. The patrol was supposed to deliver soldiers and a few media members to COP Terra Nova. When the MATVs (mine-resistant, ambush-protected all-terrain vehicles) in the convoy started moving toward Terra Nova, they reached the exact location on Route Phillies where Two Charlie's Platoon Sergeant Santos had been killed. The first IED of the Top Guns' deployment struck the convoy as the MATVs were passing under the stone irrigation bridge that crossed over the first canal.

Staff Sergeant Robertson was one of the battery's most humble leaders. He earned the respect of the men with his leadership style and willingness to go above and beyond to assist his subordinates. Robertson had vast artillery experience but was still adjusting to the battery's new routine as provisional infantrymen. He had chosen to be the vehicle's driver because he believed he had more significant experience and that being the first in the convoy made them more likely to be hit. Because Alpha was the new kid on the block, he assumed the Taliban were keeping an eye on their movements.

Robertson had combat experience in Iraq and believed that, if attacked, he would be better prepared than others. He was brilliant and one of few enlisted men in the battery who could boast of having a college degree; he chose to share this information with a select few and urge others to further their education. Most people were puzzled why he hadn't been commissioned, but Robertson enjoyed the laborious mindset of being an enlisted soldier.

Sergeant Milton was the truck commander with Robertson in the MATV. Milton was essentially just there for the ride during this movement, but it turned out to be one he would remember. Robertson and Milton's vehicle had a resupply of ammunition for COP Nolen. Their load would ultimately turn into an inferno. When the MATV struck the IED, the explosion hit with such violent fury that it sent the truck flying into the air, throwing Robertson and Milton about inside the vehicle. Robertson suffered a violent blow to his head, an injured shoulder, and a compressed spine. Because of the heavy loads soldiers must carry daily in the field, these kinds of injuries can have detrimental, long-lasting impacts on them throughout their lives. Additionally, they can have long-term neurological effects on troops throughout their lifetimes.

"Milton, are you good?"

"Not really, but as good as I can be."

"Bro, everything hurts. What about you?"

"Same here, Rob. Can you move?"

"Even if I couldn't, I'd find a way to get out of this truck."

"I hear people around us; let's try and get the fuck out of here."

"Let's go, little brother, let's go."

Security elements arrived and began assisting with removing personnel from the vehicles. Staff Sergeants McClain and Blythe were hauling soldiers out of the flaming wreckage. Captain Cabebe tried to make sense of the turmoil that had just broken out as he watched the MATV burn. The injured were tended to as quickly as possible. Although there were only minor injuries sustained by the soldiers of Alpha Battery and the reporters embedded with them, the IED had succeeded in one respect. Due to some of the battery leaders questioning whether they were prepared for the battle ahead, it had a monumental impact on their organization. One thing unites soldiers: their bond is nearly unbreakable due to their shared struggles. The Alpha soldiers were now struggling to gain traction. Enemy fighters had forged a link between themselves that would make them more resilient as warfighters and greatly enhance their mission capabilities in the future.

The soldiers of Alpha Battery were only a few days into their deployment and were already in daily contact with enemy fighters. Engagements with a faceless enemy were an almost expected occurrence for the men. It often felt as though COP Nolen was turning into the Alamo. Much like the men of Two Charlie had been concerned regarding the threat of enemy fighters setting in IEDs because they had been stagnant in Building 666, the 82nd soldiers at COP Nolen hadn't been active before the 101st arrived; ultimately, it provided the same luxury for the enemy fighters, who engaged the towers daily with harassing fire and the occasional RPG. The men of Alpha believed it was only a matter of time before their luck would run out.

CHAPTER 5

Luck Always Runs Out

> The brave die never, though they sleep in dust: Their courage nerves a thousand living men.
>
> MINOT J. SAVAGE

Falling in on their area of operation during the height of the fighting season was no easy task. The soldiers of Alpha Battery were struggling to acclimate to the sweltering heat and had already encountered their first improvised explosive device (IED). They'd witnessed several leaders hurt and one of their MATVs (mine-resistant, ambush-protected all-terrain vehicle) destroyed. Although a field artillery battalion by definition, no one in the unit was planning to lay down and die simply because they had been given another infantry deployment. Alpha had experienced previous infantry rotations. The battery had done a variety of infantry operations in the past, none of them a standard infantry assignment. Also, none were conducted among pomegranate orchards, grape furrows, and canals.

On July 9, 2010, Nūr Muhammad Kolache (NMK), a village south of Combat Outpost (COP) Nolen, was to be visited for the first time. NMK offered excellent opportunities to attack the troops of Alpha Battery and could play host to Taliban fighters. There were plenty of pomegranate orchards, grape furrows, and open fields between COP Nolen and NMK that would expose the Alpha men to attack. Given this was their first patrol into NMK, it's possible they had the element of surprise over the Taliban. Enemy fighters probed their perimeter regularly with harassing fire, but there was nothing substantial to mention. The men returned from the patrol and ate bland MREs (meal, ready to eat) in their "club," "McPattersons." The 82nd men had created McPattersons partly as an aesthetic addition to their dining facility and as a means of safeguarding the food and keeping the soldiers out of the elements as they ate. While the dinner was not particularly noteworthy, it was a minor, albeit fleeting, win in the Arghandab, and any triumph is better than none.

After spending six days on the ground, Staff Sergeant Zavala had ample opportunities to make numerous observations. Fast forward one day to July 10. Zavala had heard the cracking sounds of the Arghandab and seen the fields firsthand. Nolen was about a thousand meters away from NMK. It could take up to four hours for troops to cover a thousand meters on patrol in the Arghandab if they encountered IEDs or small-weapons fire. Without coming across an IED or enemy fighters, the members of Three Alpha managed to make their way to NMK. Soon after the soldiers positioned themselves within NMK and established rooftop security, they began to encounter probing fire, much like the One Bravo soldiers encountered at Building 666.

The intensity of the attacks soon increased, almost as if Three Alpha had discovered something meaningful to the enemy fighters. More soldiers moved to the rooftops as fighters positioned themselves with AK-47s and PKM machine guns in the orchards and started to fire more aggressively. Zavala and Private First Class Grata were on the rooftop, keeping NMK secure. The soldiers on the rooftop had been receiving instruction from Zavala, directing the location of their fires. After several hours, Zavala and Grata were relieved for a quick bite. Not long after stepping off the roof, a thunderclap was heard in the distance, although nobody paid much attention. A moment later, the building the security was positioned on took a direct strike from a 60-millimeter mortar round, which was so fast that its whistling sound was almost indistinguishable as it flew past. A hole was blown in the roof with a tremendous "BOOM." Shrapnel from the explosion of the mortar round was hurled both inside and outside the building. This was unlike the usual mortar volley fired by enemy fighters in the area; in the past, they missed their target. Zavala and Grata lay wounded and unconscious. Although they were only momentarily rendered unconscious, as they gathered their composure, they were beginning to realize all hell had broken out in NMK. Rocket-propelled grenades (RPG) soared wildly overhead, and AK-47 and PKM bullets were landing with precision. It was starting to seem like a battle for survival at NMK. Though they hadn't personally encountered it, the guys had heard tales from the 82nd about the hostile fighters' aggression. As the members of Three Alpha faced the possibility of being surrounded by this unrelenting enemy, their confidence grew. They were up against seasoned Taliban fighters who couldn't push them out of NMK. The fact that none of the men from Three Alpha were willing to give up ground and that they were standing together against an enemy who was more knowledgeable about the terrain and more equipped to fight in the Arghandab River Valley than they were giving them strength from one another.

A quick-reaction force (QRF) element was simultaneously spun up at COP Nolen. An infantry squad was assigned to every battery in the battalion. Staff Sergeant Strickland's squad was assigned to Alpha to support the field artillerymen with patrolling and any other tasks they might encounter in the Arghandab. As a QRF element, Strickland was deployed with the remainder of his squad to try to flank the enemy. The team's progress toward NMK was significantly hindered as they navigated the grape furrows and orchards.

The element ran straight into a group of enemy fighters as it approached a set of furrows. Several men were almost killed by enemy gunfire during the opening exchange. An enemy fighter was getting ready to launch an RPG as the Americans tried in vain to stop him. RPGs have historically been used against soft-skinned and armored vehicles. The soldiers were only a short distance away when this RPG was fired; it had a devastating effect on the vineyard walls behind them. Strickland suffered injuries and a concussion, but amazingly, he was not struck by any shrapnel. Some soldiers were hit by dirt as the remaining members of the QRF battled valiantly to stave off the enemy attack. It seemed like forever from the time the RPG was fired until the soldiers gained fire superiority, but the enemy eventually broke contact. With the men covered in sweat; and having been peppered by flying debris, they finally had the chance to identify the injuries sustained. Stunningly, none of the men had been hit by any of the enemy rounds or the RPG, but Strickland had been knocked unconscious during the altercation. Enemy fighters, having run out of ammunition or deciding to live to fight another day, decided to dissolve into the orchards like the ghosts of the Arghandab that they were. There was little to no doubt the Americans would be fighting these men again soon. Zavala, Grata, and Strickland were going to require a medevac due to all being knocked unconscious. They were taken to Kandahar for traumatic brain injury assessment.

It was July 12, and the QRF was again leaving COP Nolen because troops were in contact. They had just learned their first squad had sustained a casualty. Specialist Gatson had initiated a pressure-plate IED. Gatson, a well-respected member of the Alpha Battery family, was well known for his positive attitude that lifted the spirits of the platoon despite whatever craziness they found themselves in. He went above and beyond, but now it was time for his brothers to save him. When the blast went off, Specialists Torres, Persaud, and Pelayo were still on the opposite side of the mud wall that separated the patrol, preparing to cross over with the rest of the section. Despite this, when the device detonated, Persaud and Torres were knocked unconscious, along with several other men from One Alpha. Pelayo was the first to come to his feet; Torres and Persaud were buried under the rubble of the wall. Pelayo pulled the mud wall from on top of Torres and, as he slowly regained consciousness, Torres looked around, his ears ringing and his vision cloudy; he could see dirt and debris falling all around. It felt like a scene from a movie. "There's no way this shit is real," he thought to himself. "There's no way I'm here in this shit." Then, the tunnel vision faded, and he noticed Persaud was still down. Instantly, the ringing stopped, Gatson's intense screams echoed across the field, and he knew this wasn't a scene in a movie; this was real, and he needed to fucking react. When he stood up, he saw Gatson on the ground, lying in a pool of blood. He was missing his left leg as the blast had shredded it; only a portion of his quadricep, torn and frayed and riddled with dirt and debris, remained. He was left with his right leg, but it had been severely damaged and was now reduced to sharp, broken bone fragments and mangled flesh. His hands had suffered too, with a partially amputated thumb and an injury to his index finger in which the flesh and skin had been peeled from the bone. If the men were to save him, they needed to work fast. Gatson was fighting for his life and had only been in the country for a short time.

"This shit fucking hurts, man, fucking help me!" Gatson said.

"I got you, man, just hang on, I got you," Torres replied.

Despite the catastrophic explosion, Gatson was still holding firm. He was in agonizing pain and had suffered an extreme loss of blood, but he was still holding it together. Their platoon sergeant, Sergeant First Class Reese, having been on the same side of the wall as Gatson and despite having been knocked back and hit by shrapnel, was trying to direct personnel into security.

"Persaud, let's fucking go. I need your help!" Torres yelled.

"I'm coming, man!"

Both men, fully aware of the situation and the severity of Gatson's injuries, realized time was of the essence, and they could no longer wait.

"Do we have any morphine?" Torres yelled at Reese.

"No, we don't have any morphine. Get your tourniquets and start applying double tourniquets on him. Pelayo, let's fucking go, man. We need your help to get across the fucking wall!"

Gatson had already lost a ton of blood, and the fact that he was in agonizing pain was torture for the soldiers.

Torres had followed Reese's instruction. "Persaud, I'll throw a tourniquet on this leg; you get the other one; put that shit fucking tight! FUCKING TIGHT!"

"I'm so fucking thirsty, man," said Gatson. "I need water. Please give me some water."

"You know I got you. I froze this shit last night. It's ice cold, man, drink it slow. I told you before I got you."

The men applied double tourniquets to each of his limbs to preserve what they could. They applied pressure dressings to what was remaining of his damaged flesh. They continued doing everything to ensure he would be okay. The reality of war, however, is that they had no way of knowing. Gatson was temporarily stabilized, but they didn't have time to waste. They needed to get him on a bird. They didn't have a litter, so they were forced to carry him to the pickup zone.

Torres said, "Gatson, look, man, this shit is going to fucking hurt. We're going to get you there as quick as we can; you're just going to have to hold on to us."

"I need some more water," Gatson said, having drained Torres's.

"Smoke Reese replied, "Here, man."

"Come on, Smoke, I don't want that hot shit. Where is Torres with his frigid water?"

"I got you," Torres said.

"Well, fuck me, I guess," Smoke said. "Gatson, the bird is coming. Just hang on a little longer, and they will take good care of you when they get here."

Fatigue started to set in as the soldiers began lugging Gatson to the medevac, the weight of his body almost certainly wearing them out. It was becoming nearly impossible for Persaud to look away from the wreckage that was Gatson's legs. On the journey to the helicopter, Persaud slipped multiple times, almost dumping Gatson, and caused his foot to encounter the ground, which left his limb in severe pain.

Gatson screamed. "Motherfucking Persaud, pick my fucking leg up, man, FUCK!"

Persaud was exhausted and fighting back, passing out either from his injuries or other factors.

First Sergeant Hartlaub took over for Persaud to prevent him from injuring Gatson further.

"Don't drop me, fuckers. I've got enough shit going on!"

As Torres, Reese, Pelayo, and Hartlaub carried Gatson, they were all covered in his blood. They were exhausted from the ordeal.

"How long until they get here?" Gatson asked.

"Let me radio the pilots," said Reese. He sighed and said, "Gatson, they said about twenty minutes."

"Man, fuck, call them back and tell them it's me, and see if they'll speed it up."

When Reese was initially calling in the nine-line to get Gatson out of the Arghandab, a QRF element consisting of Staff Sergeant Malin and Sergeant Richards was also being assembled. Richards and Malin were moving with fury to get to the element with their reinforcements. En route, they were forced to halt. Their point man, Private First Class Kent, had a terrible feeling about continuing forward due to the safety of their element.

"Sergeant Richards, the road looks like someone has been messing with it."

"Let me get Malin to take a closer look."

Malin left to assess what his point man was telling him. On his way, he initiated another pressure plate, sending shrapnel, dirt, and dust flying in all directions. Malin was one of the most seasoned veterans of the Alpha men and had been with the 1-320th on the deployment to Taji, Iraq. His soldiers trusted him and would follow him anywhere. They knew he was experienced and had proven his resolve—they put their faith in him. Malin was in excruciating pain and struggling to contain the adrenaline running through his body. Richards sprinted up to begin rendering aid.

"Let's go! We need to put tourniquets on his legs now to stabilize him."

Richards's initial diagnosis was that Malin was going to be a double amputee, with both legs severely damaged above the knee. With the help of a few others, Richards did all he could and applied tourniquets to Malin's limbs. Seeing one of their respected leaders in such an unspeakable state was heart wrenching for the men.

"BREAK, BREAK, BREAK, NINE-LINE FOLLOWS!"

This was the cue for all radio traffic on the net to cease immediately. A nine-line was being sent up, indicating something serious had happened. After Richards completed calling up the nine-line to get Malin to Kandahar Airfield (KAF), he hoped he could get the Black Hawk that secured Gatson to turn around.

Richards radioed, "Longknife, Rock Hard Two Two Bravo. Can you turn around? We have a Litter Urgent casualty over."

Longknife replied, "Rock Hard Two Two Bravo, Longknife. That's a negative, we are already inbound to KAF."

"Longknife, Rock Hard Two Two Bravo. You are already in the air. The time it takes to get another bird in the air will only delay his care. Can you not get our casualty? They are urgent, over!"

"Rock Hard Two Two Bravo, Longknife, negative. You're not the only troops in contact, and we can't turn around. There will be another medevac inbound to pick up your casualty shortly."

"Longknife, Rock Hard Two Two Bravo. Roger. Thanks."

A hot landing zone (HLZ) had to be quickly set up. The soldiers placed Malin on the litter to transport him. They began setting up their security perimeter around the HLZ for the Black Hawk to land; they made sure each man knew he needed to provide talking guns for the mad minute as the Black Hawk began their decent to attempt to pick up "Smoke" Malin. M240s on adjacent areas of the field began alternating their rates of fire. This method of "talking guns" would keep the enemy fighters honest at a minimum for a short while and would help keep the enemy fighters' heads down, preventing them from shooting down the medevac. As the Black Hawk landed, the aid and litter team swiftly moved Malin under the cover of fire; after getting him out of harm's way, the remainder of One Alpha attempted to reset the patrol to continue the mission. As the men tried to settle their nerves, it was highly probable they would have to return to base sooner rather than later to regroup.

Reese and 1st Lieutenant Black were the leaders on the ground for One Alpha. While the men tried to settle their nerves, the patrol reconsolidated, cross-loaded ammunition, and ensured everyone had water. This would, at the very least, ensure everyone could make it back to COP Nolen. As noncommissioned officers (NCOs) accounted for all sensitive items and personnel, the patrol began preparing to push forward again.

Black radioed, "Rock Hard Main, Rock Hard One Six. We are continuing with the mission."

The patrol prepared to move out. The QRF element, including Kent, who had come into the fields to assist the troops in contact, stood up, and immediately, another IED was initiated; the blast shook the earth beneath their feet and knocked several of the men on their backs. The explosion from an IED isn't something one can train for. It's an unbelievable force that hits with energy that, at best, will take your breath away and, at worst, leave you lying in a pool of blood, dead.

Some of the men were unable to react due to being disoriented; others were knocked unconscious. This put the element in a compromised position, as very few could respond quickly or effectively. The patrol still hadn't maneuvered very far from COP Nolen and had now hit their third IED of the day. Team and squad leaders quickly worked to account for their men over the radio. A cry was heard across the field.

"MEDIC!"

Kent was down; he became the first triple amputee from Alpha, losing both of his legs and part of his hand. Sergeant Richards, "Doc" Russ; and several others were in the immediate vicinity and quickly began rendering aid to Kent, who was in grave danger. His body was much like Malin's: it was peppered with shrapnel, but above that, attempting to prevent infection due to the environment was getting increasingly more difficult. Tourniquets, pressure dressings, and other lifesaving measures were furiously applied. Another nine-line was called up; luckily for him, the Black Hawk carrying Malin was still close by. This time, they successfully got it to turn around. Once One Alpha got Kent off the HLZ, the survivors regrouped and returned to COP Nolen. They managed to navigate through the IED-laden fields on the way back to the COP, but it was now becoming the concern of several NCOs as to whether they had enough men to complete their mission.

Two days had passed for the men at COP Nolen. Two days doesn't seem much, but for those in the Arghandab, two days might as well be two months. It was July 14, and the soldiers enjoyed one of the most remarkable days since their arrival. It was 108° Fahrenheit, cooler than it had been on most days. Life in the Arghandab had started becoming repetitive for some soldiers who were part of the initial push to COP Nolen, but in no way were they becoming complacent. It was becoming standard data that after Fajr, the morning prayer, at approximately 5:45, radio traffic on the ICOM would be picked up by the interpreters. Fajr takes place at the time of dawn before the sunrise prayer call. Muslims can pray the Ishraq prayer, also called Duha, when the sun rises. This is usually between 8:30 and 9:30 am. This was generally when enemy fighters would begin probing the compound with small-arms fire. It was common for the towers to be engaged not long after assuming their shifts. The crude towers left behind for Alpha Battery would often be littered with shell casings from ammunition the men had fired into the pomegranate orchards.

Throughout the day, Alpha pushed out patrols to keep a presence in their new area of operation. They patrolled in the wildly long grass that stood up to six feet at some points. They snaked through the fields so as not to present an easy target for Taliban fighters. The grass provided plenty of concealment, and they could've walked up to the rear of any compound they wanted and gone unnoticed. They ventured into the orchards and sat in overwatch positions, but the patrols were uneventful. Following each patrol, the guys returned to

Nolen, their sleeping quarters, and their protected area. Given Alpha's recent history at Nolen, quiet patrols were viewed favorably. So much had happened in a short period, and it was hard not to be impressed by the resilience of the soldiers. They had assisted in potentially saving three of their brothers who were hit by IEDs that could have decimated a vehicle.

The men had eagerly awaited the end of the blackout so they could finally reconnect with their relatives back home. For the soldiers, and even more for their families, any time a blackout happened was unnerving. Deployments are stressful times for family members. When they are unable to communicate with their soldiers, it's even more challenging. Communication blackouts are enabled so proper channels can be notified in the event of a soldier's death. The MWR (morale, welfare, and recreation) was placed in a plywood structure that met up with a mud wall. While this may not have been the best internet café they'd experienced in their short lives, it was the best they had experienced in the Arghandab.

The men pulling guard in the towers at COP Nolen were getting to experience the sweltering heat and how it amplified with their gear on. Every man's life was in their hands each time they positioned themselves in the towers. The towers consisted of plywood and 2×4s, fortified with sandbags, but were otherwise very rudimentary. They were in serious need of refurbishment, but until the supplies arrived, they would make do with what they had. The men of Alpha had been on their own and away from the 82nd for only a few days. Leadership focused their attention on the safety of their men in the orchards, ensuring they had enough litters, tourniquets, and medical supplies. First Sergeant Hartlaub and Captain Thomasson were figuring out what supplies were needed around COP Nolen to make the men in the towers more secure and the COP more secure overall. Sergeant Wilke had just changed out and transferred the authority of sergeant of the guard (SOG) to Sergeant Richards. SOG ensures the proper protection of troops and equipment and is essential to maintaining a secure and safe perimeter for an outpost. Before entering the towers, Richards checked with his guards to ensure they were adequately equipped for their duty. He then sent the men to their respective towers. Those stationed in the towers had radios to communicate incidents within their designated areas. Private First Class King was in Tower Three on the southeast corner with the Mk 19 grenade launcher. He was positioned facing the orchards. He had a casualty producing and had minimum standoff from the enemy. He had a casualty-producing weapon that could range up to 2,212 meters into the orchards if necessary. Private First Class Descoline was in Tower Two on the southwest corner with the 240B machine gun, surrounded by orchards, and had the village of NMK within striking range. Sergeant Torres was in Tower One on the northeast corner with the M2 .50-caliber machine gun; he had a more open field of fire to inflict more damage on anyone attempting to approach Nolen. As the furious sun began setting in the Afghan sky, the towers were finally getting relief from the heat. As the sun faded away, the silhouette of the men blended with their surroundings more.

CRACK!

Heard throughout COP Nolen, Richards initially thought it was a bottle in the burn pit that had busted, then concern it was possibly a single shot grew.

"Tower One, SOG, radio check, over!"

Torres replied, "SOG, Tower One, read you, Lima Charlie, over!"

"Tower Two, SOG, radio check, over!"

Descoline replied, "SOG, Tower Two, read you, Lima Charlie, over!"

"Tower Three, SOG, radio check, over!"

"Tower Three, SOG, RADIO CHECK, OVER!"

Descoline and King were the best of friends and rarely seen apart; not hearing his brother respond was excruciating. Richards ran from his rooftop perch to where Tower Three stood. He found King dead on the floor of the tower—in a pool of blood, brain matter, and bone pieces—after being shot in the head.

"MEDIC!"

As everyone hurried up to the tower, it was discovered King had been shot by a sniper, who had hit him just below his helmet. The shot was precisely placed; he was killed instantly.

"He's gone, let's get him down," "Doc" Russ said.

"Sergeant Richards, I'll pull guard for King," Private First Class Mendiola said.

"Mendi, look, I'll cut open a sandbag and pour it on the floor; so you don't slide all over the place," Wilke offered.

"Thank you, I appreciate it. If this motherfucker comes out, I'll get his ass."

Mendiola would be standing guard in blood until the sun came up, enduring its metallic smell as he scanned for the sniper with his M4 while trying to redeem his buddy. Following King's death, the brigade commander visited Nolen and Tynes to assess their defense situation. The battery and battalion command teams were forced to adjust and add mosquito netting.

The soldiers in the towers never received precisely placed sniper fire after that point.

CHAPTER 6

Battle for Bakersfield (COP Stout)

The only hope you have is to accept the fact that you're already dead. The sooner you accept that, the sooner you'll be able to function as a soldier is supposed to function: without mercy, without compassion, without remorse. All war depends upon it.

1ST LIEUTENANT RONALD SPEIRS, EASY COMPANY,
502ND PARACHUTE INFANTRY REGIMENT, 101ST AIRBORNE DIVISION

A few short weeks had passed since the troops of the Top Guns Battalion arrived in the Arghandab River Valley, a lifetime in those days. As impressive as the men from Two Charlie had painted the valley, it had already lived up to their hype. Though the battle was still in its early stages, the Top Guns were the piercing point of the 30,000-soldier advance expected to affect the counterinsurgency in Afghanistan significantly. The area still looked insurmountable. Combat Outpost (COP) Nolen was still in contact daily; they had lost several soldiers, including some of their seasoned leaders. COP Tynes had squads patrolling east, pushing the needle ever so gracefully toward Babur; and south toward the river, flooding the orchards and grape furrows with soldiers, but still had minimal success as they bogged down.

An overwatch position had been created in the grape furrows south of the second canal, where the One Bravo element set up their patrol. Sitting in the shadows in the furrows, they watched as some of the farmers went about their daily business, mowing fields, but they also watched as several fighters gathered to launch what seemed to be a concerted attack. The patrol was positioned around one hundred meters south of the small mud hut where the enemy fighters were operating while the One Bravo element remained hidden in the furrows. Staff Sergeant Fontenot had the Afghan interpreter, Nabil, translate what they were saying,

"Sir, they are planning to gather men to attack when patrols are in the fields eventually."

However, One Bravo intervened before the enemy fighters could round up enough soldiers. One of the rules of engagement that hindered the Top Guns was that an American soldier could not engage a Taliban fighter if he were not armed or an engaged combatant. Despite knowing the soldiers were mustering to attack a patrol leaving from either Nolen or Tynes, the men from One Bravo still weren't allowed to engage unless the enemy fighters had weapons on them.

Despite having little information, "Smoke" Tatro used his knowledge and judgment to make a wise choice. After conferring with Fontenot about whether Specialist Bibb possessed the BAT (Biometrics Automated Toolset) and HIIDE (Handheld Interagency Identity Detection Equipment) systems, he decided to stop the enemy fighters, take their photos, and enter them into the systems. The BAT and HIIDE systems allowed soldiers to identify if an enemy combatant had been previously detained by locating them through biometric information. The American soldiers had a database at their fingertips that could provide information such as whether someone was a high-value target, village elder, or imam. A retina scan was recorded and entered into a database alongside other data; a record of up to 45,000 people could be stored. Bibb was called forward since he had attended the course and learned to correctly enter locals into the system. They knew these men were fighters, whether they had weapons or not, and Nabil had given them vital information to enter into the database. They knew without a doubt they would run across these men again. The soldiers from One Bravo were compelled to let the Afghans go once Bibb entered them into the database, however, because they had no solid justification for keeping them in custody any longer.

"Smoke, I don't feel good about those guys," Bibb said.

"Bibb, neither do I, but we couldn't hold them."

"There needs to be something better. If we know these guys will turn around and attack us, then why do we have to let them go? That doesn't make any sense to me."

The One Bravo patrol had just departed the area when the Afghans left; fortunately, they had already picked up and moved from the position because, shortly after, indirect fire started falling from the sky on that exact position. Regardless, it was a violent show of force from the men in the fields; that the Americans had just set free, who took notice of their presence and their inability to engage.

As the patrol was getting ready to cross the first canal, Parker came to a point that looked like dark, thick mud; he explored the area, knowing the patrol could clean off once they entered the first canal. However, he had not encountered the typical mud of every other patrol. Parker had found a shit pond that led right into the first canal; and led the patrol right into it. The men found humor in the situation, with a few soldiers sounding off.

"Well, this is a shitty patrol," joked Bibb.

"We're up shit creek now, fellas," Specialist Cooper contributed.

"Hey, shut the fuck up," said Fontenot before continuing with "Parker, get us the fuck out of this shitty situation."

The men chuckled under their breath. While they entered the canal and were able to clean off their boots and pants, it was also a welcome opportunity to cool off.

After leaving the orchards, the patrol headed west to Terra Nova to resupply. Most of the time, especially if they were only going to Terra Nova, patrols out of Tynes collected supplies without needing vehicles. Assault bags were converted to transport food, mail, or other inbound supplies; soldiers were used as mules. On one such occasion, Sergeant Junkin had identified that Terra Nova had ice cream in their freezers. He procured a gallon of ice cream in such a way which could be returned to Tynes in a half-melted container to share with others. When it was later identified he had taken the ice cream, some of the battalion leaders were unhappy.

When the patrol arrived at Terra Nova, they discovered the battalion's compound was significantly more developed than COP Tynes. Terra Nova had massive towers around its perimeter, and it had complex structures throughout for the command teams to meet in, for the battalion tactical operations center, for sleeping quarters, and, hell, even their MWR (morale, welfare, and recreation) was set up like a true MWR. Some soldiers took a few minutes to attempt to say "hi" to loved ones on computers that weren't throwbacks to the Stone Age. The MWR at Terra Nova was in a large tent with tables and multiple computers that could be booked in time blocks. What was wild was that at COP Tynes, only about two thousand meters east of Terra Nova, Tynes; only had three computers that connected to the internet. The internet was mainly garbage since the Afghan National Army (ANA) usually ruined whatever chance of communication they had to get online by hanging their clothing on the equipment. At Terra Nova, they only needed to be patient and wait for the resident soldiers to finish their turn online.

While One Bravo enjoyed a break from reality, Fontenot was outside reconnecting with his old buddy, Sergeant Stout. At age twenty-five and from Texarkana, Texas, Stout met Fontenot in unusual circumstances when the latter first arrived at Fort Campbell. Stout had just endured a "freak accident" in which he suffered a broken jaw. They were both privates the first time the men met, and Fontenot had just gotten his barracks room. Some guys showed him around and introduced him to Casey and Stout. There was an abundance of drinking going on and some video play, and, in typical fashion, Stout tried to talk to Fontenot despite being heavily sedated and his mouth wired shut.

As Stout and Fontenot reconnected, Stout continued filling his magazines with 5.56-millimeter rounds and grabbed several high-explosive grenades to set in pouches. They talked about how the tempo was unbelievably fast throughout the area of operation and how Alpha Battery was still in the fight after taking hit after hit. The conversation then shifted to how HHB (Headquarters and Headquarters Battery) was progressing.

"Fonty, bro, honestly, I'm exhausted. We never have a chance to rest, and we are just jumping from one patrol to the next. If we don't slow down soon, someone is either going to die from the heat or die because they step on an IED. Either way, something bad is going to happen soon."

"Well, Stouty, let's hope that it's neither one of us, man. Look, bro, focus on your guys, one day at a time, one moment at a time, and we'll be home before you know it."

One Bravo was preparing to leave Terra Nova to return to Tynes, so the men said their goodbyes.

"Stout, be safe, bro."

"Stay angry, Fonty."

One Bravo stepped off for their movement back to COP Tynes through Jelawur and made a short stop in the town to do a key leader engagement. Captain Ward was big on interactions with locals, so the men tried to facilitate these meetings. If nothing else, it allowed them to get a pulse for the area. The problem with the pulse of the locals was they lied more times than not. They were fearful of the Taliban fighters as they threatened their families with death, threatened to rape their daughters, and threatened to kill their livestock if they helped the Americans at all. Therefore, the locals were seldom honest. After the short interaction, the patrol headed back to the sanctuary of COP Tynes. The men had an opportunity to improve their towers with netting, which provided concealment and more shade. They also fortified the towers with more sandbags to provide ample cover from the 7.62-millimeter ammunition enemy fighters used in their assault rifles.

It was the evening of July 29, a muggy night in the Arghandab. Everyone started looking forward to evenings simply because it wasn't as hot. Inside the mud walls at COP Tynes, it was dark, musky, and gloomy. The men had been patrolling nonstop, and the sun had beaten everyone into the ground. Tower One had just called down to the sergeant of the guard to let him know a patrol from HHB was entering the compound through the southwest entrance. Shortly after, Stout, along with Captain Shaffer and Sergeant First Class Lyons, were speaking with leadership to get information about what routes the Bravo patrols had taken previously. Ward and Shaffer talked in detail about what routes had been burned (to try to steer clear of those). One of the issues the Havoc (HHB) element was going to face was they would be heading into the same orchards and the same area where One Bravo had encountered the unarmed fighters a day earlier. As a founding member of Bravo Battery during the Operation *Iraqi Freedom* 2007–09 tour, Stout was reconnecting with old friends and conversing with Creighton, Fontenot, and the other Bulls soldiers. They told him to stay alert and to avoid the area of the field immediately within the second canal where they had already come across hostile fighters. The Bravo soldiers let Stout know they would be available at any time if they were needed.

While conducting their recon at the intersection of Routes Mariners and High Life, Shaffer and his Havoc element learned One Bravo had made heavy contact with the compound nearby during their relief-in-place (RIP) engagement with the Two Charlie men, and on the patrol a few days prior. Although the strategy wasn't entirely obvious when speaking with the Havoc leadership, the battalion wanted to seize that territory, clear it, hold it, and use it as an Afghan National Police checkpoint. Shaffer was advised by Bravo leadership that, while they would be happy to accompany him to the location to get eyes on the objective, reconning it at 3:00 or 4:00 am would be ideal; to account for the tactics and sleeping patterns of the Taliban. Bravo knew everything was terrible from 7:00 am to 4:00 pm, but recons, and local and national engagements; were usually suitable from 3:00 am until roughly 7:00 am. There was a high risk of improvised explosive devices (IED) and direct fire if engaging in combat between 4:00 and 8:00 pm but, other than that, nothing new would be learned. Shaffer decided not to continue the patrol for the rest of the night because he was happy with the intelligence the battery leadership supplied him.

Later, at the battalion command's request, Shaffer, Stout, and Lyon made a second trip to COP Tynes. Due to manpower constraints, COP Tynes lacked a quick-reaction force (QRF) element, so sending out a patrol would be extremely risky.

"Top Guns Main, this is Bulls Main, over."

"Bulls Main, Top Guns Main, send it."

"Top Guns Main, Bulls Main. We do not have the manpower to facilitate a QRF element for this patrol you are requesting."

"Bulls Main, Top Guns Main We acknowledge, but we must focus on the objective."

"Top Guns Main, Bulls Main. We also want to confirm that you know that air is red over."

"Bulls Main, Top Guns, Red air means it's pilots' discretion."

"Top Guns Main, Bulls Main, we just don't want to find out that these pilots' discretion is not to fly when we have guys with bullets in them over."

Knowing there was a very high chance this recon would go awry because of the time of the day it would take place, Captain Mark from Three Bravo leaped on the net, and 2nd Lieutenant Pantaleo got in the towers to try to control their machine-gun fires. It didn't take long for the patrol to step outside the main gate of COP Tynes before there was a notable increase in enemy radio chatter.

"They're coming, the Americans are coming right at us, we are almost set up," one Taliban fighter said.

A second fighter replied, "The ambush is ready. They're right in front of us."

The first rocket-propelled grenade (RPG) went off with a mighty "BOOM" as the patrol approached the first canal's grooves. Subsequently, two PKM machine guns fired at the Havoc element, around six hundred meters south of Tower Two. Bullets were striking COP Tynes, and RPGs were soaring as the gunners on the towers started to return fire in response to the enemy fighters' overflowing fire. After being thrown off his feet by an RPG that had struck the Hesco barrier, Pantaleo was desperately trying to recover control of the fires. The Afghan National Army (ANA) first sergeant arrived with a mounted Dushka heavy machine gun on a Ranger pick-up truck. Just as Pantaleo stood back up, the Dushka began firing. Only a few meters separated the massive Dushka from Pantaleo's face; he was knocked down again by a single concussion. The ANA was shooting into the fields mindlessly, having no idea where the American or Afghan forces were. Pantaleo got to his feet, realizing what had just happened, and threw his helmet at the ANA sergeant, knowing that both Havoc and Bulls friendlies were out there.

"This is the fucking second time this has happened. If you fire another shot without me fucking telling you that it's safe to shoot, I will fucking shoot you myself!"

The firefight continued for another 20 minutes until the Havoc element, and Shaffer eventually broke contact and returned to COP Tynes. Once everyone had safely returned to the wire, Mike, the Bulls interpreter, informed them of ICOM chatter as they debriefed.

"Enemy radio chatter is stating the Americans failed; we are going to set up more IEDs."

In the early hours of July 30, HHB and the 1st Kandak, ANA, began clearing a known Taliban enemy stronghold at the intersection of Routes Mariners and Highlife for a significant offensive known as Operation *Dragon Strike*. The area would later become known as "Objective Bakersfield." The battalion command team determined Bakersfield to be a critical site in the Arghandab because of its position. Bakersfield connected Nolen, Terra Nova, Tynes, and Jelawur. For years, Taliban insurgents had used this spot in the Arghandab as a critical piece of terrain in their battles with Russian and American forces. Seasoned fighters had discovered that Taliban fighters used this strategic position to create homemade explosives (HME). The Taliban could attract religious students from Afghanistan and Pakistan who were eager to arm themselves in the name of combating the West. The Arghandab, specifically Bakersfield, enabled Taliban insurgents to launch swift and successful coordinated attacks utilizing IEDs before disappearing into the orchards and furrows like ghosts.

Shaffer, Staff Sergeant Tivao, 1st Lieutenant Hopper, and Sergeant Naquin were members of the HHB assault unit that would enter the orchards early in the morning under cover of darkness. As the moon poured a dim blanket of light across the valley, the shadows from the pomegranate branches appeared to be arms reaching out to the HHB soldiers as they navigated through the orchard. As the assault element progressed south of Jelawur, grape furrows covered them, and the men disappeared behind mud barriers.

Despite having technology, it was getting increasingly difficult to track where guys were. Night-vision goggles are a great instrument, but using such technology in the orchards was nearly impossible due to the incredible maze of branches and lack of lighting, especially while attempting to cross the IED-infested minefields. Naquin, the first squad leader, would spearhead the opening advance into Bakersfield. He had patrolled in Iraq with HHB before, and his experience would be helpful here. Nobody anticipated how crucial this mission would be to their success in the Arghandab. Bakersfield would become a critical component and a watershed moment for the Top Guns.

Naquin, or "Cajun," was a young man from South Louisiana with a thick accent who brought with him leadership skills and a taste for crawfish boils that made him a favorite among the Top Guns. His squad was charged with being the lead element to breach into Bakersfield. Once inside, they were to establish a foothold to set the remainder of the clearance operation in motion. As Naquin and an ANA soldier descended into Bakersfield, they came across the mission's first IED. The ANA soldier experienced a once-in-a-lifetime panic, but he also achieved his first operational win when the IED failed to detonate. Though the men didn't always have luck, they were content to accept a victory when possible. They would need every soldier, Afghan or American, for this mission.

The men kept pushing into Bakersfield while attempting to take up a support-by-fire position. Just past the first canal, Naquin uncovered a second IED on Route Mariners while setting up the position. Underneath the IED was an 82-millimeter mortar. The results would have been disastrous if he hadn't found the IED the way he did. Naquin and his soldiers advanced the HHB element's whole entry point a few meters to the west. The issue with moving the entry point to the west was it changed the entire trajectory of the mission because each squad would have to adjust their entry. The unit's standard operating procedure for the operation was going to be that when an IED was found, the soldier that identified it would mark it with either a chem light or a VS-17 panel with a rock attached to it. Using identification techniques enabled the element to proceed and eventually arrange for the explosives ordnance disposal team to return to detonate the device. This would permit Stout and the second squad to pass through and Naquin and his men to set up security.

The difficult assignment of performing site exploitation in the compounds south of the first and second canals fell to the second squad, scheduled to arrive shortly after Naquin's men. These were the identical mud huts thought to be HME factories. With the IEDs discovered by the first squad, the second squad moved into the grape fields east of Route Mariners, placing Stout in the same area where One Bravo had found the enemy fighters the day before.

The first and second squads of 2nd Platoon were now in the orchards, the former set up in a support-by-fire position. Second Platoon, Havoc and Stout were moving along in their part of the clearance operation. Platoon sergeant Tivao and platoon leader Hopper were in the formation with them and assisting in any way necessary.

Tivao had transitioned to being an artilleryman from the infantry and was one of the very few artillery soldiers to have experience in combat as an actual infantry soldier. He and 2nd Platoon moved carefully through the fields. By this point in the fighting season, it was well known that the fields were heavily farmed, so the orchards were flooded, adding additional elements to the already chaotic operation. As the soldiers from 2nd Platoon remained vigilant despite the odds against them, it was hard not to get frustrated and attempt to find some dry land. However, they understood the issue with dry land in the Arghandab—it was often heavily seeded with IEDs. The longer the platoon remained in the area, the more it appeared they were in the depths of an IED minefield. Stout identified one and marked it with a VS-17 panel. He rerouted the second squad with Specialist Gilke around the IED to ensure none of his men accidentally set it off. Just northwest of his position, the Top Gun 6 personal security detail (PSD) was coming into the area to flood the orchards with soldiers. Tivao was nearby and could be heard yelling at Specialist Ritsema to put on his eye protection. One of the leaders from across the canal waved Specialist Stansbery across as Stansbery began navigating the thick mud wall near the first canal. As soon as he had cleared it, he landed directly on top of another IED.

BOOM!

"IED, IED, IED."

The IED went off with a storm of fury, sending Stansbery flying into the air. He was cut in half by the blast. Captain McGuigan, Specialist Sample, and young "Doc" Fontenot ran over with a litter to assist him but quickly realized they could do nothing. Stansbery had been killed instantly by the blast. Unknown to most of the soldiers across the battalion was that he had just arrived at Fort Campbell. When he requested to be stationed with the 101st, he unknowingly marked on his reenlistment paperwork that he would waive his dwell time. This meant he would be on the ground with the Top Guns as soon as he could be put on a plane to a combat zone. Upon finding this out, First Sergeant Brown made it a point to provide him with a four-day weekend to spend time with his family because the Top Guns were scheduled to leave shortly after, and the battalion wanted every man or woman with a pulse on those planes. The men did what they could to recover Stansbery's body and his sensitive items; and moved him to a casualty collection point where they would later call in a nine-line. Ritsema was also injured in the explosion when he received shrapnel to his face. He may have lost his eyesight if Tivao had not told him to put on his eye protection moments before. While fortunate not to lose his eyesight, he was later placed on a medevac.

Naquin was checking on his soldiers after the explosion to ensure no one had any second-order effects from the shock waves of the IED. At that point, enemy fighters began attacking from the south and west with small-arms fire. Minutes later, a complex ambush exploded in the orchards. The enemy fighters were utilizing the chaos from Stansbery's IED to regain the advantage. Naquin directed his squad's fire to suppress the enemy to the west while also attempting to control the attached ANA squad's fires. Controlling the ANA during a firefight was much more complicated than it would appear. Most barely spoke English, so voice commands were nearly obsolete; hand and arm signals played a critical role. While Naquin was directing the fire from his element, the men from the second squad were moving from west to east on the objective when another IED detonated. It was so fierce it shook the mud walls at COP Tynes a thousand meters away. The men at the outpost ran to the Hesco barriers only to see dirt and debris filling the air, not knowing what happened.

Stout set off the IED. It had caused irreparable harm to him, and he was struggling to hang on, fighting like a true warrior. He had lost both his legs, the remnants ending in torn flesh and shattered bone fragments. His right hand was gone, ending at his wrist, and he had suffered a deviated septum. Hopper was the first to get to Stout and rapidly assessed the situation. He began applying tourniquets and combat gauze and began coordination for medevac support. Tivao, now knowing a friend of his and one of his men was in harm's way, also ran out to assist. Despite the potential for secondary IEDs, several other men moved quickly to help. Hopper, Doc Fontenot, and Tivao were all rendering immediate aid to Stout when the relentless enemy tried to take advantage of another compromised scenario in which the HHB soldiers found themselves. Tivao directed 2nd Platoon's fires east of the objective toward Druia and Babur as enemy fighters began taking potshots at the soldiers helping Stout. They must have felt like they had the HHB element on the ropes with the two effective IEDs and were now executing a complex ambush. However, the HHB fighters were unwilling to give up any ground, knowing they would indeed be overrun if they did.

The medevac was on its way to get Stansbery and Stout. Tivao, Doc Fontenot, and Hopper were trying to keep Stout engaged to keep him from slipping into shock. The soldiers postured into security as the Black Hawk came down, prepared to conduct the mad minute.

"Smoke, make sure my guys get the fuck out of here," Stout implored.

"We will, Stout. Just hang on, bro."

The medevac landed, and the aid and litter teams loaded Stansbery and Stout onto the helicopter. They knew they had already lost Stansbery, and things looked bleak for Stout, but they did everything they could to help him. As the Black Hawk lifted out of Bakersfield, the men of HHB knew they would be in a battle for the foreseeable future.

As the men from COP Tynes looked on helplessly, all they wanted to do was help HHB in any way they could. Unfortunately, they could only wait for the word to move south. Although HHB had avoided stepping on further IEDs, they were still under constant enemy attack from both small-arms fire and mortars. The company fire team established a defensive perimeter on the south side of the objective, with dismounted soldiers and mounted weapons systems. Enemy fighters continued to attack the perimeters of the HHB security over and over with both small arms and RPGs. The determination of the HHB men continued to be their saving grace as they successfully repelled multiple attacks.

Master Sergeant Pittman was attached to the 1-320th as an advisor from the Asymmetric Warfare Group. He had retired from the 5th Special Forces Group out of Fort Campbell only a few months earlier and was eager to help the soldiers in the Arghandab. During the RIP with Two Charlie from the 82nd, he was in the element that was on the patrol when Specialist Moon was killed. He was also on the patrol initially when the men went down to Building 666. Pittman was originally with the men at COP Tynes but chose to realign himself with HHB, who were in contact with them in the fields south of the first canal. He understood he was a leader and a combat leader so; being a force multiplier, he moved into the fields with HHB to be an asset to the operation moving into Bakersfield. Pittman epitomized the value of selfless service; he positioned himself with Naquin's support-by-fire position and took up a spot on a mud wall as a rifleman to help assist where he could.

"Naquin, I'm no longer here to advise. I'm here to fight with you guys. Where do you need me?"

"Master Sergeant, I need to check on my guys. Just hang tight in my spot for a minute if you want to."

"Easy enough, man, check on your guys."

Naquin left to troop the line and check on his men. Pittman slid into Naquin's position to cover down on his sector to ensure there were no gaps in the security. A few seconds after he had replaced Naquin, Pittman was struck by a single round that hit him in his collar bone, ricocheted straight down, and struck near his heart. The men in the support-by-fire element immediately provided cover for Pittman while others provided aid. The men were positioned on the mud wall surrounding a primarily open area. While under enemy fire, Captain Haith, Doc Fontenot, and Private First Class Rosario chose to expose themselves for over 100 meters to get to where

Pittman had fallen. Rosario was the first to get to Pittman; upon arrival, he began providing assistance and was instantly alerted to the fact that Pittman had been hit by sniper fire. Rosario diligently worked to stop the bleeding without hesitation until more help got to him. He understood the immense danger he was under, as the sniper could now be targeting him, but he was willing to risk it. Once Doc Fontenot arrived, both men began vigorously working as enemy fire increased and RPGs flew overhead.

Haith called up the nine-line medevac request. Still, out of concern, the Black Hawk wouldn't be able to land due to the volume of enemy fire, so he bounded back across the open field to their initial starting point to set up a fortified defensive position. Upon reaching the Mk 19 grenade launcher, he focused its fury on the western compound wall to help secure a pick-up area.

The Black Hawk approached the hot landing zone (HLZ) as it began its descent, it was hit by an onslaught of enemy fire from the south, west, and east. The pilots had a near-fatal miss when the Black Hawk narrowly escaped an RPG that appeared to have the aircraft zeroed in. The men picked up the pace, trying to secure the HLZ and prevent the scenario from becoming even more extreme. Rosario and Fontenot, on several occasions, found themselves looking left and right as rounds impacted all around them as they attempted to get Pittman to the helicopter. However, the Black Hawk was still unable to land. The soldiers along the mud walls engaged the enemy fighters but could not get the incoming fire to diminish. The pilots were forced to land over a hundred meters from where the initial pick-up would have been. Rosario volunteered to help transport Pittman's litter to the helicopter. He understood every man on the aid and litter team would be exposed and vulnerable to enemy fire, but attempting to get Pittman on the medevac was paramount. Doc Fontenot took charge of moving Pittman's litter toward the HLZ. The young soldiers were defiant and determined to get him on the Black Hawk. Fontenot and Rosario took a knee in the middle of the field; as the medevac raced toward them, they were getting pummeled by dust, rocks, and debris from the fields. Rosario covered Pittman, shielding him from the fury of the rotors and incoming fire. With Fontenot, he ensured Pittman was quickly moved forward and secured in the helicopter. The pilots wasted no time lifting off due to the intense engagement and the amount of time it had taken just to be able to touch down. Shaffer had pulled Tivao and Naquin in and given them the unpleasant news that Stout had succumbed to his wounds at Kandahar Airfield (KAF). The leaders, not wanting to tell their men, knew it was their responsibility and the right thing to do. Naquin and Tivao returned to the platoon to pass on the sad news. The reality was that most of the men on the ground who had seen Stout already had a sense he might succumb to his wounds, but no one would admit it. Naquin and his support-by-fire team then moved to the southern security screen to hold off the enemy during resupply operations. Enemy fighters attempted to maneuver on Naquin's position, but his squad and ANA fighters continued to engage them with small-arms fire. The cracking sounds of machine-gun fire all around the area became part of the soldiers' backdrop; they were acclimated to the persistent threat and the constant intense engagements. During the time they were positioned in the southernmost sector, Naquin discovered another IED to the southeast of Bakersfield and narrowly prevented an ANA soldier from initiating it. It was a blessing to have narrowly escaped another IED, at least for today.

Once again, Shaffer knew his leadership would have to deliver unsettling news to the men on the ground after a long and grueling day of fighting. Despite this, he briefed the leadership of Pittman's death so they could alert the soldiers on the ground. As leadership alerted the men of Pittman's passing, a sense of dread came across their faces; despite the fear, however, there was also a sense of determination they would stand in defiance of the faceless enemy in the shadows of the orchards.

On July 31, Objective Bakersfield was officially renamed COP Stout; this was the beginning of a new era for the soldiers of HHB. While they had been enduring wave after wave of enemy attacks for the past few days, which included IEDs, small-arms fire, and RPGs, they were still standing strong. Early afternoon of the 31st, COP Stout began receiving accurate indirect fire from a 37-millimeter grenade launcher. The enemy had an immediate impact on this attack and inflicted four casualties. Hopper, 2nd Platoon's leader, exposed himself to enemy fire while calling in the nine-line and helping where he could treat the casualties. With little cover, COP Stout attempted to move the wounded to any fortified cover, imperative to their survival. While the noncommissioned officers were busy positioning soldiers in security positions that wouldn't leave them exposed to indirect fire, another mortar attack came in. Hopper was hit in the leg by shrapnel, subsequently performing self-aid on himself. The medevac bird initially requested had arrived; however, before Hopper climbed aboard, he ensured the other wounded were loaded first and that there were no additional casualties on the ground. With the Black Hawk climbing into the clear blue skies of the Arghandab en route to KAF, the soldiers of COP Stout continued holding their ground, anticipating reinforcements soon.

The battalion called in reinforcements after several heavier attacks from RPGs and small arms. Elements from COP Tynes began arriving in force, and an element from One Bravo was now postured with an ANA squad in a southern security position. Three Bravo was postured as an eastern element with their infantry squad attached to them behind Druia. They were conveniently positioned behind the Afghan graveyard that had been dug up over the years by jackals and wild dogs. Their position was set in at the entry point to the grape furrows. This position could cut off the entire northern side of the fields. The only way the enemy fighters would have access would be to come from the east because COP Nolen was covering the west. Two Bravo and Four Bravo would rotate in and out every 12 hours, so there were always fresh men in the fields. The Taliban fighters were slowly having the lifeblood squeezed out of them, and there was a sense they were beginning to get desperate and were going to attempt to do something big to make a move to regain their land. Sergeant First Class Tivao was sitting in gun positions he had identified in the wide-open fields south of Stout; he was tirelessly working to reposition his most casualty-producing weapons, but due to not having the proper equipment since their infill, he only had an E-tool with him. The E-tool, or entrenching tool, is a digging tool used by military forces for various purposes. However, it is small and makes a doable job difficult. Tivao had to do this work during daylight, which exposed him and allowed enemy fighters to observe as he and his interpreters moved around freely.

Tivao had two interpreters with him because he had identified that, when he addressed his ANA, it appeared half of the formation didn't understand. He later determined this was because he had some who spoke Pashto and some who spoke Dhari. Private First Class Talbert and his interpreter picked up enemy ICOM traffic that they were maneuvering on the American and the two interpreters. Shortly after the ICOM traffic, all hell broke loose. The enemy fighters began bounding on Tivao and the interpreters' and the ANA's positions. The Kiowa helicopters hovered above their positions and unloaded on the Taliban fighters, showering the Americans with brass casings. Tivao and his soldiers observed numerous enemy elements attempting to move into some of the buildings around COP Stout. Tivao again identified several fighters running past a small opening in a wall just north of their location. He effectively directed several Kiowas to the station to conduct gun runs, ultimately eradicating the enemy team attempting to assault their position. Once 2nd Platoon had established fire superiority, they had Apache gunships come in to engage the building with Hellfire missiles, which decimated all enemy opportunities.

The additional support from Tynes had helped to make an impact and had slowed the bleeding at Bakersfield. The HHB element was finally getting needed resupply, and items were brought in to help them set up what would eventually become the final product of COP Stout. As all four platoons from Bravo Battery rotated through Bakersfield, it was apparent Three Bravo was beneficial due to its attached infantry squad. However, not long after being in Bakersfield, Staff Sergeant Anderson was hit by shrapnel from a 37-millimeter grenade and was one of the soldiers lost to his injuries for a few days. One Bravo was used in the southernmost security position with ANA fighters attached to it, and it rotated with Three Bravo at the graveyard east, located south of Druia. Specialist Miller was positioned on the M240B machine gun in a south-blocking position along Route Mariners, an avenue enemy fighters had utilized frequently. Cutting this route led to maximum animosity.

Staff Sergeant Fontenot and 2nd Lieutenant Pantaleo were patrolling with a group of men just south of the first canal to assist HHB with their security. Bravo Battery had an MRAP (mine-resistant, ambush-protected) vehicle, with an M2 .50-caliber machine gun mounted in the turret, just north of the first canal. Private First Class Dulaney was the gunner in the turret and was pulling security east toward the grape furrows of Druia. It was a clear day in the "Devil's Playground," which enabled COP Stout to finally get a much-needed delivery of gravel to help them quit stomping around in the moondust that had accumulated from the men constantly moving to attempt setting up their security defenses.

Fontenot and Pantaleo moved north of the intersection at Route Mariners and the first canal to intercept the vehicles delivering the gravel. They could see Dulaney in the gunner's hatch, pulling security as they crossed the bridge toward the MRAP. The sky opened at that moment and mortars began raining down; Pantaleo and Fontenot were in the open and running in a zigzag pattern, attempting not to get peppered with shrapnel. They could see "Smoke" Krabbenhoft and Captain Mark from Three Bravo just north of their position, also running for cover, trying to escape the barrage of mortars. Dulaney had ducked down in the hatch to protect himself. When the mortars were exhausted, the screams of "Medic!" from inside COP Stout could be heard south of the first canal. Someone had been hit by shrapnel, but, ultimately, it was determined to be minor, and no one was lost due to this attack. Shortly after, the enemy attack calmed, and the skies quieted, and the vehicles were inbound with gravel for COP Stout. As the two crude dump trucks approached, there was nothing shockingly specific about either; one was white, and one was black. As the vehicles turned toward the first canal, they did so in a sweeping fashion, with the black vehicle going first and the white vehicle trailing; as they turned together and almost in line with each other, they were now facing

COP Tynes in a manner that allowed them to back into COP Stout to dump the gravel. By all accounts, this seemed very normal. As Pantaleo and Fontenot began walking toward the vehicles, they were within about twenty-five meters when the white truck detonated. It was a vehicle-born IED or (VBIED); the blast sent shrapnel from the vehicle flying east toward Pantaleo, Fontenot and the MRAP, which contained Dulaney. Dirt and gravel from the back of the truck contributed to the carnage. Pantaleo and Fontenot were knocked on their backs by the blast but, miraculously, both escaped being hit by shrapnel; as the dust began to settle and everyone was attempting to account for each other, the two drivers of the vehicles were seen fleeing west into the furrow just north of COP Stout. The soldiers were disoriented when they began the chase and had already lost too much ground. Fontenot and Pantaleo went to check on Dulaney as he was no longer in the gunner's hatch; they found him on the floor of the MRAP. He had been hit on the back of the head with a piece of shrapnel and knocked unconscious. It was his lucky day, however, as the shrapnel had lodged in his helmet and hadn't penetrated. When he came to Fontenot asked, "D, are you okay, man?"

"I've got a wicked headache, Chief."

"Fuck, Dulaney, I'm thankful that's all you got, bro."

Despite the severity of the attack; and how deadly it could have been, the men had walked away with nothing more than a nasty headache. For four straight days, the enemy continued to attack with snipers, indirect fire, small arms, IEDs, and another VBIED, but the combined platoons from HHB and Bravo Battery remained resolute. With the success of Bakersfield, this was the first time Taliban forces had been denied freedom of movement in the Arghandab. COP Stout was in the early stages of being established at the intersection of Mariners and Highlife, at the first canal, and would now interrupt weapons movement throughout the "Dab." The Battle for Bakersfield had taken its toll on the Top Guns. After five days of fighting, the battalion had suffered two killed by IEDs, and another by sniper fire, eight wounded within the next few days, and another 12 injured during the security and establishment of COP Stout. Still, in the end, the Top Guns held their ground, and COP Stout was established where the Taliban once called home.

CHAPTER 7

The Boys of Babur (COP Babur)

> Courage is not the absence of fear, it is the realization that some things are more important than what you are afraid of!
>
> MEG CABOT

Welcome to the eight-hour rotation cycle life at Combat Outpost (COP) Stout and COP Tynes. Bravo and Havoc Batteries have all four platoons working themselves to complete exhaustion on rotation cycles. The workhorse that is the Top Guns Battalion continues to move forward despite suffering multiple casualties. The Taliban either has a mortar team or an indirect-fire weapon system that has inflicted six more casualties on American forces, including the beloved chaplain Captain Tietje, and, at some point or another, that team must become a primary focus of the battalion. It has become standard to see Apache and Kiowa helicopters continuously for the past several days, and rarely does a period go by when a soldier finds an opportunity to gather his thoughts without a mortar round, indirect fire, or a rocket impacting close by. The Strike Brigade has pushed a tremendous amount of assets to the Arghandab; however, the dog teams have been worked to exhaustion, and PsyOps (Psychological Operations) have been blurting wild and exotic shit over loudspeakers. At the very least, it's entertaining with everything from playing "Drowning Pool" and "Iron Maiden" to messages to enemy fighters to have them come out and fight like men. Twenty-man platoons are just not cutting it; the manpower isn't sufficient to take and hold ground as well as patrol, but somehow, the Bulls and Havoc elements are finding a way day after day to do just that. The Arghandab has rightfully earned the namesake "the Devil's Playground" and had genuinely become "the Valley of Death."

The men from Four Bravo had been embedded with Havoc at COP Stout for several days and had seen constant action. They experienced several of the most intense engagements the Arghandab had to offer but were standing strong. Staff Sergeant Corcoran, having been positioned in a blocking position on Route Mariners, watched as a rocket-propelled grenade (RPG) impacted the rear cage of his MATV (mine-resistant, ambush-protected all-terrain vehicle) as it pulled security. When the RPG impacted the MATV, it set fire to gear in the back of the vehicle but, thankfully, no one was injured. On another occasion, during an intense altercation with enemy fighters, Specialist Rivera was engaged with a fighter when, out of nowhere, an RPG flew close enough to tear open his uniform, but not detonate.

Four Bravo had been patrolling in the orchards and the furrows and had encountered a relentless enemy that was constantly attempting to overrun the perimeter at COP Stout. They had yet to sustain a casualty and were beginning to feel almost invincible. Four Bravo had seen several of the HHB (Headquarters and Headquarters Battery) men leave via medevac, but were still standing tall as a platoon. Being in the orchards with the soldiers of HHB provided many opportunities for Four Bravo; it allowed them to refine the patrolling skills they worked on at Fort Polk, Louisiana. Scenarios at the Joint Readiness Training Center (JRTC) were always thrown their way in the most extreme ways possible; when they would win against "Geronimo," there was always the feeling of "Well, we finally beat Geronimo." However, there was no real emotion or feelings attached to the scenarios. It's easy to dismiss loss when there is no real loss of life associated. On August 1, 2010, Four Bravo were witnesses as First Sergeant Brown and Sergeant First Class Lyon, and a squad from 1st Platoon HHB were tasked to secure a sapper squad employed to clear Route Mariners of explosives and reduce structures and enemy obstacles on the eastern side of COP Stout. Enemy fighters began engaging Lyon and his squad, as well as the sappers, with accurate small-arms fire within fifty meters of their position. Lyon responded by bounding forward under enemy fire and assaulting the enemy position. His squad followed him forward, and he directed them to occupy covered positions where they were able to repel the enemy attack. This enabled the sappers to complete their obstacle reduction unimpeded. On August 2, after nearly forty-eight hours of constant contact with enemy fighters, Brown and Lyon again began receiving small-arms fire from southwest of COP Stout. They directed multiple gun runs by A-10s that destroyed the enemy position. Later in the day, while taking more sustained fire from buildings to the southwest of COP Stout, Brown, and Lyon directed the aviation attack onto the targets, personally coordinating the destruction of the enemy position with Hellfire missiles and 37-millimeter fire.

The Babur mission had continued to get pushed back repeatedly for reasons outside the view of the soldiers. They continued to go about their day-to-day activities of patrolling and pulling quick-reaction force (QRF) and force-protection duties but all they knew was the deployment was heating up, both with the unimaginable temperature, and the height of fighting season.

At COP Tynes, things appeared to be a somewhat normal day. One Bravo was preparing for a patrol heading out toward Babur to recon the western area, soldiers were in the towers conducting force protection, Three Bravo was on QRF, and the sector was eerily quiet for the most part. Lieutenant Colonel Flynn had been recently informed that the Top Guns' mission had become the focus of Afghanistan and that assets were being pushed to the area of operations (AO). Across the Top Guns' AO, the interpreters picked up enemy radio chatter. A Taliban commander was heard to say, "Today was a very bad day, many of our brothers died. God help us all."

For once across the battlefield, it was becoming evident to the artillerymen that they were able to stand toe-to-toe with the seasoned Taliban fighters in their backyard. Staff Sergeant Fontenot had his guys in the briefing room discussing the route they would take for the day's patrol. It would take them out toward Babur—that always brought inherent risks, then the plan was to head south toward the first canal and into the furrows. As Fontenot was going over the route, the men began discussing possible scenarios regarding what they would do if they were to hit an improvised explosive device (IED) on Route Red Dog or somewhere else. What would their plan for a medevac look like … BOOM! The earth shook, the walls of COP Tynes shook, and dirt and debris fell from the ceiling.

"What the fuck was that?" asked Fontenot.

Sergeant Junkin, the sergeant of the guard (SOG), came in with news. "Someone just hit an IED in Druia; I'm trying to figure out what the hell is going on from Tower Two, standby. Tower Two, Tower Two, SOG, what's the SITREP!"

"SOG, Tower Two, it looks like about 20 zombies walking towards us right now."

"Tower Two, SOG. What the hell does that mean?"

"SOG, Tower Two. An ANP Ranger had about 20 ANP in it, and they hit an IED on Red Dog about 200 meters from Tower Two, there's dead guys on rooftops, BREAK! The other guys are like zombies walking toward Tynes, requesting further guidance."

"Tower Two, SOG. Keep an eye on them, we will get the guys from One Bravo over there to help along with the medics."

Second Lieutenant Pantaleo, Fontenot, Corporal Parker, and the rest of One Bravo quickly left, heading to the front entry point of COP Tynes to intercept the Afghan Nation Police (ANP) approaching the front gate. The ANP were known to the 101st men as Taliban sympathizers. They were getting paid to act as if they were working on behalf of the Afghan people, but; unlike the Afghan National Army (ANA), which may stand on its own when the Americans left, the ANP would defect back to being Taliban, which is what they were before becoming police. This was well known around the Arghandab and was shared with the 101st by the 82nd during their relief in place by the interpreters. As the casualties came in the gate, "Doc" Stegehuis identified and separated them and pushed them to different people to be treated. Pantaleo began working on two separate casualties; one was still alive but peppered with shrapnel and was being carried in by two of his colleagues. The other was in and out of consciousness. Stegehuis was going back and forth, trying to do what he could to keep them alive. One of the men had a dime-sized hole on one side of his chest and another on the other side but it didn't require immediate attention. The other young man was completely fucked up: a piece of his ass was missing, his right forearm was gone, his head was gushing blood, and he probably had between 100–150 pieces of shrapnel along his entire left side. Pantaleo was patching him up, and just as he turned to check the man with the two small holes, he noticed he wasn't breathing anymore. He turned to the other soldiers working on him and said, "He's dead, bag him and help the others." The man's eyes were wide open; he was only around seventeen. A piece of shrapnel had passed right through his heart; he was dead from the start; his body didn't know it yet. Fontenot was treating another ANP man peppered with shrapnel throughout his arms and was in much the same condition as the casualty who had just died. The young man had a hole in the back of his head, and Fontenot was attempting to bandage it so his brains weren't falling out of his skull. He wrapped the head ever so gently as not to put unnecessary pressure on the brain, laying his head on his side; the young man raised his arms in the air for Fontenot to treat them but there wasn't anything Fontenot could do. He poured water on his arms to help cool him off from the burning shrapnel. By this point in the deployment, Pantaleo and Fontenot had become inseparable and were like brothers despite their ranks; they were positioned next to each other, treating two casualties, and were each facing their share of hardships.

Pantaleo was fighting to save the young man's life, but it was an uphill battle as the wounds appeared to be getting the best of him. Fontenot tried to reassure his casualty to relax, to put his arms down, and that they were going to call in a medevac to get them to Kandahar as soon as possible. Shortly after, he heard Pantaleo yelling at the casualty he was working on. "Don't fucking die on me, man, come on, keep breathing, man, don't fucking die on me, God damn it!" At that very moment, the man took his final breath and spit blood directly into Pantaleo's mouth. Pantaleo looked over at Fontenot with this look of frustration and disgust and, in his Jersey accent, said, "Fuck, this sucks."

The rest of the men had continued to work on the other casualties while Junkin had been working to call in a nine-line to get birds inbound to pick up the casualties. This was the first mass casualty Bravo Battery had to address. The Kiowas were flying overhead, identifying the dead ANP on the rooftops. The tactical operations center was reporting it up to Top Guns main to see how they wanted to proceed—did they want One Bravo to reroute their planned patrol to collect casualties or to continue with their previous mission and let the ANP collect their own dead? Ultimately, the decision made was to allow the ANP to collect their own, and One Bravo would regroup; after the casualties were on their way to Kandahar; and head out on their patrol. Shortly after, the 160th Special Operations Aviation Regiment arrived to collect the ANPs that were still alive and take them to Kandahar. The dead men were sadly lined up with their heads facing Mecca, and prayers were said on their behalf as gunfire, IEDs, gun runs, and firefights continued for the remainder of the day.

On August 6, Captain Smithson and Sergeant First Class Toon got word that they would be the focus of the clearing operation heading into Babur a few days later. They had been in the orchards conducting patrols and partnering with the soldiers and leaders from HHB for several weeks, and were already tired. Smithson and Toon knew the upcoming operation would be taxing both emotionally and physically. Smithson was newly promoted and would soon be assuming the executive officer role but was currently relishing his time as platoon leader of 4th Platoon. Toon was the Four Bravo platoon sergeant; he was excited to be back with the troops after having been an air-assault instructor for a while, having his primary focus on Pathfinder and air-assault instruction. Smithson was the calm, and "Smoke" Toon was the storm. Together, they made a great team, especially when it came to patrolling. They had a platoon of seasoned noncommissioned officers. However, they had initially thought they were coming to the Arghandab to be the artillery platoon for the battalion, so when it was time to give up soldiers before deploying, they selected some of their most physically fit colleagues. Now that they were walking in the valley of the shadow of death, Smithson regretted giving up some of his Allstars.

Four Bravo meticulously planned routes; and contingency plans during and after their 24 hours of refit from being on the line at COP Stout. Smithson had made rules for himself while he was at JRTC because he never wanted to fail his men in combat. Some of those rules would play a pivotal role in the weeks ahead as the challenges began to arise in Babur.

GREEN BOOK AAR – NQ 02135 45364

1. If something is fucked up address it, don't let it go. Bad training leads to bad habits.
2. Ensure I know what's going on, I can't expect soldiers to know what's going on!
3. Never Allow My Flank to get rolled up again.
4. Create a PLT SOP to Signal Everyone is ok Day and Night if comms are lost.
5. Rehearse
6. Execute what you Rehearse!
7. Establish SQD SOPs
8. Situational Awareness
9. Tactical Proficiency
10. Leaders Need to Ensure Soldiers are what they want.

The Top Guns had made it to the second week of August, and the weather in the Arghandab had continued growing more intense with each passing moment; the days were now beginning at a sweltering 110° Fahrenheit in the shade. The Top Guns had earned a small victory during the Battle for Bakersfield despite suffering the loss of Sergeant Stout, Specialist Stansbery, and Master Sergeant Pittman, as well as several of those wounded in action, during the establishment of COP Stout. The men were still steadfast at work and diligently pushing forward. The Four Bravo element was nearing the execution of their clearing operation that would cover the brigade's furthest eastern sector in Regional Command South. The Strike Brigade was the main effort for Regional Command South. Now the "Boys of Babur" were going to be covering the furthest and most exposed sector facing Pakistan, already synonymous with taking the life of sniper Specialist Christopher Moon less than a month earlier. It had become a primary focus of the battalion and brigade and was seen as a piece of key terrain that both echelons were driven to take and hold at all costs. The village of Babur was once a vibrant farming community; but it is now nearly desolate. When the Top Guns first arrived in the Arghandab; and the leadership patrolled north into Druia, they could see farmers north of Babur tending to fields. However, the Taliban had forced the locals out of the village to use it as a fighting base. It was well known to military intelligence that Babur and the villages of Charqolba Olya and Khosrow Olya were also being used as homemade explosives (HME) factories. Babur was once known for being the armory for Mullah Naqib's fighters; therefore, it was expected that Four Bravo would likely face resistance as they moved into the town. Babur is strategically located next to the Shuyens, suspected of housing most of the Taliban fighters in the Arghandab, which was potentially another hurdle for the Four Bravo element as they moved into their new AO. The key areas of the Shuyens were known as Shuyen-e Olya, Shuyen-E Vosta, and Shuyen-E Sofla. Prior to the 82nd and the 101st coming into the Arghandab 1-17 IN the 1st Battalion, 17th Infantry Regiment, also known as the "Buffaloes," suffered the highest casualty rate of any US infantry battalion in the War in Afghanistan. During their deployment from 2009–2010, 22 Buffaloe soldiers were killed in action due to the high rate of IEDs they encountered in the area during the short time they were there. They also fell victim to two DUSTWUNS at one time which is horrific for any unit, so the Bulls had their hands full going into this area. The Bulls also faced another major hurdle, due to rising tensions within the chain of command, their beloved First Sergeant Banister was fired by the battalion command sergeant major; due to "disloyal statements against the Battalion," so now Captain Ward and First Sergeant Baca, the replacement who was an infantry man, were eager to get the men into Babur to begin setting up the new combat outpost and start a fresh chapter for the Bulls. The COP would find itself approximately a mile east of COP Tynes and approximately four miles east of COPs Terra Nova and Nolen. It was positioned directly on Route Red Dog and, much like COP Tynes, would be exposed to fighters moving west from Charqolba Olya and Khosrow Olya and those coming west into the Arghandab from Pakistan and the Shuyens.

As the men of Four Bravo began their assault into Babur during the early morning of August 8, they prepared for the "Miserable Mile," the movement that would carry them through the northern side of the Arghandab north of the Menorah Canal (also known as the first canal). The first canal had become known as the hotbed for enemy fighters. They knew any movement south of the canal would likely result in enemy contact. Khosrow Sulfa was directly south of Babur, south of the first and second canals, and housed Taliban fighters and HME materials. The men heading toward Babur were briefed during their short stint at COP Tynes and, during their time assisting in the fields at COP Stout, about what type of fighting was happening south of the first canal toward Khosrow Sulfa. It would come as no surprise when they eventually found themselves in direct contact with enemy fighters. Upon leaving COP Tynes, the men headed northeast and crossed a waddy; when it rained, the waddy became a river of its own. During the movement into Babur, the men had expected to be hit by IEDs; despite their concerns, they only encountered small-arms fire. Sergeant Estep, one of the Four Bravo team leaders, was moving along their planned route when his MRAP (mine-resistant, ambush-protected) took an RPG to the door. Fortunately, there was no damage or injuries, so the convoy kept moving right along. Specialist Mazariegos was one of the drivers in the convoy; he thought that initial information flow was very limited. The soldiers on the ground felt they were going in blind and were just going from place to place as required. They trusted in their leadership and believed they would only be sent where they were needed.

Due to not hitting much resistance, the men were overly cautious about entering their new home. Once Four Bravo got into town, the leaders set up a security posture and set up a shura with the local elders. This allowed them to purchase a local compound to set up the new outpost. The compound the men inherited, and thought would become COP King, was a large structure with potential for development. The walls erected around the compound provided a great deal of security with the exception of the eastern side of the compound. On the east side, there was low ground that dipped so low locals could see inside. This made it a strategic nightmare and Hescos were going to need to be fortified so their defense would be sufficient, but that was going to take a while.

The men of Four Bravo were finally going to have something to call home. They had been living like gypsies, moving from Forward Operating Base Jelawur to COP Stout, to COP Tynes, and now to their new home in only a few weeks. When they moved into Babur, they initially thought their new home would be called COP King. They would later discover that, due to politics and personal biases regarding perceived circumstances surrounding PFC King's death a few weeks earlier, their new home would not be named after him; rather, it would be called COP Babur. Many across the battalion took offense to this outcome and always believed that the COP rightfully should've been called COP King after their fallen brother.

Over several weeks the "Boys of Babur" continued working diligently to fortify their security. The men had encountered a big issue with the ANA that they hadn't anticipated. Their setup of COP Babur had fallen during Ramadan. Ramadan lasts for 30 days and is when many Muslims abstain from eating and drinking from dawn to dusk, celebrating with pre-dawn breakfasts and nightly feasts. This caused issues due to dehydration and weakness for the Afghans, who would be attempting to work and patrol with the Americans. When Four Bravo initially went into COP Babur initially, the ANA refused to go with them. They chose to sleep outside of the COP in tents and on cots. During the initial infiltration into Babur, the men from Four Bravo were also reinforced by Charlie Troop, 1st Squadron, 75th Cavalry Regiment (1-75). The men from Charlie 1-75 were there to supplement the artillerymen with whatever they were going to need but, to Four Bravo's surprise, they were only there for the first few days of the operation. Once the 1-75 had left COP Babur, Captain Smithson felt as if the "Boys of Babur" were alone in the middle of no-man's-land. Left with empty Hesco barriers, and about twenty-one American soldiers, things looked bleak. Being supplemented by Afghan soldiers who were in the middle of celebrating Ramadan didn't help their situation at all; if anything, force protection and patrolling were out of the question, as COP security was paramount. After about two days on the ground, a blessing arrived in the form of a front-end loader from the Seabees.

The machine was going to help them fill their Hesco barriers in a quick and efficient manner. It began filling the Hescos, but not long after, COP Babur took indirect fire from 37-millimeter grenades and an RPG, which hit the front-end loader and blew the tires, rendering it useless. The "Boys of Babur," not really having many other options, resorted to filling the Hescos with sandbags. However, they didn't realize that to fill one Hesco takes roughly fifteen hundred sandbags, which would take them about seven hours if they had soldiers working nonstop; in the Arghandab heat, that just wasn't feasible. Specialists Atwell and Brow, "Doc" Dozeman, and Specialist Solemonik began working on wiring up the partition walls the Seabees had helped the men construct. It wasn't much, but it was more than they had when they arrived. Unfortunately, the men were still forced to go two men (on alternating shifts) to a cot due to a shortage. That was just life at COP Babur for the time being.

Part of the force protection set in place to secure the perimeter of COP Babur was to set up an MATV with a common remotely operated weapon (CROW) station at the western sector along the waddy facing Druia. This allowed the gunner to monitor the sector with the thermal system inside the turret with a machine gun. The "Boys of Babur" were equipped with crew-served weapons, so their CROW system was equipped with an M2 .50-caliber machine gun. The gunner monitoring the waddy at the edge of Druia was Specialist Branch. He was able to spot four enemy fighters placing an IED on the edge of the last building of Druia. This had become a common spot for IEDs that were being hit by vehicles clearing through Route Red Dog while attempting to provide supplies to COP Babur; or just route-clearance vehicles. This was also the same spot where One Bravo and Two Charlie had narrowly missed a radio-controlled IED. As Branch identified the fighters digging the IED in, he engaged them with the M2 .50-caliber machine gun. He shot multiple volleys, but they had no effect as the fighters were unaffected and just kept digging. Noting the rounds wouldn't hit them, they immediately picked up the pace of their digging. In their haste, one of the enemy fighters stepped on the IED. With a mighty blast, dirt and debris were sent flying across Route Red Dog. The enemy fighter was sent flying in the air toward the compound behind him, missing one of his legs. One of the other fighters immediately grabbed him and sat him on a nearby motorcycle to get him out, not wanting the American soldiers to be able to take advantage of their situation. As quickly as he had hit the IED, the Taliban fighters were gone from the area. The remainder of the shift was uneventful, but that blocking position proved to be effective as it prevented other IEDs from being positioned in the future.

Later that day, Top Gun 6 and Top Gun 7 came out to COP Babur to tell the men that they would soon be getting air-conditioned tents. As the news was delivered to Smithson, he thought, "Wow, the men will be excited," but the excitement quickly eroded. Lieutenant Colonel Flynn explained that because it was Ramadan, the tents needed to be given to the Afghan soldiers. Smithson was taken aback and lost as to what he would tell his men. Flynn explained that after Ramadan, the Americans could move into the tents, but that would be easier said than done, not to mention the conditions in which one culture lives in compared to the other. Smithson was baffled as to how he would sell this to his soldiers to get them to buy into the fact that, even though there were air-conditioned tents, they would continue to sleep in the dirt and build their own structures. Even as the weeks went by, the "Boys of Babur" continued to live like gypsies with no cover from indirect fire or mortars.

COP Babur began setting up blocking positions throughout the AO and started pushing out patrols once a day. They didn't have the soldiers to facilitate multiple patrols or provide force protection in the towers. During this time, Staff Sergeant Howard was driving his MRAP through Babur and took an RPG to the gunner's hatch. To everyone's amazement, however, the RPG didn't detonate. Howard and his crew returned to COP Babur to remove the RPG. Top Gun 6's personal security detail was still at the COP and saw the RPG. "You can't have that in the COP." "I was just going to take it out myself," Howard replied, at which point he was told, "No, you need to call EOD." An explosive ordnance disposal team was soon en route to blow it in place.

After the incident with Howard's MRAP, Captain Ward called to bring Two Bravo to COP Babur to reinforce Four Bravo and assist in patrolling and whatever else would be needed. First Lieutenant Dabrowski was the platoon leader, and Staff Sergeant (Gunny) Torres was the platoon sergeant. Torres had been with the Top Guns for multiple deployments and was well respected throughout the battery. Now that COP Babur had reinforcements, they were able to push out multiple patrols a day. The men felt they may have been blessed and were beginning to feel invincible. They had taken on some of the biggest battles the Taliban could throw at them and were still standing and eager to fight.

Three weeks had now passed—it was August 27—and Four Bravo was going to be pushing out another patrol to conduct what the men humorously called a "Facebook" patrol, going from compound to compound to identify fighting-age males. This would give them a feel for who lived where and what occupation they said they had; in the future, they would know who was telling the truth and who was lying. During the patrol, they had dismounts that were covered by vehicles. Captain Smithson was the platoon leader, or the senior leader on the patrol, which meant "Smoke" Toon was on the radio listening to the patrol if they encountered anything. "Doc" Dozeman had been going out on every patrol because the other medic was on mid-tour leave, so Smithson had instructed him to take the patrol off. He didn't anticipate they would encounter anything anyway. Shortly after the patrol started, the first CRACK was heard, then another, and another, and it kept coming; the men were in a steady firefight with an enemy positioned along the first canal. Enemy fighters were attempting to bait Four Bravo into the orchards, into the IED minefield they had waiting for them. Smithson had spotted a suspected IED emplacement; as he and several Four Bravo soldiers went to confirm it, enemy fighters engaged the squad with machine-gun fire, utilizing a complex ambush from two positions. From a third position, an RPG was fired. Smithson had Sergeant McCloud in his MATV return fire with the M2 .50-caliber machine gun. McCloud effectively engaged three enemy fighters who were all confirmed KIA. Shortly after, Specialist Atwell was able to get *Longknife* on station; once attack aviation had checked in, they attacked multiple enemy positions with Hellfire missiles. Atwell then called in a Predator drone, which had positively identified an enemy fighter who continued to harass Four Bravo with PKM machine-gun fire and had attempted to fire an RPG. The Predator engaged with a missile as the men continued to push forward toward the position. It was confirmed the drone strike killed him, and Four Bravo was tasked to document and recover his remains. Specialist Branch, Smithson, and Sergeant Pohlman began placing what they could find into an MRE (meal, ready to eat) box as there was nothing more than small pieces of flesh, bone fragments, and tissue. Smithson was primarily concerned with identifying the man's face and fingerprints so they could attempt to identify him using the BAT (Biometrics Automated Toolset) and HIIDE (Handheld Interagency Identity Detection Equipment) systems. Pohlman attempted to use the fingerprints, but they were badly damaged. The men were also tasked with capturing photos of the scene for higher echelons to ensure the engagement was conducted correctly. At the same time, Staff Sergeant Corcoran identified an Afghan male carrying an RPG, so a group of soldiers maneuvered and captured him and another enemy fighter who a local had seen running into a compound. Smithson had his men regroup at this point, then he had his soldiers stay with the two detainees. They brought them back to COP Babur; "Doc" Dozeman stayed with them while the rest of the team began to search the compound. During the search, they uncovered multiple explosive-making materials such as fertilizer, detonation cords, crushed cans, pressure plates, yellow HME jugs, and other devices. At the end of the patrol, Four Bravo had been on mission for over ten hours, approximately six of the ten in direct contact with the enemy. They accounted for eight enemy-confirmed KIA and two prisoners; and uncovered an IED-making compound. The "Boys of Babur" had once again had a successful day in the Arghandab and continued their trend of feeling invincible. When all was said and done, they had to release the two detainees; "Doc" Dozeman had an eerie feeling when he released the two men. "Something doesn't feel right about letting these guys go."

CHAPTER 8

The Longest Day

> The ultimate measure of a man is not where he stands in moments of comfort and convenience, but where he stands at times of challenge and controversy.
>
> MARTIN LUTHER KING JR.

There was no wind to stir the trees into dancing. The sky was as blue as the purest ocean waters, the clouds drifted placidly above the peaks of the mountains, and the air was as dead still and unresponsive as the victims the Arghandab had claimed years and years before. As they prepared to be QRF (quick-reaction force) for a significant operation involving Alpha Battery, the soldiers from One Bravo were loading up at Combat Outpost (COP) Tynes on their way to COP Nolen. The operation entailed a lot of risk and was headed toward Nūr Muhammad Kolache (NMK). For One Bravo to participate in the preparation of the operation and be on the ground when it began, it was planned for them to arrive a few days early. The goal was to leave under the cover of darkness to make the most of the night. The troops were no strangers to enemy fighters; in the 11 weeks since their arrival in the Arghandab, they had been engaged several times and had learned to seize every opportunity that came their way.

Four miles away, the "Boys of Babur" were readying a patrol and were scheduled to meet some of the locals to continue their "Facebook" patrols. After conducting their pre-combat checks and inspections, Sergeant First Class Toon, Staff Sergeant Corcoran, Sergeant Durham, and the rest of the patrol were prepared to carry out another task in their newly designated area of operation. It was August 28, 2010, and the day was already showing signs of being unrelenting in its determination to drain the soldiers' last reserves of energy. The intense heat lingered just above the earth's surface, engulfing them like a wool blanket and stifling every degree of heat that reached their bodies. The men moved slowly and methodically through Babur but hadn't made it far since setting out. The patrol had been out just under 45 minutes when the radio-telephone operator reported to Captain Smithson at the command post that the 4th Platoon element was being engaged by small-arms fire from the southernmost point of Charqolba Olya, just south of the first canal. The QRF element, made up of their Two Bravo element, which was already short-staffed due to guard positions, was instructed by Smithson to prepare to leave. In the distance, the sound of PKM and responding 240B machine-gun fire was constant. The "Boys of Babur" were once again in the hotbed of the Taliban, fighting a battle with an unlimited timeline. Concussions from the 40-millimeter projectiles Durham was lobbing from his M203 were occurring frequently. As Specialist Atwell, the platoon forward observer, got ready to put in work, Smithson was trying to get *Longknife* in the air.

"Doc" Dozeman, Private First Class Storti, Specialist Pepper, Durham, and Specialist Castro were all in contact at the end of Babur. The troops could continue to fight the enemy from the nearby wheelhouse, which could shelter two individuals, and the nearby narrow alleyway, from which Durham could fire his M203 with precision. Castro told Dozeman to take Pepper and Storti and move to the alleyway to the west; he would stay with Durham. To prevent opposing fighters from having a chance to engage from the alley, Dozeman, Pepper, and Storti moved to guard the next one down. Meanwhile, QRF continued to assemble soldiers. COP Babur was around seven hundred meters from the patrol when an abrupt, loud explosion was heard. Everyone could see at that point that one of the platoon's soldiers had detonated an improvised explosive device (IED).

The blast occurred immediately before an open space that led to Charqolba Olya and the Shuyens near the end of Babur, next to the final compound. A narrow corridor descended to the first canal, where enemy fighters were battling Four Bravo.

"IED, IED, IED!"

The sound of the leaders calling out could be heard all around Babur. Squad leaders used their radios to ask their men to check in, but Durham and Castro were missing. The two soldiers were positioned close to the wheelhouse in the eastern position. Durham had been having an issue with his M203 grenade launcher.

"Four Seven, this is Four One Actual. I have a jam in my 203. I'm going to clear it and be back in the fight shortly."

"Smoke" Toon replied, "Four One Actual, this is Four Seven. Roger."

"Castro, I'm going to step behind you, and you step here and shoot down the alleyway so we can keep them from coming up this road. I'll clear the jam; it'll just take a second, then I'll get back in position."

"Too easy, man, let's go," Castro replied.

Durham moved into position and began clearing his M203. Like he had said, it only took him a few seconds to clear the jam, and he was back in action. "Okay, man, let's switch positions."

As Durham stepped behind Castro to get back into position, he initiated the IED. He was known as one of the Bulls who always had a smile and a dip in his lip. A 24-year-old native of Chattanooga, Tennessee, Durham had a unique talent for making everyone around him happy. He had an unrivaled love for music and was a devoted soldier and father. In a place where hate reigns supreme, he would frequently take out his acoustic guitar to spread a little love, but on this day, love was nonexistent.

"Smoke" Toon and Corcoran were searching for Durham and Castro through the dust and falling debris. When they reached the location where Durham was found, the dust covering his body prevented them from seeing him, but; as the dust gradually lifted, they were able to determine he had been killed in the explosion. Dozeman was able to determine Durham must have been wearing his belt of 40-millimeter ammunition because it appeared to have exploded in the blast. Due to this, he was cut in half above the waist. "Doc" looked at Durham helplessly, knowing he could do nothing for him. Durham's body remained in the crater that claimed his life.

They still hadn't found their intelligence analyst, Castro. Even as they continued to take shots from the orchards, the guys were calling out and trying to find him. Smithson was still at COP Babur and successfully contacted the nine-line to request the medevac. *Longknife* was now in the air and had one of their Kiowas flying above the men to provide aerial cover. One of the pilots called down, asking if they had an American soldier in the compound next to them. Knowing they didn't, it became the priority to get inside the compound no matter what it took.

"Gunny" Torres, Dozeman, Pepper, and Private First Class Patton went down a small alleyway to the west of the compound until they found an entryway. They went inside and were able to get to Castro. "Doc" identified that he had a hole approximately ten inches in diameter on the right side of his chest. He administered morphine to ease his pain, then packed the hole and applied a pressure dressing; at that point, however, Castro had already suffered a tremendous loss of blood. His right leg was mangled and turned into disfigured muscle. It was unknown what other injuries he may have sustained from the concussion of the blast, but the morphine blunted any pain he may have felt. When the IED went off, Castro had been blown over a 10-foot wall and flown another 10 to 12 feet inside the compound. The impact on his body and the shockwave from the blast was enough to have killed him, yet he was still alive and fighting. His right arm had been severed almost surgically, so much so that Doc couldn't put a tourniquet on it. Torres ran up to Staff Sergeant Bigelow.

"Bigelow, have Maz drive that fucking truck through that wall so we can get Castro the hell out of there."

"Mazariegos, I need a hole in that wall right now!"

Mazariegos was in the MATV (mine-resistant, ambush-protected all-terrain vehicle) along with Specialist Siedlik in the gunner's hatch and Specialist Melbourne as a dismount; everyone was yelling in the vehicle as they were trying to figure out what to do. Mazariegos was the driver and already in a frenzy. He turned to Siedlik and Melbourne. "SHUT THE FUCK UP!"

He backed the MATV up and drove through the wall as hard as possible. Once the dust settled, he saw Castro and the men working on him and went into a state of shock. Once he snapped out of it, Mazariegos looked around the truck and everyone had the same look on their faces, complete and utter disbelief. Regaining his composure, he pushed the MATV into reverse to allow the soldiers to reenter the area under security.

Castro, a 20-year-old Californian, was well known for his ability to make light of almost any circumstance and for being a prankster who enjoyed playing cards. He had offered to accompany the forces on this mission as an intelligence analyst to gather information to help them in future operations. When Castro was at COP Tynes, the soldiers often joked with him because the locals thought he was one of them due to his dark skin and beard.

Torres attempted to keep him engaged and alert to prevent him from going into shock.

"Gunny, I can't feel my arm."

"Castro, just focus on me, buddy."

"Gunny, am I going to die?"

"No, man, you're going to be okay."

"Castro, I'm gonna give you some morphine, man," Dozeman said.

"Castro, who's your favorite musician?" Torres asked.

"Bob Marley, Gunny."

"Great choice, man. Hey, repeat after me, every little thing is gonna be alright."

Castro said faintly, "Every little thing is gonna be alright."

To protect Durham's body, they covered him with a warming blanket. Smithson arrived to assist with the aid and litter team. After that, they transferred Castro and Durham to the landing zone. The men got Castro on

An Afghan National Army Soldier was told to pull security. This was the position he selected. It's ironic that no matter what side of the war a soldier falls on, in the end they fall in this exact position.

Dabrowski, "Doc" Dozeman, and an ANP servicemember enjoying chai tea in Babur. (Nate Dozeman)

During a joint mission to the village of Nūr Muhammad Kolache. Zavala directed fire to a sniper who had them pinned down during "Smoke" Manley's medevac. (Elliott Woods)

An Alpha Battery soldier gets a few minutes of rest while at Nūr Muhammad Kolache. (Elliott Woods)

Santoro with a local boy during a Top Gun 6 PSD patrol. (Geoffrey Santoro)

SGT Durham preparing to step off for another patrol from COP Babur. (Victor J. Blue)

Parker, during a clearing operation in Druia, attempting to find a mortar tube the Taliban continued using.

Pittman from the Asymmetric Warfare Group during the last patrol with Two Charlie, 82nd Airborne.

A patrol heading down Route Phillies toward Tarok Kolache during Operation *Bakersfield II*. (Nathan Miller)

One Bravo patrol heading into the pomegranate orchards from Strong Point Stansbery.

"Doc" Fontenot patrolling in the canals south of COP Stout. He was one of the medics directly responsible for treating casualties and saving multiple lives. (Mark Patterson)

Junkin, after a patrol with Three Bravo in which the patrol was ambushed in the furrows. (David Creighton)

During the initial setup of Strong Point Stansbery, Creighton pulled security to the north side of the orchards.

"Smoke" Tatro's MATV was destroyed during the QRF mission following Durham and Castro's IED. All soldiers evaluated were subsequently cleared to return to patrolling.

Durham during a patrol in lower Babur. (Christy Durham)

Junkin and Fontenot sharing a frozen drink at COP Terra Nova.

Stout at COP Terra Nova preparing for Operation *Bakersfield*. (David Creighton)

A. J. Castro during a key leader engagement in Jelawur with One Bravo.

Cheatham during an overwatch patrol in north Jelawur. (Nathan Miller)

Naquin serving as sergeant of the guard at COP Stout. (John Naquin)

Some of One Hotel pose for a photo after a close-call night operation in Takia. From left to right: Terrazas, Kinsel, Casey, Ester, and Walt. (Chris Kinsel)

Casey, Kinsel, and Lyon. Shortly after, Kinsel arrived at HHB and joined One Hotel. This was a small kill team assembled to swim down the second canal and place a demolition charge to clear the view for a tower. (Chris Kinsel)

Perrault and Deatherage conducting preventive maintenance checks on an M249 light machine gun before a patrol from Strong Point Weaver. (Chris Kinsel)

Tebaldi (with the orange VS-17 panel), Flynn, and Fontenot following the ambush in Druia.

Casey and "Doc" Shannon in the fields near COP Stout. (Chris Kinsel)

Fontenot and Pantaleo at the main mosque in Jelawur. This patrol was to observe the mosque to ensure elders weren't recruiting for Taliban fighters.

Fontenot and Sturgeon with an entourage of children in tow during a patrol in the Shuyens.

Babcock ensured the medevac for Chavez and Strickland from Strong Point Manley was successful. (Elliott Woods)

Tower Two at Strong Point Stansbery. The picture was taken to show how soldiers stood guard throughout the night to ensure the rest could sleep.

Returning from a miserably cold mission, "Doc" Stegehuis clears the last open area before entering back into COP Tynes.

Combat outposts weren't allowed to fly the American flag, so this one was flown at COP Nolen facing Strong Point Lugo. (Nathan Miller)

Vehicle-borne IED that hit during the establishment of COP Stout.

Aerial view of the grape furrows, pomegranate orchards, and compounds that the soldiers would attempt to navigate over the next year. (David Parker)

During a joint mission to the village of Nūr Muhammad Kolache, soldiers of Alpha Battery make contact, engage, and maneuver on enemy fighters. (Elliott Woods)

An ANA soldier engages enemy fighters at Nūr Muhammad Kolache with his RPG while Alpha soldiers continue repelling the attack. (Elliott Woods)

Wilke and Alpha Battery soldiers engage enemy fighters in the orchards outside the walls at COP Nolen. (Elliott Woods)

Kelly enjoying a smoke break during the fighting at the "Alamo wall." (Elliott Woods)

Pantaleo and A. J. Castro during a key leader engagement in Jelawur.

Soldiers salute at the ramp ceremony at Kandahar Airfield for Durham and Castro, both killed in Babur, August 28, 2010. (Victor J. Blue)

Soldiers rotate on a work/rest cycle during the construction of COP Babur. (Victor J. Blue)

Atwell, the forward observer for COP Babur, and "Doc" Dozeman prepare to head out for a night patrol from COP Babur. (Victor J. Blue)

Howard leading his squad during one of the infamous "Facebook Patrols." (Victor J. Blue)

Bigelow checks the towers at COP Babur during sergeant of the guard as a patrol leaves the wire to react for QRF. (Victor J. Blue)

"Smoke" Carrol, Wilke, Kelly, and Boxley engaged in a firefight outside COP Nolen. (Elliott Woods)

SGT Flowers repelling an attack on COP Stout. (Robert Plotkin)

SGT Kyle B. Stout and a local village boy during a patrol in Jelawur. (Caleb Talbot)

"Doc" Fontenot bandaging up an Afghan man injured by shrapnel. (Robert Plotkin)

Battlefield Cross Ceremony where "Doc" Stegehuis, SPC Sullivan, SSG Fontenot and SPC Webb paid respects for SPC A. J. Castro and SGT Durham. (Chad Webb)

SPC Bennett and SGT Jackson while SGT Jackson was providing Bennett his sector of fire.

"Doc" Fontenot and "Doc" Shannon at the COP Stout aid station. (Joseph Shannon)

SGT Tebaldi during a patrol in Lower Babur, outside of Strong Point Stansbery, embracing the freezing water. (David Parker)

SPC Dru, and PFC Luke from Two Charlie of the 82nd Airborne, with SSG Fontenot during a firefight after SPC Moon was hit with an IED. (Brian Mockenhaupt)

SPC Joseph calling for more ammunition during a firefight in Babur. (Nathan Joseph)

"Doc" Fontenot cares for a Havoc soldier as SPC Terrazas stands guard. (Robert Plotkin)

SPC Reivadeneira fires his M320 during a MEDEVAC at COP Stout. (Robert Plotkin)

"Smoke" Tivao during a firefight at COP Stout. (Robert Plotkin)

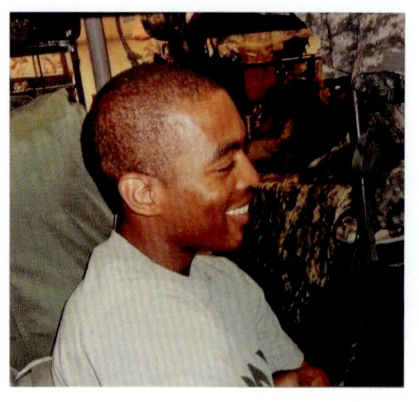

The last photo taken of PFC Brandon King. (Mrs. Carolyn King)

COP Babur was separated by a waddy that would turn into a stream that vehicles struggled to cross during the rainy season. (Victor J. Blue)

One Hotel at Strong Point Weaver. (Joseph Shannon)

Roses may dry and wilt, the paint on the bricks may in time crack and fade, but the memories of the men who have their names inscribed on them will always be remembered as long as Free men remain Free.

the Black Hawk, and the flight medics started working on him immediately, but not before he flatlined. They knew Castro didn't have time on his side. The Black Hawk lifted off toward Kandahar. The "Boys of Babur" had lost someone for the first time in the Arghandab; amid a once peaceful blue sky that was now turning a somber gray.

They knew at this point that Castro was not expected to make it and that Durham was gone. Now they were on the ground, the men from One Bravo's QRF assisted in relieving the patrolmen who had been aiding with the medevac and helping with the aftermath of the explosion. Having to recover Castro and Durham, the "Boys of Babur" had suffered greatly. When Smithson arrived back at COP Babur, the sergeant of the guard (SOG) instructed the towers to keep an eye out for possible enemy approaches while One Bravo worked on recovery. Smithson radioed the towers to be especially vigilant when observing the structures close to the medevac site. He saw that the soldiers and noncommissioned officers (NCOs) on the patrol were emotionally disturbed as they made their way back to the COP. Some were still drenched in blood from their work on the aid and litter team, others from helping to deliver life-saving assistance. Some were so exhausted, both psychologically and physically, that they were throwing up; others exhibited fits of rage; still others just put their heads in their hands, unable to believe what had just transpired. They were furious and desired retribution. They wanted to exact revenge for Castro, who had grown to be a member of their family since coming to Babur, and Durham, one of their cherished team leaders. Troops conversed among themselves, detailing the types of wounds Durham and Castro had sustained as well as the atrocities they had gone through. Until all the returning men had a chance to clean up, Smithson decided to leave the soldiers on tower duty. He received an alert from the SOG informing him of an urgent situation in one of the towers. Upon arriving at the tower, Smithson discovered a soldier holding a rifle to his mouth. To defuse the situation, the captain entered the tower.

"What's going on?"

"I don't want to do this anymore."

"Do what?"

"Sit around and wait to die in this place."

"Do you really believe that this is where you'll die?"

"Yes, based on what I saw when Durham and Castro were blown up. I believe I'm going to die here."

Extreme post-traumatic stress disorder forced the man out of the tower; Smithson's platoon was now essentially combat-ineffective. While they could understand the soldier had experienced stress and might want to check out, the others at the COP couldn't imagine wanting to do that. On the other hand, they wouldn't want to go on patrol with someone who would be doubting himself, so, in a way, it was a blessing.

Once on the ground, Sergeant First Class Tatro and 2nd Lieutenant Pantaleo told Staff Sergeant Fontenot to position his soldiers in security while they planned their next move. There hadn't been much guidance given to the leadership; all they knew going into Babur was that Durham had been killed, Castro was on his way to Kandahar, and shit had gone south. On top of that, One Bravo was rapidly losing daylight. Fontenot positioned Specialist Cooper and Corporal Parker on an alley just west of the compound where Castro was recovered. Specialist Bibb was positioned further toward the west side of town on another alley, Specialist Miller, "Doc" Stegehuis, and Staff Sergeant Beaudrie were in Tatro's vehicle, and Private First Class Dulaney was positioned with the 240B machine gun where Durham had been killed to provide cover over the open area toward Charqolba Olya. Staff Sergeant Peltier was patrolling Route Red Dog and monitoring the security. Because of the high heat, he was extremely attentive in checking on hydration and verifying everyone was aware of their sectors. The remainder of the platoon remained mounted in their vehicles, awaiting further guidance. Major Raymond, the battalion's executive officer, was the highest-ranking officer present at Babur at the time.

"Fontenot, I need you and your guys to do your best to secure Durham and Castro's sensitive items [SI]. I understand the time restraints you and your guys are under and that you're losing light, but I need you to find their SI."

"We'll do what we can, sir."

Fontenot let Pantaleo know what the major wanted. "Sir, you know that Major Raymond wants us to search for Durham and Castro's SI, right?"

"I am now."

"Okay, well, I'm gonna take a team, and we'll start looking around. It'll be me, Parker, and Coop-a-loop."

"Alright, just try to stay where route clearance has cleared."

"Sir, of course, you know me."

"Yeah, Fonty, that's why I said that."

Fontenot and his team had cleared Route Red Dog primarily and the blast site area. They were losing the benefit of the sunlight and would soon be under night-vision goggles (NVG). Understanding the severe IED threat around them, everyone was already on edge, the leadership especially. Fontenot went to "Smoke" Tatro and Pantaleo for guidance on continuing their search.

"Smoke, we looked at the blast site, around the compounds, and we've found a lower receiver, plastic from somebody's weapon, but other than that, we haven't found much."

"Well, Chief, you know, understanding the damage that Durham sustained, we aren't going to find much. As far as Castro, I don't know, you know."

"So, do y'all want us to keep looking, or what do y'all want us to do?"

"Have y'all looked on the north side of Red Dog just along the road?"

"No, sir, honestly, we stayed primarily south."

The explosives ordnance disposal (EOD) and route-clearance NCOs were nearby and overheard the discussion. Both said emphatically, "Do not go hunting for sensitive items until we can clear the area tomorrow." Fontenot replied, "At the very least, we need to attempt to find something."

It was now nightfall for One Bravo; they had lost all daylight. With Cooper at the farthest eastern position and Parker furthest west, Fontenot deployed his troops into a night as dark as charcoal. As the team began clearing under NVGs, they struggled to see due to a lack of illumination. They had hardly gone about fifty meters off Route Red Dog when Fontenot felt a dreadful sensation in the pit of his stomach. He instructed the team to take a knee, go white light, and look through their ACOGs (advanced combat optical gunsight); the ACOG would magnify what they were looking at. As they began scanning from their stationary position, Cooper called Fontenot over.

"Chief, I got something."

"Coop, what you got, man?"

"I don't know, Chief, look about 150 to 200 meters out."

As Fontenot looked through his ACOG, he saw several wild dogs eating part of Durham's leg. In that moment, he felt an extreme rush of anger like never before. Maybe it was adrenaline, maybe it was just frustration, but Fontenot couldn't fathom having his soldiers go looking for one of their buddies' SI and picking up body parts or, worse, watching animals eating those body parts. At that point, Fontenot decided he wasn't making his guys go walking through the IED-filled desert in the dark.

"Coop, we're pulling back, man."

"Parker, pull back."

Fontenot got on the radio. "One Seven, One One."

"One One, One Seven," Tatro replied.

"One Seven, One One. Hey, we see stuff about 200 meters out, I'm pulling my guys back."

"One One, One Seven. Acknowledge all."

"One Seven Delta, One Seven," Tatro called Miller.

"One Seven, One Seven Delta."

"One Seven Delta, One Seven. Move the MATV into a blocking position north of Route Red Dog, north of the route-clearance vehicle."

"One Seven. Roger, we're moving."

Parker, Fontenot, and Cooper started pulling back, and the MATV began moving into position. Tatro was walking toward his truck to talk to his guys when, BOOM, an enormous explosion rocked all of One Bravo. Fontenot was on one knee in the middle of the road, being pelted with IED shrapnel and engine parts. As he looked north, all he could see was a cloud of dirt flying toward him, and he could hear screaming in the distance. "SMOKE! SMOKE! SMOKE!"

"SHUT THE FUCK UP!" Fontenot yelled back.

Trying to get a grasp on the scenario, Fontenot got on his radio. "One Seven, One One." There was no answer.

"One Seven, One One."

"One One, One Seven." A faint voice came over the radio in a real country accent.

"One Seven, One One, where you at?"

"One One, One Seven. I'm down in the middle of the road; give me a minute to let me get my bearings."

"One Seven, One One. I don't have time for that; I'm coming to get you," said Fontenot, then to his men, "Everyone keep fucking pulling security, I'm going to get Smoke. Parker, I need you to check on everyone and ensure they're alright."

Fontenot headed to the last spot he had seen Tatro; and there he was, slumped over in the middle of the road. He had been concussed in the explosion and pelted with shrapnel and, like Fontenot, Parker, and Cooper, was only about twenty-five meters from the truck. Fontenot helped him off the ground and got him to the route-clearance vehicle.

"Look, I need y'all to keep an eye on him. Smoke, are you good?"

"Yeah, Fontenot, I'm good brother."

In the meantime, Pantaleo was calling up a nine-line for "Doc" Stegehuis, Miller, and Beaudrie. "Doc" Dozeman listened intently to the radio at COP Babur, and as he heard the injuries, fear crept into his mind. Chaplain Tietje was at the COP due to the incidents that had unfolded earlier in the day; Dozeman figured he should take this opportunity to speak to him.

"Would it be okay if I spoke with you for a moment, Chaplain?"

"Of course, Doc."

"Doc Stegehuis and I are friends back home, and I promised his mom I would bring him home safe; I don't know what I'm going to do if he's dead."

Chaplain Tietje, attempting to comfort "Doc," replied, "Wait for everything to happen before drawing any conclusions."

Meanwhile, Fontenot continued trying to communicate with the guys in the truck on the radio, but to no avail. He saw that the MATV had been lifted from the spot where it had struck the IED and was now lying adjacent to the crater. The front of the vehicle was a twisted heap of metal. The back passenger door had burst open, leaving someone dangling halfway out and their weapon barrel-first into the ground. The passenger on the driver's side rear of the vehicle was slumped over and not moving, while the driver was aware.

"Miller, are you okay?"

"I'm okay, Chief, but I'm stuck in the driver's seat."

"Check on Doc and Beaudrie; I'm coming to get y'all."

The route-clearance NCO told Fontenot, "You can't go over there; there's probably a secondary IED."

"SHUT THE FUCK UP. Those are my guys. I'm going to get them!"

Fontenot went to the truck and checked Stegehuis's vitals; he was good but was unconscious. Fontenot grabbed Stegehuis and tossed him over his shoulder. He grabbed his M4 and carried him to the route-clearance vehicle. From what he could tell, Doc was knocked unconscious in the explosion and had likely suffered a concussion. When Fontenot returned to the MATV, he knew time wasn't on their side.

"Miller, how are you pinned in the driver's hatch?"

"Chief, I think I can get out, but; between the way my body is twisted and the radios and shit, I'm just stuck."

"See if you can start breaking shit. I'll be right back. Let me get Beaudrie out of here."

Fontenot climbed through the MATV, pulling Beaudrie from the opposite side. He successfully maneuvered him through the truck, threw him over his shoulder, and brought him to the route-clearance vehicle, where they began assessing him. When Fontenot returned the third time, he needed to help Miller get out. The fire-retardant system trapped Miller.

"Miller, can you remove your gear and use your helmet to break the system?"

"I think so, Chief, just give me a second. I don't have any fucking room in this bitch."

Miller was finally able to climb out. He was the last soldier out of the MATV; Fontenot supported him to the route-clearance vehicle. Fontenot eventually returned to recover the radios and SI to ensure nothing was left behind. It was determined the One Bravo soldiers would head to COP Terra Nova to see the medics and be evaluated for symptoms of traumatic brain injuries (TBI).

Fontenot went to COP Babur with his men to ensure their safety. When he entered the COP, he saw Howard. Before the deployment, Howard and Fontenot had an issue with each other but neither seemed to know why; at that moment, they were brothers and that's all that mattered.

"How are you doing, bro?"

"Pretty terrible, honestly." Howard replied.

"I'm sorry about Durham and Castro."

"Do you know what makes all this even worse?"

"What, man?"

"Today's my birthday."

"Man, I'm truly sorry."

They discussed the day's events before Fontenot left with his soldiers. The day was far from done for the guys of One Bravo.

The next day began with the sun cresting over the Babur sky and the men were positioned like targets anxiously awaiting the enemy fighters eager to engage them the day prior. However, they never came. Route clearance cleared the remainder of Route Red Dog at first light to ensure what men had been walking on for the past 24 hours was not going to suddenly kill them. The passageway "Gunny" Torres, "Doc" Dozeman, Pepper, and Patton had entered to secure Castro had been a death trap. Fontenot had positioned Parker and Cooper in the same alleyway all night, believing it was clear, but he had placed his men practically right on top of an IED. At first light, they discovered it buried not far from where Parker was positioned; this was the second IED in less than 24 hours that Parker had narrowly survived. The EOD team was contacted to clear it so, in anticipation of their arrival, One Bravo sat in the scorching sun, waiting for the IED to be destroyed or to be engaged by enemy fighters, whichever came first. After hours of cooking in the unforgiving heat of the Arghandab pressure cooker, the men were finally relieved. The IED positioned in the alleyway had two mortar rounds buried beneath it, which would have been disastrous for the soldier who discharged it. The "Boys of Babur" had had a difficult day before, as had One Bravo; initiating another IED would not have made their life any easier.

One Bravo had Tatro's truck towed to COP Babur and hauled to Forward Operating Base (FOB) Jelawur's boneyard. The platoon planned to recover everything they could from the MATV later in the day, but first, they needed to stop by the battalion aid station at COP Terra Nova for cognitive tests. Each soldier close to the vehicle was brought in for testing because they didn't have the necessary equipment to do official TBI testing; the medics did what they could with what they had, which wasn't much. They didn't have the technology official facilities such as Kandahar or Bagram Airfields had, and they weren't even able to document any injuries the soldiers had sustained, so it was more or less just letting each man know to "Take care of this when you get home if you remember." Fontenot sustained a holed eardrum, the guys in the truck had concussions, and others suffered similar injuries, but they were eventually deemed they were "good enough to return to duty." The guys from One Bravo made jokes about it for the next three days. They were fortunate, given the magnitude of the explosion.

One Bravo made its way to FOB Jelawur and the boneyard. It was eerie to see Tatro's truck among the others destroyed in explosions in the Arghandab.

"Crazy to think that people walk away from some of these vehicles looking the way they do," Sergeant Creighton said.

"Hell, crazy to think we walked away from Smoke's vehicle looking the way it does," agreed Miller.

A few of the soldiers took photos of the destruction of the MATV, amazed no one was killed in the explosion.

"Smoke, man, your truck looks so much worse in the daylight than it did in the dark," said Pantaleo.

"Sir, how the hell Parker, Cooper, Fontenot, or I weren't fucked up when we were so close to the blast? I'll never know, but I thank God we weren't."

The men climbed through the cab, grabbing headsets, hand mics, and other gear they considered useful to crossload. They made certain the first-aid equipment and litters were grabbed. Given they were still on QRF, they expected to need those. Their next destination was COP Nolen. Some guys were working without much sleep, and their day was still going strong. While most of the junior soldiers slept for two or four hours, leaders, like Fontenot and Peltier, remained in the lines and refused to sleep. While driving from FOB Jelawur to COP Nolen, Fontenotwas in the MRAP driven by Parker. Fontenot accidentally bit his tongue when he nodded off for a moment. This made him so angry he took off his helmet and started smashing it against the dashboard.

"Chief, just take a nap for the love of God," implored Parker.

"Parker, just fucking drive the truck. I'm not taking a fucking nap."

"Damn it, Chief, you're so fucking stubborn!"

They understood a new dark fate lay ahead of them as they proceeded into the Arghandab desert. If there was one thing COP Nolen was renowned for, it was its reputation for being hazardous and unpredictable and, sure enough, that is exactly what it would turn out to be. The men arrived at the COP by driving along Route Phillies. After parking their convoy in the motor pool at the designated spot, they entered the building to receive an orientation on the next day's patrol. The platoon leadership walked inside to receive a briefing regarding the mission to depart for NMK early the following day. Along with Tatro, 1st Lieutenant Babcock, Pantaleo, and the squad leaders from both elements, "Smoke" Manley was there. Sergeant First Class Manley could see from glancing at the One Bravo leaders that they had gone through a lot in the past few days. He was aware they had visited Babur and helped with Durham and Castro's site following their medevac, but he was unaware Tatro's MATV had been struck. His first impression was that the men appeared shocked, but he knew they would pull through. Babcock briefed the routes and the QRF plan on what would happen if something went wrong. Following the briefing, the men strolled outside to enjoy the lovely, hot, fresh air courtesy of the Arghandab River Valley. Shortly after walking outside, another gunfight broke out, and the towers began firing as if they were defending the facility from an enemy seeking to overtake it. The M240B in the southwest tower was firing cyclically, and the Alpha Battery soldiers were immediately gearing up and jumping onto the outside walls.

The impact of 40-millimeter grenade rounds in the orchards was felt repeatedly. The firefight, which appeared to be more of a probing attack meant to elicit a reaction from the Americans, didn't last long, though. These kinds of encounters had practically made the Alpha warriors numb. Everyone descended the walls and the towers and returned to their regular security shifts. Beaudrie and Fontenot strolled back toward the sleeping quarters, thinking they would try to get some rest. The funny thing is, if trying to sleep in the Arghandab, something usually happens that raises the adrenaline. While the men were discussing the previous 32 hours, an RPG passed over the wall and landed between their feet, failing to detonate. Fontenot and Beaudrie exchanged a look.

"Man, what the fuck!" Fontenot exclaimed.

The idea one's time in the Arghandab could end at any second was becoming increasingly clear. In this moment, it was apparent it wasn't their time. It also wasn't their time to sleep. The men returned to the vehicles, relieving the guys pulling security for the trucks because they weren't getting sleep now. They sat back, relaxed, and enjoyed a moment of calm and privacy while the rest of the platoon rested in preparation for Alpha's departure in the early morning.

During the patrol brief, One Bravo had learned the motive for the mission to NMK was due to COP Terra Nova getting hit by mortars a few days earlier. COP Nolen happened to be the crossing route between the suspected mortar tube and Terra Nova. Therefore, Two Alpha would be the lucky bastards to camp out at NMK for three days. During this time, the main objective was to find the mortar tube. As the platoon stepped out in the middle of the night, the movement wasn't going to be anything that would be mind-blowing. Standard movement techniques would get them from point A to point B with minimal issues. Movements at night in the orchards were always eerily quiet; when the men were lucky, the moonlight would guide them along their routes under their NVGs.

They had made it about two hundred meters from COP Nolen when Staff Sergeant Strickland stepped on an IED. Much to his and the rest of the patrol's amazement, it failed to go off. It was a blessing in disguise; they marked the IED and kept moving. The patrol couldn't afford to lose precious time while attempting to get into NMK; they knew what happened when they lost time.

As the sunrise began to crest over the trees, Two Alpha sent out a few patrols. It hadn't taken very long before the locals were visually and verbally upset because some of their grapes had been damaged during the infill of the soldiers. The patrol moved into a compound with walls that were approximately fifteen feet high. There was a stairway that went up to the next level and it had several goat pens in it. The Top Gun Six personal security detail team showed up along with Captain Zastrow, the battalion's Physician's Assistant, and it was almost on cue that Two Alpha began receiving harassing fire. Two Alpha consolidated their water and gear, knowing they would be there for 72 hours. Shortly after, there was another volley of enemy fire, and one of the Afghan National Army (ANA) soldiers standing on the stairs was shot in the face. The round had gone in one side of his mouth and exited the other with minimal damage. Although he was bleeding excessively, his wounds were not considered life-threatening, so he was carefully evacuated in an ANA Ranger pick-up truck.

Two Alpha found themselves in the same unfortunate position that the "Boys of Babur" found themselves four miles away while setting up their COP. The ANA soldiers were celebrating Ramadan and had used all the soldiers' water to wash their feet and hands; they were only 12 hours in. Zastrow recommended dropping a speed bag with water, especially with the ANA going through it as fast as they had. At approximately 2:00 am, two body bags were dropped in, each weighing about two hundred pounds apiece. The men ran out to grab the bags, which required four men each to carry. Manley was concerned that, due to the weight of the bags; and the weight of the men carrying them, if there was an IED in the vicinity, they were going to set it off trying to get the water back to the compound.

As sunrise came on August 31, "Smoke" Carroll pushed out a patrol in the orchards. Carroll was known as being the glue that held the battery together; he was the one constant, and the men trusted his leadership ability above anyone else. They maneuvered through the orchards and found the enemy fighter with the mortar tube. As soon as he was located, it was like the floodgates had opened, and every enemy fighter in the Arghandab was on speed dial to begin attacking to protect their mortar team. Two Alpha and every other American element started taking contact. Manley had just gotten up and thrown his body armor on. He looked out of the courtyard; there was a five or six-story building not far away, and he could see an enemy fighter with an AGS-30, the Russian equivalent of a Mk 19 grenade launcher. Manley attempted to radio Sergeant Little, who was their forward observer, to call in a Kiowa, but in the process of doing so, the enemy fighter fired a 30-millimeter grenade. Manley was hit in the face by shrapnel, the round hitting about eighteen feet in front of him. His nose was crushed as he was blown back roughly ten feet. When Manley was blown backward, he had a dip in his lip so the first thing he needed to do was clear his mouth. He spit out the tobacco, but this was immediately followed by blood. His cheekbone had been broken where the radio had impacted his face. He tried to lift his arm but couldn't because it was broken. To top it off, he had also lost his trigger finger. Manley had been peppered with shrapnel in his left leg, leading up to his groin, but had been spared anything going higher. His left shin was broken, and he was lying in an impact crater about a foot deep.

Trying valiantly, he attempted to crawl into the next room where the medics were, but due to his wounds, it was a slow process. When the medics realized what had happened, they grabbed him by the carrying handle of his vest and dragged him into the next room. They began sticking him with morphine to try to relieve some of his pain. By this point, it was all-hands-on-deck, the medics and other personnel helping to position tourniquets on him; they were doing what they could to place them as high as possible on his thigh to help with the shrapnel going into his stomach. Manley was communicating with the medics and others working on him that he wanted them to tell his daughter that he loved her. What those who were diligently providing him with lifesaving aid weren't aware of was that Manley felt, that as of the day SPC Kuehl was hit his fate had been sealed.

Specialist Kuehl was one of Manley's soldiers and was the first he witnessed being taken out of the Arghandab on a litter. The significance of this event for Manley was that his platoon had been in the courtyard for about 20 minutes, and the area had been cleared by a bomb crew led by their dog team. During that time, they hadn't found anything. Manley had gotten attacked by wasps inside his vest and was tending to that issue when ... BOOM!

"IED! IED! IED!"

Kuehl had initiated the device. He was missing his left leg, and his right leg was severely damaged. His brothers rushed to assist him, doing what they could to help. They administered tourniquets on both legs while a nine-line was being called up. Both of his arms had been peppered with shrapnel, so pressure dressings were administered to help prevent infection. Manley was on Kuehl's aid and litter team to help ensure he was carried to the Black Hawk safely. Ultimately, the fact remained he had seen one of his soldiers in harm's way, and it had haunted him since that day. After the medevac was complete, Manley returned to the courtyard to search for Kuehl's leg but never found it. Now, it was Manley who was being cared for; he found himself in much the same situation as Kuehl. As his men placed him in a body bag to medevac him out, coincidently, it was one of the bags that had been dropped in the middle of the night to deliver water. Each time the pararescue team came in to attempt to get Manley, enemy fighters would start shooting RPGs, mortars, and PKM machine guns at the helicopter. The pararescue helicopter returned with miniguns blazing, but they couldn't get in to get Manley out. Strickland and the remainder of the aid and litter team recommended putting him in another field. They feverously moved him, and the pararescue helicopter didn't bother landing; the crew jumped out, grabbed Manley, threw him into the helicopter, and flew away. As the men from Alpha withdrew into the orchards, another one of their beloved and respected leaders was gone; his status was unknown, and there were many lingering questions the soldiers had that needed to be addressed for the betterment of the battery who would step up to take his place and, ultimately, would he be okay?

CHAPTER 9

Hard Right Over the Easy Wrong

> Again, I looked and saw all the oppression that was taking place under the sun: I saw the tears of the oppressed and they have no comforter; power was on the side of their oppressors, and they have no comforter. And I declared that the dead, who had already died, are happier than the living.
>
> ECCLESIASTES 4 NIV

One thing that was constantly changing in "The Devil's Playground" was the days on the calendar. They may have changed slowly but they changed, nonetheless. The men from Alpha Battery had now descended south into Nūr Muhammad Kolache (NMK), the men of Bravo had moved east into Babur, which was unfathomable in the past. The warfighters of HHB (Headquarters and Headquarters Battery) had done the unthinkable. They pushed into the orchards and furrows south of the Menorah Canal to set up Combat Outpost (COP) Stout. Although there had been a presence in the killing fields in the past from the Americans, it was minimal. Each time units attempted to go further into the orchards in the past they would withdraw after taking casualties. Enemy fighters had become accustomed to seeing patrols that had taken casualties, calling in medevacs, and then withdrawing to the safety of their COPs. The HHB soldiers had suffered numerous losses, but due to the battalion leadership's continuous guidance, they were resolute to hold the line. Initially holding that line looked as if it were going to be treacherous and see men losing their legs daily. Patrols continued moving out under the leadership of Sergeants First Class Tivao and Lyon, and 1st Lieutenants Hopper and Weaver, along with seasoned noncommissioned officers (NCO) Staff Sergeants Casey and Reed, Sergeant Naquin, and others. One thing had been identified in the Arghandab: this was a squad-level fight. Squad and team leaders were crucial to the success of any organization; if a battery had strong NCOs, they would be successful. HHB had strong NCOs within their ranks and strong officers; their soldiers, although shell-shocked, trusted their leaders and were resilient enough to continue pursuing success in the Arghandab.

One Hotel received Weaver recently, and he was a huge asset to the team. He was Ranger-qualified and highly recommended by Colonel Kandarian, the brigade commander. Weaver was a hard worker who refused to cut corners; he was steadfast and persistent in executing tactics and quickly instilled an unparalleled work ethic in his soldiers. The men fell in line with him, and Lyon, his platoon sergeant, loved working alongside him. With One Hotel having a multitude of different military specialties among them, getting an asset like Weaver was enormous.

The unoccupied Hesco barriers that encircled their perimeter were one daily obstacle for the HHB soldiers. There were problems for those inside its hollow walls since the Hescos were too high, and silhouetted those inside. The commander at COP Stout realized the shield separating them from the enemy was a facade. Much like the leaders in Babur, those at COP Stout faced the same dilemma: how to fill the Hescos while waiting for assistance from the Seabees. They still didn't have M2 .50-caliber machine guns because they had walked into the orchards during Bakersfield and had yet to be reinforced with necessary equipment. They weren't expected to get higher-caliber machine guns until the Seabees showed up weeks later. This would be when supply lines opened, towers built, and barriers finally filled. The soldiers on the ground experienced a notable improvement in morale when even small tasks like filling Hescos were completed. Much like the Babur soldiers, they had attempted to put sand in the barriers, but it did nothing more than hold the Hescos in place. The soldiers lived in moon dust and continued receiving indirect fire from a suspected AGS-30 grenade launcher again and again. They took consistent rocket-propelled grenades (RPG) daily for about five days after COP Stout was set up. One of the 30-millimeter rounds found its home when it landed inside the compound, and shrapnel hit "Smoke" Tivao in his neck. It hit dangerously close to his carotid artery; as "Doc" Fontenot worked on him, the men shared a conversation and tried to make dark humor of the incident, as soldiers typically do.

"Doc, how bad is it?"

"Well, Smoke, when I remove the shrapnel, it'll probably feel better, and I'll be able to bandage you up, or you'll die. It'll certainly be one or the other, but I'm unsure yet."

"Damn it, Doc, don't tell me that."

The two men just chuckled after that. Fontenot was able to remove the shrapnel from Tivao's neck, but he had been lucky; just a few millimeters left or right, and it could have been fatal. Shortly after, the soldiers from HHB finally got a reprieve from the front line. They had an opportunity to return to COP Terra Nova, where they were initially positioned, to enjoy a hot shower. They were able to relax for a few days, free of being shot at or worrying about indirect fire. The stay was short-lived however, and when they left, it would be for good. They loaded up their gear, and reality began to set in that this would be their final exfil from Terra Nova; they would no longer have the fortress with the large mud walls surrounding them, and fully erected towers protecting them. Instead, they would be waiting for the Seabees to arrive and relying on each other until the foreseeable future. As the men prepared to head back, two of their soldiers had seen enough; they were artillery soldiers and hadn't signed on to be infantrymen. They had officially quit on HHB and were reassigned to guard the gate at COP Terra Nova. As it turned out, this might as well have been a reward, considering the circumstances.

As the soldiers from COP Stout edged closer to September, they observed the orchards continuing to spring to life and acting as a ferocious enemy. The fields constantly presented the men with something fresh, regardless of whether they were doing a routine patrol or dealing with explosions audible throughout the Arghandab. The heat finally gave them a bit of a break as it eased to a mere 90° Fahrenheit days, which was monumental and nearly felt like winter compared to the 116° days the soldiers had fallen in on. The men from HHB were not all 13Bs (cannon crewmembers) like Alpha and Bravo, as they were a hodge podge of military specialties like weathermen, forward observers, and human-resource specialists. This had given their leaders a variety of combat arms and soft-skill military specialties to attempt to overcome. Youth was also another hurdle for the Havoc leaders. The troops' morale was on life support; it had a pulse, but it was hard to find on some days. Some of the soldiers performed like a dog that had been beaten—timid and worried. By this point, "Doc" Fontenot had treated every casualty hit at COP Stout and was doing his best to stay upbeat. Like many troops, he had times when it was impossible to remain positive and he needed to let it out. Tivao overheard Fontenot venting to Private First Class Talbert about some things happening in the sector. Tivao pulled him aside.

"Doc, I need you to get your shit together, guys are depending on you, make sure you have the proper equipment. Guys need you to be on your game, you are their lifeline. They depend on you every day."

"Roger, Smoke, I'll get it together."

As "Doc" began tearing up, Tivao didn't know if it was because he was overwhelmed or if his message had hit home. Fontenot was an 18-year-old from Port Barre, Louisiana. He was full of vigor and ready to help every soldier instantly. His dad was an Operation *Iraqi Freedom* veteran and was killed in Baghdad during his third tour when "Doc" was 16 years old. Doc wanted to prevent other families from losing their husbands, fathers, brothers, and sisters. He had already seen some of the most catastrophic things a combat medic could see, and he was only a few months into the deployment.

They didn't have enough manpower to get the men enough rest efficiently, and they were pulling from other batteries to replace some of the lost soldiers. Staff Sergeant Casey had been pulled from Two Bravo to help supplement One Hotel with experience and lethality. Sergeant Lucas was sent to be Sergeant Stout's backfill. He was a communications specialist and for the most part, Tivao hadn't seen him very often. He mostly stayed inside the MRAP (mine-resistant, ambush-protected). Unfortunately, Lucas had little experience and was tasked with filling massive shoes with the loss of Stout. As a result, Tivao positioned Specialist Gilkey in Stout's role for a while. Still, due to their mission's enormous responsibility and dangerous nature, the position had to be temporary and carried out by someone with more experience. Eventually, Staff Sergeant Dinero, an infantryman, filled the role permanently. The soldiers from Two Bravo were having a tough time readjusting after Bakersfield. Two Hotel had lost Stout, one of their platoon's critical components.

Tivao sat alone inside COP Stout before a patrol, attempting to gather his thoughts while figuring out how to get his men to regain their confidence in the orchards. The real question was what would get his young team to gel in these harsh conditions. Before their deployment, they hadn't had much opportunity to build a battle rhythm or trust in each other like most infantry units do. Initially, Tivao was in Alpha Battery, and his team was set the way he wanted. Then, he was told he would be heading to HHB to take over a platoon. When he found out he was leaving Alpha, a wave of emotions came over him.

"Why is this happening to me? Why now? My team is set."

Tivao immediately resisted; he argued with First Sergeant Hartlaub, Captain Thomasson, and Command Sergeant Major Barrios about the move. He didn't want to leave the team he had built over the previous 12 months. He probed Barrios with questions, trying to identify who his leaders would be and whose team he would be inheriting. When asked who his squad leaders would be, he was told, "Sergeant Naquin 'Cajun' and Sergeant Stout." He knew both from their time in Iraq. Tivao and Naquin had worked together on the personal security detail team in Iraq, and he had seen Stout around in garrison. Tivao called Naquin to get a pulse for what he was walking into.

He wasn't happy about the move, but as is typical with most leaders, he would do his best. Tivao believed that, if nothing else, he was given good squad leaders. Two Hotel went to the Joint Readiness Training Center together for their Combat Training Center rotation. The rotation was lackluster at best and didn't bond the men or create a sense of pride like a unit ramping up to deploy needs. When they returned from Louisiana, they would head out on leave immediately, followed by a round-trip flight to the Arghandab, they hoped. Now, Tivao was sitting in the Arghandab without Stout and attempting to figure out how to get everyone back in the fields. He wargamed how to inspire his soldiers to continue to fight another day, much less the next 10 months. Most of his guys had never been in combat and were between 18 and 19 years old. They were on the ground and had already witnessed Stansbery, Stout, and Pittman's deaths, as well as a multitude of other casualties. Tivao decided that; to earn his soldiers' confidence and expedite their return to patrolling, he would lead them as point man using the mine detector. Patrol after patrol, he realized that, although this method was working, his platoon may be decimated if he were hit because they would lose another critical ingredient. Tivao began supplementing their patrols with Afghan soldiers. They were utilizing many techniques during their movements and implementing them into their schemes of maneuvers. He had his leaders focus on training the Afghan soldiers on weapon safety and basic patrolling to ensure they understood how to move alongside the Americans effectively. Two Hotel began avoiding choke points that once may have haunted them; they became fluent with movements, were experts at climbing walls, and stayed away from main roads at all costs. Main roads, also known as "hard balls," had become a point of contingency in the Arghandab. Those who attempted to use them met a grim and gruesome fate. They were now setting up effective overwatch positions that provided valuable intel across the Arghandab. Patrols began noticing when Taliban fighters placed markers in the fields to identify where they had hidden improvised explosive devices (IEDs). During one overwatch position, Two Hotel observed a Taliban fighter unhook a 9-volt battery pack from an IED, which allowed them to intervene before anything detrimental happened. Two Hotel appeared to be back in the saddle, moving along and gaining steam. However, things aren't always as they seem. Tivao observed Naquin attempting to play superhero by taking point on every patrol. He was forced to reel him back in; he knew it would only cause more chaos if the platoon lost another senior man. Tivao was an experienced leader and knew how much a core group of leaders meant to his team. Due to this, he was determined to preserve his group at all costs. He understood each man attempted to cope in his way. Tivao believed Naquin was beginning to do the same thing he had done, but he couldn't risk losing him.

On September 8, Tivao and Naquin prepared to push out a patrol northwest of COP Stout. The patrol would navigate them alongside an area where they knew the terrain would be rough. They were going to be passing through grape furrows and open areas. In the past, enemy fighters had utilized shooting holes in mud walls to ambush American patrols as they attempted to maneuver through the fields. One of the routes the patrol planned to take would lead them to an area with an enormous wall visible from COP Stout. As the patrol neared the area, Tivao radioed, "Tower One, this is Havoc Two Seven. Can you see our patrol from your tower; over?"

"Havoc Two Seven, this is Tower One. Negative, over."

The patrol continued maneuvering through the unforgiving terrain, snaking around the area until they encountered a few locals behind the massive wall. What seemed odd to the men was that behind this wall was nothing more than a tapered-off area that enabled enemy fighters to engage American soldiers and then disappear like the faceless enemy they had become. Tivao sat down with a local farmer to sip chai tea with him. He spoke through his interpreter to make small talk while trying to build rapport. Tivao asked several standard questions from his days in Iraq, like "What can we do to improve your life here?", "What can we do to help secure you and your family?" and "Is there anything you and your family need?" After a few minutes of conversing, the farmer had this look of concern come across his face as he listened to the ICOM traffic that came across as broken static on the radio.

The farmer informed Tivao's interpreter, "They're here."

"Who's here? Taliban?" asked Tivao.

"Yes."

One of the reasons for the extreme look of concern from the farmer was because it was well known across the Arghandab that those who helped the American fighters would face the wrath of the Taliban. Afghans would be subjected to beatings, as well as the rape or murder of their family members.

With a complete disregard for the lives of the Afghan farmers in the vicinity of the American soldiers, the first CRACK was heard. Then, it was like the floodgates had opened. The men of Two Hotel had walked into a hornet's nest, and the hornets were furious. As Two Hotel desperately fought to gain fire superiority, they were clearly encircled by a relentless enemy that had baited them into the area. The patrol continued to repel the assault with every ounce of energy they had. They knew that if they could repel this volley, they could return to COP Stout. They also knew from Bakersfield that losing ground could be catastrophic for their element. Tivao decided the best thing to do would be to live to fight another day. The patrol slowly began bounding back one element at a time, with one team providing overwatch while the other maneuvered rearward. The persistent enemy attacked with PKM machine-gun fire and the occasional RPG. The patrol had now been in the furrows for several hours in the blistering heat, trapped in their gear and being hunted. After a furious back-and-forth match, Two Hotel eventually made it back to the solace of COP Stout without sustaining any casualties. It would come at a cost. Tivao had chosen to break contact, which wasn't something the leaders of HHB were used to doing. When Two Hotel found a safe space inside the makeshift barriers surrounding COP Stout, tempers elevated to fever pitch. Sergeant First Class Lyon and Tivao got into a heated dispute about whether the patrol should've broken contact or stayed in the furrows and continued to fight until reinforcements arrived. At that moment, neither Lyon nor Tivao was willing to budge on their stance. It was ultimately determined the leader on the ground needed to be trusted to make the call they believed was best for their soldiers and the unit; Tivao made that call while encircled.

Night crept in on the soldiers of COP Stout, and there was an almost anxious feeling in the air due to the happenings from the patrol earlier in the day. Several of the NCOs from One Hotel sat down with 1st Lieutenant Weaver to wargame their plan for the next day's mission. Staff Sergeant Casey had been recovering from dysentery for the past two days, had gotten an IV for the last day just to get rehydrated, and was finally able to hold food down. Weaver jokingly came in and was giving Casey shit about him not wanting to go on the patrol the next day.

"Casey, if you didn't want to go on the patrol, you could've just said you didn't want to go."

"Sir, you know I'm down to go on the fucking patrol. Let's fucking go."

"I'm just messing with you, Casey. I know you're always down to go out. I want you to be ready to go. We need you out there."

Staff Sergeant Reed was the second squad leader for One Hotel. Much to his dismay, he wouldn't be going out because he had injured his shoulder breaching a wall on an earlier patrol. Instead, Reed would remain inside the tactical operations center (TOC), keeping an eye on the radios so he could react quickly in case the patrol needed help. Lyon, Casey, and Weaver wanted to ensure they could avoid choke points. Due to a shortage of available Americans, they decided to supplement the patrol with their Afghan National Army (ANA) counterparts. The plan was to set in an L-shape ambush northwest of COP Stout along a bridge they believed they had good imagery of. They planned to utilize the imagery; and lessons learned from speaking to Two Hotel; to make a few adjustments. They knew the patrol would be complex and relatively unstable and that climbing walls would be time-consuming and slow. Additionally, they were aware from earlier encounters that they needed to account for the shooting holes in the walls. The wall facing the patrol as they were to begin their infill to set in their machine-gun team was an 11-foot barrier that had these holes. Multiple patrols had been ambushed at that site. The leaders from One Hotel knew where they intended to set in their ambush position, but COP Stout couldn't provide any cover whatsoever.

It was September 9, and the men from One Hotel had conducted a map reconnaissance and reviewed contingency plans; they felt confident and intended to establish a foothold in the area for yet another win against the Taliban. They had the pleasure of having a sapper squad with them to assist in clearing buildings. The sappers were crucial to the success of the clearance of obstacles at COP Stout and would also be involved in future operations. The use of some of the demolition explosives from the sapper team came into play as they were trying to figure out exactly how they were going to set the bait for the Taliban fighters. Lyon and Weaver figured that, at some point, they would be ambushed; once they had encountered enemy fighters, they would bound back into the furrows, and then they could detonate the C4 they had acquired from the sappers. This would make it appear that one of the soldiers from One Hotel had initiated an IED. In the past, anytime an IED would go off, ICOM chatter would light up, fighters asking, "Who's IED was that?" and then they would attempt to do a complex ambush on the troops in contact. This time, the plan would be to bait the Taliban rather than be baited by them.

Before stepping off, as the team leaders conducted their checks, Lyon took a step away from his troops to think about where they had come from and how far they'd come in a short period. He thought back to the infill of Bakersfield and how they walked into the fields with only the gear on their backs and the ammunition they were carrying. He smiled, knowing the Strike Brigade had provided them with overwhelming support to ensure COP Stout had resources to facilitate its security and establishment as soon as feasible due to the environment. Lyon understood the One Hotel squad had been assembled and trained using tactics, techniques, and procedures right out of Captain Shaefer's Ranger handbook since Lieutenant Colonel Flynn had the foresight to do so a year before the deployment. Now he looked at his soldiers, who had been through a range of conditions since they were dropped in, had seen some of the atrocities of war, and were holding ground not previously held by any other element. He found peace in the thought that his platoon was solid with their knowledge base, and they were now being reinforced by Colonel Kandarian's top lieutenant, 1st Lieutenant Weaver.

Although there weren't many ways to bring the patrol to the desired location, they would try to proceed via the route of most resistance to arrive at point A and reach point B without incident. The patrol stepped off at 3:00 am. Everyone appeared optimistic; the weather was much more relaxed than they had experienced, and they settled into a cool 86° Fahrenheit morning, which, to the soldiers, was near perfect. As the patrol began negotiating the furrows, it was apparent to everyone that, although they had grown so much in the past few months, the terrain in the Arghandab was still as unforgiving as ever and was treacherous even for the most seasoned of fighters. Unbeknown to One Hotel, they were navigating a similar route to Two Hotel the day prior. The patrol left COP Stout under the cover of darkness and moved under the green glow of their night-vision goggles (NVG); the movement was slow and methodical as most movements in the Arghandab had become. The night prior, Weaver made his NCOs and soldiers rehearse the patrol repeatedly; he insisted they perform the patrol to standard and believed that, with enough rehearsals, when they encountered contact, the men would instinctively react and prevent further casualties. Weaver was adamant about the guys doing infantry tactics the right way, and he was doing his best to ensure he and his NCOs were training the lower enlisted soldiers accordingly. He became famous for constantly preaching the importance of taking "the hard right over the easy wrong." Lyon, "Doc" Shannon, and the platoon's forward observer, along with their security element, were going to be positioned with their Bravo team roughly eighty meters south from where Weaver would be meticulously sitting in his machine-gun team. Casey was with Alpha team, and Weaver, with the weapons team, would have a dog team and a camera crew.

The dog team had been called forward and checked the area but hadn't hit on anything; Casey followed suit and scanned one last time with the mine detector, once again finding nothing. They also checked a wall next to a nearby tree using the mine detector; it was clear. At this point, the teams were still under NVGs. Casey was having problems with his, so he took his helmet off.

"Sir, I can't see shit with this on, hold it for me." Shortly after having Casey's helmet in his hands, Weaver began thinking about the sniper threat level of the past.

"Casey; put your helmet back on."

Weaver pointed out a better spot for the patrol to set up their gun crew, but they would have to traverse over a neighboring wall to get there. Casey had worked to ensure they had knocked down part of the wall that was next to them and had jumped on top of the wall. Straddling it, he looked back toward the team that was planning on moving over with him.

"Hey, LT, are you coming with me?" he asked sarcastically.

"Yeah, I'm coming."

Weaver took one step toward Casey and initiated the IED. A blast erupted like none of the soldiers had experienced up to that point in the deployment. Not even the blasts during Bakersfield compared to the ferocity of this one. Casey was blown from the wall into a ditch about 30 meters away. After what seemed like forever, he awoke face down. His face felt like he had been in a boxing match, and it felt like all his teeth had been knocked out of his mouth; he reached his hand up and felt with amazement as his teeth were still there. He called over the radio.

"IED, IED, IED."

As he clumsily stumbled back to his original position and stepped over the wall, he saw the crater where Weaver had stood moments before. Terrazas and Long were with Casey at this point. His first instinct was to set in security to ensure they didn't get ambushed. He scanned the area to see if he could see any sign of his platoon leader but had no luck; what he did see, however, was a weapon hanging in a nearby tree. He assumed the M4 must have been Weaver's. Casey and a few of his soldiers desperately looked for Weaver. They maneuvered approximately one hundred meters from the blast site when they encountered their forward observer, Private First Class Walters. He was shocked and bewildered about how to help Weaver, who had been blown so far from the initial blast site that he landed near Walters. When Walters checked on the lieutenant, he realized he was already mortally wounded. Weaver was one of Walters's role models; he was a Superman to him, and seeing him this way was unfathomable. Weaver was a quadruple amputee, suffering above-the-knee amputations of both legs and shrapnel throughout his body. In contrast to the other casualties, Weaver had suffered a severe injury to his neck and head, which the soldiers were attempting to treat. They were all in a state of shock. They had not anticipated such a disastrous event, particularly involving Weaver.

Weaver was 26 years old and had already had a profound impact on both his soldiers and the world around him. He initially volunteered as a soldier and was deployed to Iraq before commissioning and attending William and Mary College, where he graduated with honors. He grew up in four different countries and was culturally knowledgeable. He was well known for his humor, leadership, athleticism, and fellowship, but his legacy would live on through how he carried himself as a leader and a father. As his soldiers hovered around his body, they were stunned at how this could have happened to the best among them. How could this have happened to Weaver? He was a Ranger. He was the best soldier in HHB. He was the epitome of perfection. As some soldiers began to tear up, Casey said, "Hey fucking snap back into it. We need to get him back to Stout now; the birds can't get him here."

At that point, nearly 18 minutes after the blast had passed, the Lyon and Bravo teams finally arrived. They were smoked from taking the path of most resistance, attempting not to hit a secondary IED. They had honored Weaver's plan and went over every grape furrow to get to him, but it had taken them forever. The medevac request had failed; it was identified that the jungle penetrator couldn't be dropped to help them. The soldiers attempted to place Weaver on the Skedco (a flexible stretcher designed to be dragged across the ground), but it was too dense in the furrows. Casey, Terrazas, and Walden tried to move him on a pole-less litter, but they only made it about eighty meters before they realized it was pointless.

"What the fuck are we going to do if his head falls off?" one of the soldiers asked.

"We'll pick it up and bring it with us. Nothing will be left behind," Casey replied.

At that point, they grabbed Weaver's body and began carrying him. They moved him briefly until they ran into Tivao and some of the Two Hotel soldiers who could help get Weaver to Stout. When they finally got settled at COP Stout, an ANA soldier was heard laughing about something unclear to everyone.

"Today's the worst day of my life, if you don't stop laughing, I'll fucking kill you," Casey growled. The ANA soldier could've been laughing at anything at that point. Afghans see life very differently. Lieutenant Colonel Flynn anxiously waited for the patrol to return to Stout. Once back, he asked the obvious question.

"What the fuck happened?"

Casey replied, "We believe it was a pressure plate IED that he initiated. We believe that it must have been made of Styrofoam because the mine detector didn't pick it up, and it wasn't RCIED detonated."

Everyone tried to figure out how the fuck their Ranger-qualified infantry leader got hit, and yet they were still here. More of the soldiers no longer wanted to patrol. Leaders were again figuring out how to get the guys back in the orchards. Ultimately, the platoon would be subjected to getting replacements. Reed felt guilty because he wasn't on the patrol and wondered if it would've been different if he had been on the ground. A large majority of his guys were in the fields during the patrol, and he was stuck in the TOC listening to the radio; it was killing him to know he wasn't there and couldn't help or even truly understand what they were going through.

A few days later, the soldiers from COP Stout moved back to COP Terra Nova to pay their respects to Weaver in a battlefield cross ceremony. The ceremony brought leaders from across the brigade, such as Colonel Kandarian, Sergeant Major White, Flynn, and many others. The soldiers from One Hotel were there in full support to pay their respects to their fallen platoon leader. He was their leader, their shining light, their light in the darkness, and he was taken from them. As the ceremony began, there wasn't a dry eye in the formation; the soldiers shared heartache at the loss of their leader and were in disarray about how they would proceed. Weaver's death was one that One Hotel wasn't ready for; many of the soldiers were unable to comprehend how they would continue. The mood of the men at COP Stout was somber, the outlook bleak, and morale grim and mournful.

After the ceremony, Colonel Kandarian introduced 1st Lieutenant Kinsel to Lyon. The Strike commander advised Lyon Kinsel to replace Weaver. Kandarian also spoke to 1st Lieutenant Ivey, a close, if not best, friend of Weaver's. The colonel gave him the courtesy of alerting him that Kinsel would be there to help Havoc in Weaver's absence. Kinsel was White's number one lieutenant. He knew he had enormous boots to fill but was willing to take the job on. Kinsel had nothing but respect for Weaver, but he didn't attempt to be him as he knew that was impossible; he just came in knowing the platoon needed a leader, and he would be just that. Kinsel knew the assignment was going to be extremely hard. He believed he was placed in the position for a reason; he would do his best to help One Hotel pick up the pieces and carry on the mission the way Weaver wanted it done.

CHAPTER 10

Welcome to the Havoc

We may encounter defeats, but we must not be defeated.

MAYA ANGELOU

With all the excitement going on in the orchards with the Havoc men, Three Bravo had been having their fill on their patrols around the area of operations (AO). There was talk of them spearheading the operation for what would become Strong Point Babur, but nothing was solidified. They were supplemented with an infantry squad, so it would only make sense for them to be the spearhead. It was September 22, 2010, and Three Bravo was preparing to conduct a night patrol to set in an ambush on the first canal. This patrol would oversee and intercept enemy fighters attempting to enter Druia to place improvised explosive devices (IEDs) on Route Red Dog. Unlike small kill-team patrols, this movement would include approximately twenty-six soldiers, including their Afghan National Army (ANA) counterparts. Three Bravo left Combat Outpost (COP) Tynes under a full moon. The sky was clear, so they had the moon to light their way other than the stars. Illumination was perfect for their night-vision goggles (NVG) and ensured the movement would be smooth, and spacing was not an issue due to visibility. Three Bravo had patrolled this area for the past four months; the patrols were becoming routine. This one seemed a little different from the outset. Maybe it was because of the element's size, or perhaps the universe was letting them know luck was not in their favor that night. Private Penton was the point man for the patrol and oversaw the work with the Vallon mine detector. He also had one of the Thor III packs for extra protection against radio-controlled IEDs. The patrol was also fortunate enough to have a dog team with them. The dog and his handler were next to Penton, clearing the way.

As Penton steered closer to the canal, he took a knee along with the remainder of the patrol so the dog team could clear the site before entering the field. Penton followed close behind once the dog had cleared through. The dog team and Penton circled where they intended to set up the ambush site to clear the area. When crossing the first canal, Penton came to his first choke point, and his senses rose drastically. The day prior, Three Bravo had located an IED buried beneath an MRE (meal, ready to eat) box conveniently placed on the first canal. Choke points had long been a point of contention for the Top Guns. Penton decided to Vallon the wall next to the choke point; as he did so, the earth erupted beneath him.

"IED, IED, IED!"

Penton luckily fell away from the blast and toward the east side of the canal. As he attempted to regain his composure, all he could see was black smoke and the full moon painting a radiant sky. Sergeant Huber sprinted to Penton's location and pulled him into the canal to get him out of the initial blast site. He would start his triage there to ensure the private had no significant injuries requiring a medevac. Private Cheng was blown into a nearby tree, but hadn't been injured either. Despite being hit by a toe-popper IED, Penton was more fortunate than most; it hadn't torn him apart like others who were impacted in the orchards, but it did leave him with minor cuts and a possible concussion. This IED resembled a warning from the Gods to keep their heads in the game. After the blast, 1st Lieutenant Ivey decided to cancel the patrol. The quick-reaction force (QRF) arrived to secure Penton, and he was transported back to COP Tynes for further evaluation. Maybe it was due to the universe casting a blessing of a full moon on patrol, or perhaps it was just one man's luck, but Penton was most fortunate; he could walk away. The near miss, or the warning, was considered, but it wouldn't slow down or hinder the Bravo element from moving farther soon.

The soldiers of One Hotel experienced a significant event on September 9 when they lost their leader, 1st Lieutenant Weaver. The Strike Brigade had, however, ensured they were quickly provided another leader with vast knowledge and experience in the form of 1st Lieutenant Kinsel. The Army is like a conveyor belt: one soldier or leader expires or retires, and the next one steps up and takes their place. No one misses a beat, soldiers pay their respects, and that's it; they are not forgotten, but soldiers continue moving forward with the mission. Although Kinsel did not deploy with the Top Guns, he deployed with the Strike Brigade. He served as a rifle platoon leader in 2nd Platoon, Alpha Company, 1st Battalion, 502nd Infantry Regiment (1-502), which provided him with valuable experience as an infantry platoon leader. Following four months of combat with his platoon at Forward Operating Base Wilson, in Iraq, he was informed that his time with the 1-502 was ending, and he would be assigned to the 1st Battalion, 320th Field Artillery Regiment, the Top Guns, to assume command of a platoon at COP Stout. That was all he knew at the time; earlier during the deployment, he recalled hearing about this significant offensive that a field artillery battalion was conducting, that they had taken ground from the Taliban, and had lost several soldiers. Everyone was bewildered as to who the unit even was. Kinsel was blindsided entirely by the fact that he was leaving. He was on a bird on his way to the Arghandab with some of his buddies, asking if he would consider adding them to his Soldiers Group Life Insurance, almost before he knew it. A helicopter from the 101st Aviation Regiment dropped Kinsel off in the back of COP Terra Nova; no sooner had they dropped Kinsel off than they had flown away. The lieutenant sensed a voice approaching from behind him in the pitch black. He immediately grabbed a grenade, thinking, "Not today, Motherfucker!" He turned, and it was the battalion's executive officer, Major Raymond.

"Woah, buddy, it's Raymond. I'm the battalion XO."

"Nice to meet you, sir."

They went inside Terra Nova for a quick meet-and-greet with Lieutenant Colonel Flynn. Kinsel's initial impression was that the COP was massive. He reported to the battalion commander, and no sooner had he done so than the phone rang.

"It's for you."

"Hello?"

The voice on the other end of the line said, "Lieutenant Kinsel, do you know who this is?" "No, sir."

"This is Colonel Kandarian."

"My apologies, sir."

"Lieutenant Kinsel, do you know why you are there?"

"No, sir, not really."

"Because you are a well-trained soldier according to the Ranger Creed. There is an abundance of hostile enemy fighters in that AO, and you are the leader I hand-selected to lead that platoon in Lieutenant Weaver's absence, do you understand?"

"Yes, sir."

"Now, put Lieutenant Colonel Flynn back on the line."

"Roger, sir."

After the battlefield cross ceremony for Weaver, Kinsel was taken by convoy to COP Stout. When he arrived, the outpost was under attack, so he tried to take in his surroundings as quickly as possible. From what he had heard, the fighting the 320th was encountering was akin to the Vietnam War. When he arrived, he saw that his new residence was bordered tightly by canals, pomegranate orchards, and grape furrows; the foliage was also exceedingly dense, and the heat and humidity were almost intolerable. With his platoon under attack, he figured there was no better time to get acclimated, so he jumped out of the truck and joined his platoon the only way he saw fit—under fire. When everything calmed down, Kinsel and Sergeant First Class Lyon sat to discuss personnel and the direction they wanted the platoon to go. The lieutenant was shocked to learn that the battery, which ought to have over one hundred personnel, only had 40. Because of this, there were as many insurgents as American troops around the AO.

He was briefed that every patrol experienced small-arms attacks, frequently occurring before American soldiers reached more than three hundred meters from COP Stout. Lyon informed Kinsel the fighting had taken its toll on the soldiers of One Hotel, so he may see some were worn out physically and others emotionally. Still, the soldiers of Havoc Battery persevered.

It is not always easy to adjust to a new platoon in garrison. Acclimatizing to a platoon that has recently lost its leader in combat is almost inconceivable. Kinsel decided to tread cautiously, day by day, and attempt to ease into his circumstances. COP Stout was not your typical Red Roof Inn, as he soon realized when he took a closer look. For the past four months, several of his guys had been living like vagrants. They made do, whether it meant sleeping in a hole in the ground with camouflage nets shielding them from the sun or sharing a cot in the bunkers. It was not until recently that they received upgrades to inflatable tents. The one constant issue with the inflatables was the indirect-fire attacks. Most tents continued to be deflated by shrapnel and were held up by 2×4s. At first glance, he felt COP Stout looked like a scene from *Apocalypse Now*. Having seen these austere conditions and the minimal staffing Havoc was working with for the first time in his career, Kinsel realized what commanders truly mean by the "Fog of war."

Lieutenant Kinsel had been with his platoon for a few weeks, and they were starting to gel. Understanding his platoon's characteristics and developing a battle rhythm was imperative. Given their apparent bond and the fact that Staff Sergeant Casey and Kinsel appeared to be on the same page, Kinsel thought he could rely on him, and he already had a bond with Lyon, his platoon sergeant.

As fall ended and winter began, everything appeared to be going smoothly, from what Kinsel could tell. He placed immense importance on developing a solid battle rhythm and getting to know his soldiers. Everything for One Hotel was beginning to take shape as the AO continued to come into focus. It was early in the game, but Kinsel knew he was gradually bringing down walls because the soldiers were warming to him.

One Hotel received a mission to conduct a search-and-attack mission to the southwest of COP Stout. The leadership intended to use the grape furrows south of the COP to provide cover and concealment. Historically, enemy fighters had used the two compounds near the grape furrows as attack-by-fire positions. When patrols utilized movements through the grape furrows, the likelihood they would initiate an IED was lower than if they were to follow a raised path or walkway. The thought process was that if soldiers employed their Vallons correctly, and marked a lane clearly, it would be easy to defeat IEDs.

This patrol started like any other. One Hotel had been patrolling together as a team for four months. Kinsel, who was still relatively new, took a moment to watch the men's movements and was struck by how well they patrolled—especially considering they were not an infantry unit.

The platoon hadn't moved more than one hundred meters from COP Stout when they encountered a raised path. Casey began to direct the clearance of the path while the rest of the men assumed security positions. Kinsel took solace in the fact the platoon appeared competent in infantry tasks. Even though they weren't infantrymen, they were at least trying to become experts at the jobs they were performing. His platoon had shown itself to be highly adept at maneuvering through hazardous situations. Just like they had rehearsed, they started to leapfrog over the dangerous area; as soon as the area was free, they went again. Kinsel got to the danger area and began moving across. Just as he approached the other side, he heard the explosion. BOOM!

"IED, IED, IED!"

Following the blast was a blood-curdling scream that could give goosebumps to a serial killer. Kinsel was in disbelief. He turned to see a large cloud of dust and smoke just beginning to settle as the world seemed to stop. The air was heavy with the scent of explosives, scorched flesh, dust, and debris. Kinsel could see the wounded soldier not more than twenty meters from him. He was still encapsulated in the grape furrows, writhing in pain.

Last in the squad was Private First Class Macari. Three other soldiers had passed through the grape furrows; he was following them. A mine detector had cleared the area he was in, so Macari had no reason to suspect he would encounter an IED. He was a perfect example of "if it's your time, it's your time." Macari was now gripping his left leg just below the knee while lying face-up on the ground. The explosion had amputated his lower leg. The muscle in his calf had been ruptured, shredded, and torn apart, leaving the bone exposed. "Doc" Shannon and several soldiers immediately attached tourniquets to the leg. Shannon didn't have morphine for him, so they were working as quickly as possible to try to prevent Macari from going into shock. Kinsel called up the nine-line and could hear Lyon directing the casualty evacuation. Although mayhem occurs because of an IED, the soldiers from One Hotel managed to keep the chaos under control. Upon confirmation of receiving the nine-line, the platoon started to retrace their steps across the path to provide safety for the litter crew heading to the landing zone (LZ). Bakersfield was not long enough ago that they had forgotten the history of their surroundings. They were still near enough to enemy positions to know they wouldn't have much time until they were engaged in firefights with enemy fighters.

Casey and Staff Sergeant Reed began setting in security for the LZ. They had to concentrate on the threat they knew would materialize when the Black Hawk approached. While attempting to acclimate himself to his new surroundings, Kinsel found that his environment and the intense scenario were borderline overwhelming. Regardless, he knew his men counted on him; time suddenly caught up with him, and he almost lost track as it began running twice as fast. The heat was unbearable and suffocating to the young lieutenant.

"Macari, hey man, hang on, buddy. The bird will be here soon. They're on their way."

"Hey, sir, how far is this fucking medevac?" Lyon asked.

"They're fifteen minutes out."

"Okay, let's get him positioned so we can load him up as soon as they land. This kid is sucking right now, and he needs to get on the bird."

The aid and litter team began to carry Macari through the grape furrows, some of which were up to five or six feet tall. Soldiers were starting to fatigue due to the patrol, the heat, and the weight of Macari's body. They stopped, rotated roles, and reevaluated Macari. Soldiers inside COP Stout sprinted out to assist; most didn't even bring their M4s. They ran with only their gear to ensure Macari got to the medevac.

"Look, guys, we need to pick it the fuck up, I know everyone is tired, but at this rate, we are not going to make it in time for the medevac," Kinsel said.

He was concerned that if his platoon had started taking contact on the way to the LZ, their efforts to get Macari to the medevac would be for nothing because the Black Hawk pilot would not land without them there. The platoon would have to construct another LZ and relocate Macari again, and he would lose valuable time getting to the hospital in Kandahar. Kinsel paused, realizing he was overreacting and needed to relax. Let everything settle down, and everything will work itself out.

"Havoc Main, this is Havoc One Six, over."

"Havoc One Six, this is Havoc Main. Send it, over."

Kinsel radioed, "Havoc Main, this is Havoc One Six. Initiate QRF to secure the south side of the LZ."

"Havoc One Six, Havoc Main. Acknowledge all, Launching QRF time now, over!"

The time spent waiting for a medevac to arrive always feels like forever. Time stands still. The casualty is in pain, and all anyone wants to do is take that pain away. One Hotel reached the eastern edge of the grape furrows and could see the edge of the LZ. QRF still needed to be found, and time was running out. Kinsel knew soon the Black Hawks would be inbound. Like something pulled from a horror movie, a hand appeared over the grape furrows before Kinsel. It was "Smoke" Tivao from the QRF. The cavalry had arrived, and One Hotel had the much-needed assistance in case they were ambushed. They could fight off the enemy as the medevac cared for Macari. The QRF soldiers were positioned across the south side of the LZ.

"Macari, the birds are five minutes out, man, and you'll be out of here," Kinsel assured the private.

"Sir, I'm ready to go, this shit sucks."

Battery leadership, with the battalion commander, were waiting at the gate as One Hotel returned from the patrol. As was standard for an incident such as this, everyone gathered to discuss the events and be debriefed by Lieutenant

Colonel Flynn. Most of the time, these types of talks weren't productive because, after impactful events, leaders want to dissect what they did and go back to attempt to fix the issue. No one wants to hear the ramblings of higher-ups; however, that's often what happens. In this debriefing, Kinsel was so lost in a cloud of his own misery—wargaming what he did, how he could have done it better, what they could have done differently—that he didn't remember much or anything of the talk.

After the motivational speech and talk from the command team, Lyon and Kinsel sat down inside the command post to speak with the battery commander and the first sergeant. There was a negative feeling in the air; like One Hotel shouldn't go on the patrol the next day. After talking about Macari, Lyon; and Kinsel said, "We are returning to finish the mission tomorrow."

They remained in the command post for hours, working on a new course of action until they finally concluded the enemy wanted to entrap the soldiers inside the COP. They determined the Taliban were attempting to shrink the sphere of security around the COP by conducting small-arms attacks. This would allow them to place IEDs closer and closer to the COP, leaving the soldiers with extraordinarily little room to maneuver. Lyon and Kinsel planned a breach effort across a historic IED belt in their AO but coordinated with the combat engineers attached to the battery to resolve the breach. One Hotel was apprehensive about returning to the same area that had just taken out Macari, but to their credit, they chose not to complain. In typical fashion, the soldiers showed courage, determination, and loyalty; they understood that the mission had to be completed and that the leaders needed them to continue the fight. One Hotel moved through the standard troop-leading procedures and executed full rehearsals just before they bedded down for the evening. The following day, the leaders woke the platoon and began conducting final patrol preparations. Ensuring the ANA understood their part in the operation was essential. One Hotel spent most of its time with its ANA counterparts, doing simultaneous mission rehearsals so that everyone, regardless of nationality, knew what to do if certain situations became a reality. This allowed the US soldiers to focus more on their responsibility during the patrol, knowing that their partners would react the way they had practiced before leaving the COP. Kinsel was planning the next day's mission and was approached by Captain Schaffer.

"Your next patrol is on a temporary hold. Lieutenant Colonel Flynn wants to come on the patrol. He believes changing your pattern and patrolling in the afternoon instead of the morning would be best."

"Roger, however, patrolling in the afternoon subjects the platoon to a wide array of new threats."

The battalion commander requested the patrol be moved to the evening, and Kinsel considered it. The attacks on COP Stout were sometimes short, 15 minutes or so. They sometimes lasted well over an hour, sometimes up to two hours. For enemy fighters to conduct an attack of this magnitude, they had to have several fighters and lots of weapons and ammunition staged. By patrolling in the afternoon, One Hotel ran the risk of walking into one of these significant elements, which meant they would be forced into a firefight with enemy fighters on the move. A firefight wasn't the issue; their knowledge of the terrain and use of IEDs gave them a slight advantage, primarily due to the excessive heat. One of the most prevalent tactics in the area was to conduct harassing attacks with small-arms fire following an IED blast. This caused American forces to attempt to save a soldier's life and move the casualty to a medevac, all while under fire. Additionally, if the American element didn't quickly suppress the enemy or engage them effectively, the fighters would remain in contact to deny using the first LZ.

Flynn arrived late in the evening on September 30; One Hotel was waiting for him at the gate. As he exited his vehicle, Lyon immediately gathered the platoon so Kinsel could provide a last-minute briefing. As One Hotel stepped off for their afternoon stroll around "the Argha-Nam," several soldiers were concerned with the element's size going into the orchards. Any time they patrolled in the past, the squads were much smaller. On this day, they had the stripped-down personal security detail team and the sappers along for the ride; they were looking at a dozen soldiers, not including the ANA. The initial infiltration route would take them down the south side of the canal that ran straight past COP Stout. Everyone in the platoon was on edge, knowing that once they approached the canal, it would not be long before enemy fighters engaged them. The platoon moved patiently through the canal for approximately six hundred meters before establishing an objective rally point. The movement was slow as soldiers were understandably cautious of their steps. One Hotel crossed multiple danger areas during the movement; one could almost cut the tension with a knife. They hoped to catch the Taliban off guard by venturing farther than usual into an unfamiliar region. This was evident in how the soldiers moved, scanned their sectors, and performed their responsibilities. The recon team determined the position of the breach, and One Hotel prepared to launch the first of two ballistic breaches across the path.

When One Hotel arrived at its destination, it was not visible from their vantage point. There was an eerie silence across the furrows while the platoon waited for approval to conduct the first breach. After what seemed like an eternity, they were finally allowed to carry on. The engineers were ready to fire the explosives as the recon team took cover. The initial charge exploded a fraction of a second after the warning.

"FIRE IN THE HOLE!"

ICOM chatter began erupting.

"Was that your IED?" one enemy fighter asked.

"No, that was not my IED. Inshallah, the next will be my IED."

The squad leader for the engineer team advanced to ensure the entire charge had detonated after the loud explosion sent dust flying. A lane had been removed across the initial section of the path; the first charge had been successful. Gunfire broke out from a nearby compound as he returned to the remainder of the recon team. It was clear that although enemy fighters were engaging the recon element, it was not the more prominent element they were trying to flank. Expediting the initiative to get the enemy fighters to break contact, the recon unit continued to engage with small-arms fire. Kinsel contacted COP Stout to get Two Hotel to employ the battery's 60-millimeter mortars on the enemy position. The Taliban were forced to break contact after about ten minutes of gunfire and proceeded southward into the densely forested "Devil's Playground."

After passing through the first cleared lane, the rest of the platoon assumed security positions in the canal. The engineers proceeded with the same techniques before breaching a passage across another path to allow the platoon to advance south. The engineers followed the lane to direct the soldiers through the cleared area. The lead squad kept advancing further south into the field. Kinsel and his radio-telephone operator (RTO), Private First Class Walters, were behind them. As Kinsel began climbing out of the canal, he found himself in a heavy shadow cast by a big tree. The tree was conveniently rooted in the middle of the path they had just breached. It ominously shadowed part of the route along the edge of the cleared lane. Although Kinsel was concerned about how loose the ground appeared, he concluded it was more than likely a result of the breach after glancing at the ground beneath it.

He told Walters, "Be careful of this loose spot right here. It looks like the breach may have damaged it."

In a moment of comic relief, Kinsel quickly darted across the path, hopping into what he anticipated was a small irrigation ditch. It was no irrigation ditch full of black sludge, which one could almost liken to tar. It was possible that Kinsel had found the same shit pond Corporal Parker had found while patrolling with One Bravo earlier during the deployment. It was thick and gooey and took Kinsel quite a while to maneuver out of. Once clear, he joined the men in the lead squad, who were now slowly clearing an area with the mine detectors. Kinsel took a second to gather his thoughts and take in his surroundings. In doing so, he began recognizing signs of IEDs nearby. The IED cells in the AO left both natural and manufactured signs in the vicinity of their devices so colleagues knew how to avoid these areas. Once soldiers became aware of the signs, they became apparent, for example, rocks stacked randomly at the beginning of a path. Something more challenging to locate was a small piece of cloth tied to the top of a tree in an orchard. According to Kinsel, a few oddly positioned rock formations were beneath trees. He continued to observe the surrounding area; his team leader, Terrazas, identified several pieces of cloth tied to treetops. Kinsel identified they had just walked into an area with, at minimum, one IED and the potential of more. He signaled to Staff Sergeant Reed that they would halt and begin exfiltration the way they came in. They needed to find another way to head south; taking the platoon through this field was not worth the risk. Kinsel knelt to communicate to COP Stout the change of route.

"Havoc Main, this is Havoc One Six, over."

"Havoc One Six, this is Havoc Main. Send it, over."

"Havoc Main, this is Havoc One Six, over. We are changing our current route. We have identified several IED markers in this field. Record this grid, 69917 63505, as a suspected field with IEDs." While Kinsel was finishing his transmission to Havoc Main, one of his team leaders briefed his ANA counterparts.

The men were in the process of marking the IED, so an explosive ordnance disposal team could blow it later, when the entire Arghandab River Valley erupted in automatic weapons fire. One Hotel had found the more prominent enemy element they were looking for. The first small-arms encounter was nothing more than a probing encounter. When One Hotel had not initiated whatever IED awaited them, the enemy fighters broke contact and reconsolidated with the more extensive formation. One Hotel was engaged by three separate PKM machine-gun positions positioned southwest, south, and southeast. The farthest of the three gun crews was roughly sixty meters from the One Hotel formation.

"Get that fucking 240 rocking now. We need to get these fuckers off our backs for a second," Staff Sergeant Casey yelled.

"Team Leaders, start positioning your men where you need them. Let's go!" ordered Kinsel. "Havoc Main, Havoc One Six. We are in contact. Vicinity of Grid 69900 63450. How copy, over?"

On multiple occasions, Kinsel could hear a round's whistle as it passed by his face. The men in the lead squad began returning fire, utilizing the M240B machine gun to suppress the enemy fighters who had pinned down One Hotel in the field. Understanding the immense noise of battle, Kinsel pulled in his leaders, took a knee, and relayed the plan.

"We are going to break contact. We need to use the irrigation canal to set up our support by fire to allow the rest of the platoon to cross back through the canal and over the path. We only have one 240, so we need to move it to where it can be as effective as possible for our soldiers coming out of the field."

"Sir, the problem we're going to face is getting to the canal without someone getting shot," Casey replied.

"I understand, but we only have one 240, and we need to get out of this field, so position it where it can cause the most damage."

"Roger, sir, I got it."

"Walters, I need you to go back to the canal. Once you're there, provide security with everyone else until I get there," said Kinsel.

Walters sprinted toward the canal; simultaneously, Kinsel bounded forward toward an enemy position to meet his lead squad. It was obvious that nothing positive was coming from being in this field, even if the lead squad appeared to match their fire rate. Something about being positioned in the field felt ominous; it felt like One Hotel was rats in a trap, and the enemy fighters were waiting for them to take the bait. Kinsel decided the time was now if they were to get out alive.

"Bound back behind me," he yelled.

Kinsel began moving forward, engaging an enemy position with his M4, the southern machine-gun position. By this point, his ears were ringing from gunfire all around him. Time seemed stagnant; everything was in slow motion, like in war movies, as he directed his soldiers out of the field. With only a portion of the lead squad remaining, he stressed the importance of getting out immediately. "Let's go, get to the canal's edge. Now!"

Providing cover for his soldiers exiting the field, he increased his rate of fire. He emptied his first magazine as the soldiers passed to his right, heading toward the irrigation canal. He continued to fire at the enemy element until he had emptied two additional magazines and then hurried to join his platoon.

Specialist Bixler handled the path markings left behind by the lead clearing team. He was at the rear of his team, leading three ANA soldiers. Much like Specialist Cheatham, Bixler had been one of the soldiers chosen to receive language training and retained a fair amount of Dari and Farsi. As the ambush continued, Bixler and his ANA counterparts found themselves caught in the middle. They were positioned behind a wall too tall to fight over and they had a berm to their backs. His team appeared exhausted from crossing the deep canal and climbing the berm. Nevertheless, the men carefully spread out, trying to find cover and fighting positions, but it was impossible. Enemy fighters had secured superior firepower during the engagement and were firing RPGs over their heads. This, coupled with a sustained rate of machine-gun fire and approximately a dozen or more fighters engaging them from a fan of about 90–120 degrees, was causing mass hysteria.

"We are preparing to call in an airstrike, move your team back," Lyon said.

Upon hearing this, one of the ANA soldiers took the initiative to run off instead of waiting for a clear path. He ran across the berm behind where Bixler and his team were located, not realizing it was littered with deep-buried IEDs.

"Turn back! Stop! There's a bomb; I'll have to shoot," Bixler yelled in Pashto.

He ran up to him and threw him back toward the cover of the berm.

Unfortunately, those were Bixler's last commands given to the ANA. The last few words he was heard yelling were "Stop, stop, stop!" in Pashto.

He stepped to pivot.

BOOM!

"IED, IED, IED!"

It was at that moment that everything rapidly deteriorated. As Kinsel turned toward his platoon, he heard the explosion compounded with a heart-wrenching scream. Clearing his head from the blast, he watched as the dust settled, exposing Bixler. He had initiated an IED at the point Kinsel had concerns about earlier, right beneath the ominous shade tree.

After the deafening silence following the explosion, Bixler could not comprehend or even clear the noise of battle from his mind. It was too loud to discern words, and everything was ringing. He began feeling for his legs, which were no longer there. He realized he was bleeding excessively, so he started feeling for tourniquets and managed to get one on a nub. He partially twisted it down so the combat lifesavers could do the rest. He attempted to put a tourniquet on his other leg but could not find a point to apply it. He was able to partially slide the tourniquet on what was remaining of his disfigured limb before he began to black out.

"Doc" Fontenot was doing his best to prevent Bixler from going into shock, getting an IV started. Other soldiers were attempting to keep him alert by talking to him. The machine-gun team had moved forward and joined the lead squad. They were trying to gain fire superiority over the enemy fighters to enable the rest of the platoon to start organizing the casualty evacuation. The IED had successfully netted one American and one ANA casualty. The ANA soldier had superficial shrapnel wounds from rocks and dirt. Bixler was a double amputee, with both of his legs lost above the knee. He lay covered in dirt and debris in the blast crater. Lyon and Fontenot quickly finished applying the tourniquets to slow the bleeding so he could be positioned on a litter.

"What the fuck did I hit?" Bixler asked.

"Bixler, it looks like a pressure-plate IED consisting of two 80-millimeter mortars. You're lucky, though. It was filled with extra shrapnel. It looks like it had a bag of nails and glass."

"Am I going to die?"

"No, brother, you'll be okay. Do you remember bitching about carrying the THOR III?"

"Yeah."

"Thankfully, it was filled with shrapnel from the explosion, all of which could have hit you. You would surely be dead if you hadn't been wearing it."

"Sergeant Lyon, give me some quick initial information for the medevac so I can send it up," said Kinsel.

Lyon replied, and Kinsel radioed Havoc Main. "BREAK, BREAK, BREAK, nine-line follows."

Once the medevac request was confirmed, Kinsel returned to the trench to control the soldiers in contact. This attack was well orchestrated, and the volume of fire only increased following the blast. Once again, the enemy fighters attempted to make a quick casualty evacuation impossible by the sheer ferocity of their fire. Fontenot was feverishly working on Bixler as he was getting pelted with dirt, leaves, and twigs as bullets flew close by his head. Bixler could only be moved after considerable time battling the enemy fighters.

"Trail squad, move across the canal, secure the far side, and assist with moving the litter," yelled Kinsel.

One of the best sounds in the Arghandab was hearing Kiowas inbound. Just as One Hotel had crossed over to the north side of the canal, two reported in.

"Longknife, Havoc One Six, over."

"Havoc One Six, Longknife."

"Longknife, Havoc One Six. We just took a casualty from the south side of our current position in the orchards and furrows. It would be appreciated if you could assist us with engaging those enemy positions south of us."

"Havoc One Six, Longknife. It'll be our pleasure."

The Kiowas flew low overhead, first engaging with .50-caliber machine guns and then rockets. The covering fire from the air assets was what the One Hotel element needed to get the remainder of the platoon back to the north side of the canal.

As enemy fire diminished, the final One Hotel soldiers could pour out of the canal into the bean field. Casey and Reed were already busy setting in their security for the hot LZ. Kinsel was on a knee assisting with directing fires when they encountered sporadic enemy fire. The Kiowas continued flying overhead like hungry vultures waiting for a meal. While waiting for the medevac, an A-10 Thunderbolt checked in. Like a kid at Christmas wanting to play with a new toy, Reed began getting approval to incorporate the A-10 into the assault. *Longknife* continued to engage and re-engage the enemy fighters until their guns fell silent. With all the excitement of the firepower in the fall sky, Bixler was still waiting for the medevac. Lyon approached with a concerned look on his face.

"What's the ETA for the medevac, sir?"

"I'm not sure; the entire battalion task force hasn't been able to communicate with the birds. No one has comms."

The thumping sound of rotor blades reached their ears, like a sound from the heavens.

"INBOUND!" yelled Kinsel.

Lyon deployed a smoke canister to mark the LZ. Kinsel attempted to get the attention of the Black Hawk pilots as they blew right past. The men were perplexed about what just happened; they watched as the helicopters hovered over COP Tynes and knew that, somehow, they had received lousy guidance on the way to their destination. Kinsel relayed through the command post to tell them to head due south, and they would see their smoke. A few seconds later, the two helicopters swiftly moved positions from Tynes into the field. Kinsel sprinted to the middle of the field to direct movement on the LZ; Lyon quickly organized two aid and litter teams to carry Bixler and the ANA soldier. They loaded the ANA soldier; as Bixler was being loaded, he heard, "Hey, you forgot this." Lyon handed him a foot.

"Thanks, Sergeant. I may need that one day."

As the medevac lifted off, the soldiers could not help but have a sinking feeling. They had withstood a hellish assault but lost Bixler and the ANA soldier in the process. The movement to the fields seemed to take hours, but the movement back took only seconds. One downfall of being a leader is taking the bad with the good. Kinsel had only been with the platoon for a few weeks now and, in the past two days, had seen two catastrophic injuries to his men, and now had to try to communicate to them compassionately in an uncompassionate environment. He stood face to face with the soldiers from One Hotel and those in Havoc Battery. They were motionless, saying nothing. The looks on their faces were piercing—angry, hurt, and furious—yet they said nothing. The looks said everything that needed to be said. Havoc had now grown to be a close-knit family. Most of the soldiers in the platoon were close friends with Bixler and could not help but shed a tear for him upon entering the gate at COP Stout. They were exhausted, mentally and physically. Kinsel and Lyon slowly herded them back to the tent area, showing a united front. Neither leader wanted to have the discussion, but they knew they needed to. The soldiers settled into the makeshift porch outside the platoon tent area. Lieutenant Colonel Flynn and the battery leadership addressed them once again. During this time, Lyon and Kinsel stepped aside to catch their breath. There was going to be the burden of reports and sworn statements that are always required following a severe injury to a soldier. The two leaders sat somberly in the tactical operations center (TOC) and discussed, in detail, the events as they had unfolded; the soldiers assigned to the TOC sat in silence and stared. Kinsel could feel everyone around him wanting them to understand that it wasn't their fault, that it was a terrible thing out of their control, but in typical Army fashion, everyone sat in silence.

CHAPTER 11

Ant Trails to the Man at the First Canal

> The world is a dangerous place, not because of those who do evil, but because of those who look on and do nothing.
>
> ALBERT EINSTEIN

The Top Guns were now at a point in the deployment where they were being allocated a multitude of assets. The towers of COP Tynes had become accustomed to seeing one of these assets, the route-clearance package, come through often. The noncommissioned officer in charge (NCOIC), Sergeant Junkin, and Specialist Branch were behind the raid camera inside the Combat Outpost (COP) Tynes tactical operations center. This provided extra visibility for the combat outpost to supplement the towers; and allowed an eye in the sky to see if anyone was digging on Routes Red Dog, Mariners, High Life, or any of the other main routes.

One Bravo was preparing to leave with a convoy of much-needed supplies for COP Babur. After the past several months of patrolling the area and watching convoy after convoy getting their vehicles destroyed on Route Red Dog, it was now well known as a hotbed for improvised explosive devices (IED). Second Lieutenant Pantaleo, Staff Sergeant Fontenot, Corporal Parker, and Sergeant Jackson decided to put a spin on the convoy. They discussed dismounting alongside their vehicles through Druia to identify anything that could've been missed by route clearance. The chances were low route that clearance would miss anything, but there was always a chance. The route-clearance package had just cleared through the village, so the threat was minimal. However, as One Bravo was getting ready to leave out of COP Tynes, Tower Two called up over the net: "One Bravo, this is Tower Two be aware I see a guy at the end of Druia with a shovel digging in the road."

Fontenot replied, "Tower Two, One One, I acknowledge all. We will check it out. Keep overwatch on our convoy as we clear through Druia."

The route-clearance package passed the One Bravo convoy, fixing to leave COP Tynes. The dismounts were positioned in staggered columns alongside the road exiting the COP, alongside the Afghan National Army (ANA) checkpoint. They watched as the route-clearance package passed them, knowing a local national buried something in the road immediately after they had just cleared the route. However, One Bravo acted as if Tower Two hadn't called up anything. In reality, it wasn't the responsibility of the route-clearance package to investigate what the local was doing. To One Bravo, things like this had become routine; it was just another day in the Arghandab. The patrol started moving through Druia, which was standard for the most part. There was minimal presence from locals and an eerie calm, which was typically a bad sign. When the patrol passed the imam's home, who was generally seen outside his compound drinking chai with other locals, he wasn't anywhere to be found. Parker was point man, scanning the south side of Red Dog, nearing the historic IED area about four hundred fifty meters outside of COP Tynes. A local was still in the area, so Pantaleo and Fontenot called for some ANA to move forward with their interpreter, Nabil, who called the man over. When they began talking to him, it became apparent he was the gentleman digging in the road. He still had dirt on his sandals and his tools nearby, so they began interrogating him as to why he was digging. Parker and Sergeant Jackson pushed farther east toward the end of Druia to pull security.

Parker came over the radio, "One One, this is One One Alpha."

"One One Alpha, One One. Send it," Fontenot replied.

"One One, One One Alpha we have a yellow HME jug with a detonation cord attached. Have the convoy back up!"

"One One Alpha, One One acknowledge all. Cordon off the area. We'll call it up."

Pantaleo radioed up to Bulls main and alerted Sergeant Junkin that they had just located an IED on Route Red Dog and would need an explosive ordnance disposal (EOD) team. The main issue that troops always face when contacting EOD is where they fall in the order of precedence. One Bravo fell somewhere in the middle, so they were looking at a few hours of cooking in the Afghanistan sun, waiting for the team to show up to blow the bomb. The convoy was sitting stagnant in the middle of Druia, the gunners rotating in turrets. They had their CROWS (common remotely operated weapon stations) systems scanning as far as possible. They also had the luxury of having the overwatch from the towers at COP Tynes. From an outward perspective, it may have appeared they were in a pretty good position, but to the leaders of One Bravo, they were sitting in a fatal funnel and that didn't sit well. Since the battalion's initial entry into the Arghandab, no one had liked sitting still on any route moving in or out of any village. Tensions were high, and the towers were on high alert. Now, they had dismounts pulling security for their convoy and had both ANA and American troops on the ground on what should have been a simple supply convoy to Babur. As One Bravo was sitting in Druia, the Top Gun 6s, the personal security detail (PSD) team passed by, dropped off two trucks to add to their convoy, and then continued to Babur. One Bravo had been sitting stagnant for approximately two hours at this point. Fontenot was growing weary and didn't want to continue being a sitting target. He advised Pantaleo that he and Parker would see if they could trace the detonation cord. They began heading south toward the first canal, crossing through an area with grape rows where they could see the detonation cord buried. The cord continued south, and before they knew it, they were moving quite a way from the convoy.

The initial IED was located alongside a wall approximately fifteen feet high and positioned right next to an alleyway on Route Red Dog. On the east side of the wall was farmland that led to a well-farmed grape furrow. On the west side, and the other side of the IED, was a small onion patch with a small mud wall approximately five feet tall. The wall separated the ruins between Druia and Babur. Just beyond was the waddy, where Specialist Moon had been killed in July, and just beyond the onion field was where a radio-controlled IED had narrowly missed a patrol during the Two Charlie relief in place. The Red Dog bypass was a narrow road that split all the farmland, the first canal, and Route Red Dog. The bypass was also known to be littered with IEDs, and therefore, the patrols steered clear of it. The one time it was used, an ANA convoy had one of its vehicles annihilated; the Taliban ensured the wreckage was left behind as a reminder as to what would happen to those who used the route in the future. As Fontenot and Parker continued tracing the "ant trail" of the detonation cord toward the canal, they could see it lightly covered in Afghan dust along the furrows. They talked about looking forward to getting home and relaxing without all the chaos of things going boom under their feet.

At this point, they realized they were on the Red Dog bypass. The bypass was close to 100 meters from the convoy. Fontenot realized they had drifted west and were now obscured from any security that could be provided. They were now facing the hazards that accompanied an open area. They were exposed to the pomegranate orchards, and neither Tynes nor the convoy could provide cover. The area they found themselves in was in the corner of a wall that would lead them down to the first canal. It offered a clear view from the first canal to Route Red Dog. Suspiciously enough, an Afghan man was sitting with his back to a tree up against the first canal; he appeared to be sleeping, but his positioning and timing seemed off.

"Hey, bro, you see that guy up against the tree?" Fontenot asked Parker.

"Yeah, Chief, he's probably Taliban."

"Parker, let's head toward the waddy so we don't take the same route back."

They began heading east toward the edge of Druia. Once they made it to the edge of the Red Dog bypass, they ensured they were clear enough to head north and back toward Red Dog. Once they began heading north, Fontenot called up their front-line trace to Pantaleo, attempting to be extra vigilant, knowing they were crossing through another open area. While Parker was crossing the ruins, he came to an area that had an enormous hole in the ground. He called back to Fontenot, who was approximately twenty meters behind, and said, "Hey, Chief, you need to see this; it looks like a tunnel or some shit!" At that very moment, it was like it was the cue for the Taliban to release their fury.

CRACK! CRACK! CRACK! BOOM!

PKMs, AK-47s, RPGs, everything all at once began going off. Fontenot and Parker were in the open and running for their lives. The worst-case scenario had happened for the two men: they found themselves with no cover, being shot at by machine guns,

Fontenot yelled, "FUCKING RUN!" Parker was one of the fastest guys in the battery, and Fontenot was one of the strongest; both men were moving swiftly; they hurdled the five-foot wall and jumped into the flooded onion field. Fontenot heard Parker cursing behind him. "Man, fuck! Damn it, man." He instantly thought Parker had been hit.

"Bro, you good?" he asked as 7.62-millimeter rounds impacted the mud wall between them, and RPG (rocket-propelled grenade) rounds flew over their heads.

"Yeah, Chief, I'm good. My fucking cigarettes got wet in this damn field."

"Damn it, bro, are you serious? Fucking fire back!"

All around the convoy in Druia were little kids and locals, but in typical fashion, the enemy fighters had no regard for the safety of the locals.

Fontenot yelled back to the trucks, "FUCKING OPEN FIRE!"

He looked back and saw that Specialist Little was on the M2 .50-caliber machine gun and was working to get it rocking to return fire. For some crazy reason, Jackson attempted to go forward to join Parker and Fontenot.

Fontenot yelled at him not to come, but he couldn't hear anything through the noise of battle. He rounded the corner of the building, hit an irrigation canal, and faceplanted. Despite being pinned down in the field by enemy fire, Parker and Fontenot couldn't help but find humor in the situation. They both looked at each other and began laughing.

"Damn it, Chief, did you just see Action Jackson faceplant? Holy shit, that was funny!"

"Parker, damn it, let's hurry up and shut these assholes up so we can get the fuck out of this field."

Parker and Fontenot both continued returning fire. With the help of the crew-served weapons on the trucks, they silenced the fire coming from the orchards. The firefight lasted long enough to draw the attention of COP Babur. Once Pantaleo called the SITREP over the net, it was like the distress signal had been sent across the Arghandab for the wolves to come to the rescue.

Right about that time, Top Gun 6's PSD came screaming across the waddy from Babur after hearing about the firefight. They came in like knights in shining armor to save the day, but the firefight was already over. Lieutenant Colonel Flynn met up with Pantaleo and Fontenot on Red Dog and got the SITREP. He then met with the platoon forward observer, Specialist Tebaldi, and Fontenot and said, "Let's go and see what we're working with."

"Are we going on a suicide mission?" Tebaldi asked Fontenot.

"I'm going to say yes!"

With that, Tebaldi, anticipating the absolute worst, placed a VS-17 panel on his back so that if they went into the orchards and he needed to call in *Longknife*, they could spot him through the pomegranate trees. Flynn, Fontenot, and Tebaldi made their way through the onion field and across the Red Dog bypass. They came to the opening in the wall where Fontenot had spotted the man sitting along the first canal.

"Where did their fire come from?" Flynn asked.

Fontenot replied, "Sir, they were shooting at us with PKM fire from about fifty meters inside the orchards. I'm not 100 percent sure exactly where they were positioned, but the guy we saw sitting next to the canal was resting against the tree about 20 meters in front of you."

At that time, the battalion commander took a moment to consider his options. He looked at their position at the Red Dog bypass and paused.

"What if we can get into the orchards? Do you think we could flank them?" Fontenot looked at Tebaldi with concern. Both men understood they had just received machine-gun fire from that exact position.

"Sir, to be honest, I think we would get mowed down if we tried to cross this open area, but that's just my assessment," Fontenot replied.

By this point in the deployment, Flynn could trust the instincts of his leaders. He understood that both Fontenot and Tebaldi were seasoned fighters, so he decided to pull back. Fontenot and Tebaldi breathed a sigh of relief. They knew that; at least this time, the commander would listen to them.

Pantaleo was dealing with a local who had a compound to the north of where the IED was located. The local was upset because one of his sheep was hit by a stray RPG. The RPG had flown over the wall of his compound during the barrage from the Taliban fighters, and shrapnel hit the animal. Trying to diffuse the situation, Flynn took his PSD team, some of the leadership from One Bravo, and the medics inside the man's compound to see what could be done. Afghan soldiers, interpreters, and medics went to the PSD team; in a humorous turn of events, the medics bandaged up the sheep. It was wounded in its hind quarter and likely could have had a long and prosperous life doing sheep things, but its fate was sealed that day. The battalion purchased the sheep after "Doc" Stegehuis and the other medics cared for it. The guys handed off the sheep to the Afghan soldiers as it now appeared a feast was being planned instead of MREs (meals, ready to eat) or the standard fare back at the COP for once.

The EOD team finally arrived on site, and not a moment too soon. One Bravo had already had their fair share of excitement for one day, and they still hadn't even made their run to Babur. They were nearly six hours into a patrol that should've taken roughly one.

The EOD team dismounted their robot and drove it to the IED so they could examine it with the robot's camera. The guys from One Bravo found this humorous, being they had walked up to it earlier. The robot confirmed it was an IED and shortly after, the EOD NCOIC asked, "Who found the IED?"

"I found it," Parker excitedly replied.

"Would you like to blow it?"

Parker, thrilled at the idea of getting to blow up the IED, of course, replied with, "Fuck yeah!"

In typical fashion, the EOD NCOIC briefed that she would say, "Fire in the hole, fire in the hole, fire in the hole," and then Parker would initiate the switch, exploding the ordnance. Parker, being so excited, was elsewhere, thinking of how incredible the explosion would be, how excellent C4 was, or just anything other than the instructions. The EOD robot rolled back out, dropped the C4 on the IED, and returned, and the NCOIC handed Parker the switch. Everyone from One Bravo, besides Parker, Pantaleo, and the NCOIC, was buttoned up in their vehicles and ready to head out to Babur finally.

"FIRE IN THE HOLE ..."

BOOM!

"You didn't wait until the third 'FIRE IN THE HOLE'!"

"Oh shit, I was supposed to wait until the third one?"

The NCOIC just nodded her head in disapproval. When Parker got in the truck, he was laughing.

"How was that?" Fontenot asked.

"Well, Chief, I think I pissed off the EOD team! You're supposed to wait until the third 'fire in the hole' before you press the switch. I pressed it on the first one."

"Yeah, man, they say it three times. Didn't you listen to the brief?"

"I heard a brief, Chief, but I missed that part."

"Man, let's get the fuck out of here," Fontenot laughed.

When the patrol finally arrived at COP Babur, "Gunny" Torres welcomed them with open arms; it was almost like a dysfunctional family reunion. Staff Sergeant Creighton and Torres were in Truck One together in Iraq. That made them as close as you can get to family, and Fontenot was like an adopted stepson to the crew and just known as "Fonty." When they got to Babur, Torres poked fun at the guys and asked, "Damn, man, what took y'all so long to drive just over a klick to drop off supplies?"

"We just had to make it exciting."

Babur was still a work in progress. The outpost relied heavily on supply runs from Tynes, Terra Nova, and Golf Company. The "Boys of Babur" were cut off from the rest of the area of operations (AO) when it rained; no one could get to them across the waddy. The ANA was frequently seen enjoying the rainy days as they would run their vehicles through the waddy. The men from Babur often waited in anticipation for them to get stuck, but they never did. The "Boys of Babur" loaded the supplies they needed to go to Terra Nova into the convoy. Having One Bravo take their supplies prevented unnecessary convoys for Two and Four Bravo on Route Red Dog. This prevented 2nd Platoon from having to go across the AO to Jelawur, turn around, and return to Babur. One Bravo wasn't thrilled about being in their trucks; the guys had become accustomed to walking everywhere and hated being confined. However, it was a necessary evil at times. The patrol had already been out for nearly seven hours, so they figured, what the hell, why not? It was better for them to head to Jelawur for their brothers in Babur than to have them do it.

One Bravo left for Terra Nova to drop off supplies from Babur and possibly "acquire" goodies for themselves but hoped it would be a quick turn and burn. Much to their amazement, it was. Upon returning to COP Tynes, the soldiers finally got a reprieve from their gear. They were able to get sustenance and start winding down. Right about that time, a squelch was heard over the sergeant of the guard's (SOG) radio: "SOG, this is Tower One. There's a kid at the front gate covered in blood!"

All the soldiers and NCOs within earshot of the SOG ran through the frail wooden hallways of Tynes to get to the front gate as quickly as possible. There are many ugly certainties of war; one of those is that civilian casualties happen. For the American soldiers, one of the things they despised seeing more than anything else was when death came calling on an unsuspecting child. When patrolling in the neighboring towns, often the soldiers would have candy and would usually befriend the kids. They would hear things like "Mister, mister, chocolate." They would stop and take pictures with the kids because, for some, it would remind them of their children, and for others, it simply brought some humanity to what they were attempting to do in the Arghandab. There were many times they heard explosions in the distance, and they never knew who or what hit the IED; it could've been an animal, it could've been a local adult, or it could've been a child. They had no way of knowing unless it was one of their own. In this instance, a young boy was standing at the front gate of COP Tynes, he was covered in blood, and no one knew why. Tynes's Afghan interpreters, Nabil and Mike, were attempting to speak to him, as he stood there in shock. "Doc" Stegehuis checked him for injuries but couldn't find anything specifically wrong other than minor scrapes and a few cuts.

Nabil and Mike continued to probe him for information but were having trouble getting anything. Nabil asked what happened. As he stumbled on his words, the boy said he and his friend were playing in the furrows. He stated that as they were running around, he was chasing his friend, and his friend entered the corner of a field, and an explosion went off in front of him. He said he was thrown backward and landed in a ditch. When he woke up, he returned to where the explosion had happened. His friend had disappeared, and there was nothing but blood on the ground. From what the soldiers could figure, the friend was more than likely turned into a blood mist. Many children crowded around the soldiers during patrols to try to get candy. Most that did were just a little taller than waist-high. Taking into consideration that when IEDs were hitting the soldiers, most of them were being amputated up to their waist, it was feasible to consider the young boy never felt anything. He had been taken away by some of the evils of the Arghandab. As the soldiers walked away from the front gate, it was with a sense of anger. They were both angry at the fact that this had happened to a child and that it could happen to an innocent victim at all. The war they were fighting was against a faceless enemy, against an enemy that refused to come out and fight them head-on like warriors of the past. Wars of the past were fought soldier to soldier. Now civilian casualties were becoming normalized because, in the eyes of God or Allah, it was considered a sacrifice to lose your life against the Americans or "Pagans." Stegehuis did what he could to clean the young boy up and ensure he would be okay. There was no need to evacuate him for better care, so they returned him to his family, then they did their best to get rest because, in five hours, it would all start again.

CHAPTER 12

Cigarette Embers, MICLICs, and Tarok Kolache

> The brave die never, though they sleep in the dust; Their courage nerves a thousand living men.
>
> BOB RILEY

The seasons were finally beginning to change for the War Dogs of the 101st. The leaves in the orchards started falling, and the furrows were slowly becoming bare, leaving nothing but mud-caked rows and fields of dying vegetation as fall approached. The momentum was shifting slowly, like watching a slug moving across a mirror, leaving a trail behind it for its victims to follow. The warfighters from Combat Outpost (COP) Stout had diligently fortified their positions since mid-July and patrolled the orchards and furrows with a fury not seen in the Arghandab before. Interpreters picked up ICOM chatter often.

Taliban leaders were heard to say, "Wait until the Eagles leave, and then we will go back in the fields." The Havoc and Top Guns soldiers had earned a solid foothold around their area of operations in the orchards, but one thing was always apparent. Good enough is never good enough, especially in war. Havoc had now taken ground that had never been held before in the history of the Arghandab. The Russians had failed to seize and hold ground against the Mujahedeen in the 1980s. Their failed conquest eventually led to the rise of Al Qaeda and Osama Bin Laden. Al Qaeda received much-needed funding from Bin Laden, which ultimately led to the World Trade Center terror attacks. Now Havoc stood on the same blood-stained ground. However, everything comes at a cost. Havoc Battery lost four outstanding leaders in gaining what was now COP Stout. This new home was truly earned with the blood, sweat, and tears of the soldiers, noncommissioned officers, and officers of HHB (Headquarters and Headquarters Battery).

The battalion was planning its next big push toward the river. The plan was to utilize its assets to minimize casualties if possible. The town south of COP Stout was known as Tarok Kolache, also known as another HME (homemade explosives) factory and Taliban stronghold. The battalion had the opportunity to utilize outside assets, such as special forces, to go into Tarok Kolache before sending in the Top Guns soldiers; this would give them a better assessment of what they were genuinely walking into. It would be a precursor to Operation *Bakersfield II*.

A patrol from Havoc was pushing out just southwest of COP Stout to investigate a small compound suspected of having possible HME-making materials in it, such as fertilizer, the infamous yellow jugs, Styrofoam plates, batteries, and other trash commonly used for pressure plates. The patrol began moving through the area; it was slowly and meticulously clearing from building to building, carefully identifying what was cleared and what wasn't. Suspecting they would more than likely encounter improvised explosive device (IED) material, the patrol was fortunate enough to have several explosive ordnance disposal (EOD) soldiers with them who would enable them to blow in place anything they found. As the patrol navigated from one building to the next, they eventually identified pressure plates. The EOD soldiers moved forward and set C4. After the detonation was completed, Specialist Verra went back into the building to take photos, and to see how the enemy fighters were rigging the Styrofoam plates, to report back to the battalion. BOOM! Verra initiated a secondary IED. The remainder of the soldiers rushed over to him to help and were quickly able to identify he was a double amputee. Verra had lost both of his legs. His brothers fought to place tourniquets on what was left of his limbs while leaders worked to get a nine-line spun up as quickly as possible. They hadn't moved far from COP Stout, so a QRF (quick-reaction force) element wasn't set. The sergeant of the guard, Staff Sergeant Casey, was spinning up Sergeant First Class Lyon and every available soldier at COP Stout. "Doc" Fontenot was once again on site and administering morphine while attempting to control the bleeding.

Verra had initiated a pressure plate that covered several mortar rounds; the shrapnel from the rounds had amputated several of his fingers, and he had shrapnel that had gone in between the plates of his vest and up his back. Although the fighting had seemed to diminish in the fields lately, this was a grim reminder that, just when it appeared safe to go back out in the killing fields, it wasn't at all. The Havoc soldiers secured the medevac and got Verra out of the Arghandab. As he flew into the pale grey sky, the men were once again returned to the savage reality that death was merely one step away.

With *Bakersfield II* looming, tensions between the soldiers and leadership were at a fever pitch. The Top Guns had reached October 3, 2010, and it was officially fall; the leaves on the trees were beautiful autumn colors, like something from a postcard. The orchards were a maze of branches, and most fields were dried up, displaying the symmetrical box structures that housed the pomegranate trees. The leaves began falling, unmasking the landscapes beneath their cover. With the next big push for the patrol cycle barreling down on Havoc and Bravo Batteries, beginning on October 5, the prominent issue leaders within the batteries would face would be manpower. The fighting season had exhausted the soldiers, and the Top Guns had taken heavy casualties leading up to this point; the fighting season had led to a substantial number of amputees wounded and killed in action. However, this was not to say the Top Guns were ineffective, as they were still in the fight and moving forward. The battalion's batteries were getting to a point where combat effectiveness could be challenged if the brigade and division couldn't supplement them with additional manpower. *Bakersfield II*, as it would be commonly known to the soldiers of the Top Guns, or Operation *Dragon Strike Campaign*, as it was known to the battalion, brigade, and higher-ups, was rapidly approaching. The Top Guns had already made a sizeable impression in the Arghandab by having HHB move south of Jelawur into the orchards. They had taken the land where COP Stout now stood, a significant accomplishment. Having Bravo Battery move east into the village of Babur and set up a combat post was also a strategic move by the battalion to take and hold ground to control the Arghandab.

Operation *Dragon Strike* had more significant goals. However, the sights of the battalion for the operation would be to incorporate the special forces, the Afghan commandos, and the Afghan Border Police; these detachments would be used before the Top Guns. The target areas these organizations would focus on would be Tarok Kolache, Khosrow Solfa, and Charqolba Solfa. These areas were already known as Taliban strongholds and potentially some of the last remaining areas in the Arghandab the Taliban still controlled. If the Top Guns could take these areas, they would control the entire Arghandab.

At the initial phase of Operation *Eagle Claw*, October 6, the operators, commandos, and detachments that attempted to go into Tarok Kolache quickly discovered the town was one big HME factory. The Taliban had placed IEDs on most of their compounds, protecting their fighting positions and their patrol bases within Tarok Kolache. They were turning the buildings into HBIEDs (house-born improvised explosive devices). Several of the operators were injured in the initial push into Tarok Kolache, so they reported back to Top Gun 6 that the initial phase of the operation was met with resistance, and they had taken casualties. At that point, it was determined the next phase of the operation would go into full swing, which was full-on assault mode. In the dark of night on October 6 and the early morning of the 7th, HIMARS (high-mobility artillery rocket system) batteries delivered over forty-nine thousand pounds of ordnance to the village of Tarok Kolache. With the reduction of the HBIEDs complete, the combined task force isolated the operations area to the north, south, and west and conducted a deliberate breach of IED minefields along Route Highlife from COP Stout south toward the Arghandab River. After this significant strike, the next phase of the operation could begin, which would include One Bravo providing immediate security to the sapper team, with their noncommissioned officer in charge, Sergeant First Class Jones, clearing down to Tarok Kolache and Khosrow Solfa, using their mine-clearing line charges (MICLIC), Mk 7 anti-personnel obstacle-breaching systems (APOBS), and explosive line charges to establish breach lanes through IED minefields.

It was now 4:00 am on October 7, and Staff Sergeant Fontenot, along with 2nd Lieutenant Pantaleo and One Bravo, was out on Route High Life to pull security for the sappers; they were prepared for a day that would last 24, 36, or 72 hours if need be. The men were briefed to be prepared for whatever may come; they were ready for multiple days of fighting. Ironically, just before One Bravo left COP Tynes the day before, there was a complete leadership explosion. "Smoke" Tatro, their beloved platoon sergeant who had been with them since before the deployment, had been having an issue with the new first sergeant of the battery, First Sergeant Baca. The problem was that Baca was an 11B infantryman, a non-promotable sergeant first class that was frocked as a first sergeant over an artillery battery. The battery had promotable 13B sergeant first class artillerymen under him. Baca was also wearing the first sergeant diamond, a point of contention for Tatro. One Bravo had returned from a patrol, and Tatro was attempting to cool down in PTs with Crocs; he was approached and told he was unprofessional because of his attire. The situation became explosive, leading to Tatro and Baca getting in each other's faces. Ultimately, because Tatro was seen as the lesser in rank, he was relieved, on the eve of a major operation, so One Bravo was going into Operation *Eagle Claw* with Fontenot as acting platoon sergeant.

As One Bravo sat stagnant in their security posture, just waiting for something to happen, they were expecting the worst; during Operation *Bakersfield*, lulls in fighting or silence generally meant that enemy fighters were maneuvering or positioning for an offensive. The soldiers hated the dead silence, and the stillness that surrounded them. It felt like the ghosts of the Arghandab were slowly encompassing their position. The sapper team signaled for them to pull back, with the first MICLIC in position and ready to be fired. One Bravo thought they would have the opportunity to sit back and watch as the rocket fired down High Life. As security pulled back about fifty meters, the sappers instructed them to get inside a vehicle because, otherwise, it might scramble their brains. When the MICLIC shot off, a pre-positioned camera caught the ferocity of 1,750 pounds of C4 on a 100-meter lanyard flying down High Life, clearing trees and anything else in its way, clear and precise destruction. The blast was awe-inspiring, and seemed to bend time and space, destroying anything in range. When the first MICLIC fired off and the fireball erupted, everyone looked around at each other; it was like everyone's hearts had skipped a beat, and they knew it was time to get back to work. The men of One Bravo would consistently be propelled back to the front of the line as MICLIC after MICLIC was fired. As with any major operation, there are always a ton of moving components that ensure its success. While the sappers were prepping the next MICLIC, One Bravo was assisting with dismounted route clearance—some of the soldiers were tasked with proofing the path, while others provided security. After the second MICLIC was shot, the first danger area and the first checkpoint were reached; this was the T-intersection past COP Stout. After the initial MICLIC was fired and the chaos had calmed the Sapper team came under fire. This slowed the rate at which the team was able to clear the area for the movement. One Bravo went into action as the security element for them and ensured that there was little to no damage that could be done. With the ferocity of the MICLIC, the Taliban were already licking their wounds and were having problems formulating any type of repel to this forward advance of the Top Guns. As One Bravo moved forward and continued to assess the blast, they reached the first bend in High Life, which meant it was time to utilize the APOBS, line charges, Vallon or VMR3 mine detectors, or other gizmos, as well as the naked eye, to clear the danger area. This was what everyone had been doing since June when the Top Guns arrived in the Arghandab; nothing new, just another day in the Arghandab.

Pantaleo and Fontenot were up front, clearing the route and providing security. All was going well; Pantaleo identified what appeared to be a small piece of wood sticking out of the ground with two familiar wires sticking out of it.

"Hey, Fonty, I think I have an IED over here."

Fontenot was clearing the right side of the road. "Hey, sir, I have one over here too."

They were standing in the middle of an IED alley and knew they had just walked into a minefield and were surrounded.

They started backtracking, hoping to make their way out without hitting anything else. Pantaleo identified a door in a mud wall to his left. As he approached the door, he tried to use caution to clear it; he recognized it was a choke point and determined it had the potential to have an IED nearby. As he stepped up to the door, he felt a familiar and deadly feeling come rushing through his body; it was like an electric current had just discharged. Fontenot was only a few meters from him and heard the "CLICK." Pantaleo's right foot touched the ground but, before putting any weight on it, he stopped; something was wrong, and his brain was urging him to stop. He stood there as pale as a ghost for a second with all his weight on his rear foot. He looked at the door, then down toward his foot, then back at the door as if something were going to change, then slowly and ever so gently brushed his foot against the ground. There it was. The one thing a soldier in the Arghandab never, NEVER, wanted to see below their foot. This pressure plate was six inches by ten inches, just big enough to buy him a one-way ticket to the promised land. Standing within ten meters of each other when he stood on the pressure plate, Pantaleo and Fontenot realized they were both cooked if this thing went off. Fontenot figured one of two things could happen: they could get blown sky-high or walk away unscathed. Ultimately, it was like playing the IED lottery.

"Jones, go get EOD," Fontenot said.

Jones quickly obliged and took off running.

"Sir, we haven't done anything without each other up to this deployment point."

"Fonty, that's a fact."

"Sir, let's see what happens, take your foot off of that fucking thing!"

Pantaleo took his foot off the pressure plate, but it didn't go off. Both men hastily retreated. This would provide EOD with the opportunity to do their job. Pantaleo had been seconds from being piecemealed by two 82-millimeter mortars directly underneath the pressure plate which would've killed both he and Fontenot. An EOD team came up with C4 and blew the three IEDs Pantaleo and Fontenot had found; the explosion shook the ground in such a way that it gave everyone in One Bravo nervous energy. This had nearly cost them their platoon leader and section chief. The mission still had forever to run; they had already nearly set off three IEDs, and had only gone about 300 meters down High Life. It was time for the mission to continue driving toward the river. Dusk had now set in, and the red glow from headlamps was becoming prevalent; night-vision goggles in the orchards were also being donned; however, it was easy to find Pantaleo. His nerves were getting the best of him. For the next several hours, he chain-smoked cigarettes, and you could find him by the burning ember of his cigarette glowing in the darkness. Parker approached Fontenot.

"Chief, you think the Sir is going to be, okay?"

"Yeah Petey, he'll be fine, he's just got a ton of adrenaline right now you know."

While the sappers were blowing a superhighway down to Tarok Kolache, special forces operators and Afghan commandos were in the process of assaulting portions of Lower Babur and Charqolba Solfa. The Strike Brigade had initially told the soldiers they would be the tip of the spear, and the Top Guns were the tip of the tip of that spear, but this was the first time it was coming to fruition. What was happening in "The Devil's Playground" was a combined arms division destruction of Taliban safe havens and caches. When the clearance package reached Tarok Kolache, a giant crater was found in the ground. The Air Force had dropped several JDAMs (joint direct attack munition) and had ensured the IEDs set on each one of the compounds were systematically disabled. JDAMs are 500–1,000-pound guided air-to-surface bombs capable of annihilating anything in their path. With the clearance package in tow and the sappers on hand, the Top Guns could clear through Tarok Kolache. They set up an eastern blocking position with a Havoc element, where Strong Point Weaver would eventually be established. One Bravo would continue providing security for the sappers for the next several days as the latter continued to push west towards Khosrow Sofa, which was the Taliban headquarters. Three Bravo moved south toward the river to set in a blocking position. Everyone pulled back once the clearance package had reached approximately 100 meters from Khosrow Solfa. The Air Force had a B-1 bomber drop 31 multi-million-dollar bombs on the heads of the Taliban. This was done to ensure the Taliban stronghold would no longer be utilized as a hub or utilized for IEDs. It was a sight the Top Guns took in and appreciated, knowing their brothers had not died in vain. This was a sight only a select few ever get to see. When the dust finally settled, the soldiers walked through the town that was going to be the new home of COP Durham and appreciated the efforts of all involved in the operation. The combined efforts of the artillery, sappers, special forces, Afghan commandos, Air Force, and engineers completed the mission with zero casualties to coalition forces. By the conclusion of Operation *Eagle Claw*, the soldiers had uncovered a total of 31 IEDs. At a minimum 31 lives were saved and 62 legs still attached. At the beginning of the operation, there was lots of pessimism based on the way things had gone in the past; but just as the leaves had changed on the trees, so did the momentum in the Arghandab.

The soldiers from Havoc and Bravo had been extremely busy on High Life while the "Boys of Babur" were keeping the eastern front secure. Once the clearing operation was completed, One Bravo was moved into a blocking position in what was Tarok Kolache. A platoon from Havoc began fortifying their new home at Strong Point Weaver as One Bravo and Three Bravo rotated on 12-hour shifts patrolling in the orchards and down the river. This allowed Havoc to focus on establishing their new operations at Weaver, which would arguably not have much standoff from enemy aggression once the fighting season kicked off. They would be positioned on a main road that cut straight through the heart of the Arghandab into Kandahar, and if there were to be enemy fighters running weapons through the orchards, Strong Point Weaver would be at the heart of that route.

Three Bravo were in the process of clearing a compound when they located a building laced with three separate IEDs. They had to secure the area and call in EOD to have them destroy the IEDs and the building. One Bravo's mission was to hold the crossing route between Strong Point Weaver and what was to become COP Durham and the 1st Battalion, 22nd Infantry Regiment's (1-22) stronghold in Khosrow Solfa; this meant the battalion now had units to the north, south, east, and west. Due to the 1-22 guys being in Khosrow Solfa, they had found 15 IEDs in a week. Thankfully, all were found with zero casualties to American forces, which continued to be a trend around the Top Guns' area of operations. With Havoc now controlling the area south of Jelawur, One and Three Bravo patrolled Jelawur and Druia, and Two and Four Bravo controlled Babur. Alpha controlled the orchards east of Jelawur and Charqolba Olya, and 1-22 was in Khosrow Sofa. The only area in the region left without a strong point was Lower Babur.

One Bravo was finally back at COP Tynes and had started preparing for the battalion's next big push. Jelawur was the most significant and stable village in Arghandab; however, it was also flooded with high-value targets, making it the main objective of the battalion during the deployment. The battalion believed that if Jelawur could be stabilized, then the ANA had the potential to deny the Taliban sanctuary in the Arghandab. With the immense impact of the operations on Tarok Kolache, Khosrow Solfa, and elsewhere, the Taliban fighters had moved into Jelawur and utilized it as a sanctuary village. The battalion was planning to surround Jelawur and clear every compound.

Essentially, the vision was to squeeze the life out of the village. While this could be a slow and monotonous task, it could have a monumental impact.

Three Bravo continued to be strung out across the orchards, pulling security for the Havoc element during the establishment of Strong Point Weaver, which would be crucial in the upcoming operations. Back at COP Tynes, One Bravo was responsible for force protection, patrolling, and QRF. Manpower continued to be an issue across the battalion, with One Bravo down to 14 soldiers to cover all their responsibilities. During the past few days, One Bravo has been trying to show a strong presence within the village in preparation for upcoming operations in Jelawur. Having a heavy presence in the area allowed leaders to identify patterns of life and any changes that may have occurred due to the influx of locals from the orchards. Ironically, patterns of life appeared normal, and patrols had been going well. It was common to see Sergeant Jackson or "Doc" Stegehuis hanging with the local kids in the village during the key leader engagements. As plans continued to mount, and with the day of reckoning fast approaching, the new tick mark on the calendar for the clearance operation was October 25. During the operation, the battalion would be looking to clear Jelawur utilizing Bravo Battery; as the battery cleared the village; and locals' attentions were focused on the events in town, a second operation would be underway to seize a crossing at the second canal just above Khosrow Olya (Objective Juarez). Once completed, units would move farther east past Babur to Shuyen-e Olya, Shuyen-e Vosta, and in early November and then Shuyen-e Sofla in mid-November. Alpha Battery, Havoc, and the newly attached Company B, 1-22, would be doing similar operations in their area to secure and clear the ground the Top Guns gained.

The Jelawur mission looked to be simplistic. The Top Guns were used to having to clear in the orchards and, for once, would have an opportunity to go from compound to compound rather than walking through flooded orchards. Due to this being done in an area where rapport had been built over several months, the battalion believed the threat level to be low. However, if there were any Taliban left, they would be an issue, and the clearance operation would become a firefight. One thing was sure: based on the historical aspect of the Shuyens, there was an extremely high IED threat.

As the battalion neared its five-month point in the deployment, the soldiers were reaching a breaking point. Operation after operation, with rarely any refit or rest to be mentioned, the soldiers' morale was degraded despite the many wins of late. Many leaders were losing the joy in what they were doing, which was starting to show in the form of complacency. Complacency is one of the worst things that can happen to a soldier. Once it sets in, it becomes a virus to the host and those around it.

With the battalion speeding toward the end of October, the men felt they were holding on for dear life. Tarok Kolache and Khosrow Solfa were successful missions and set the following objectives to secure the Arghandab in motion. The problem was that the battalion was now on a roller coaster that appeared out of control. There was rarely any predictability for the soldiers; operations planning had gone out the window. When the area became more secure, typical garrison-style things happened, like patrols and missions just coming down for the most random things.

The Jelawur clearance mission was finally coming up. Bravo would put this operation behind them, but then the battery had already been notified they would be on standby for the next operation. It had become a guessing game as to what came next. Would it be the Shuyens, Lower Babur, supporting Alpha, supporting Havoc? Who knew? As of late, there had been next to no engagements from enemy fighters; there was intel they were leaving and going to Pakistan to recruit students to fight. As leaders overheard conversations around their respective areas of responsibility, it became apparent the soldiers were becoming adrenaline junkies. They spoke of how firefights had become a blast as long as no one got hurt. They discussed how, initially, emotions were always high, and everything was tense, but as the tables turned and they earned fire superiority, it became an adrenaline rush.

Soldiers in garrison are forced to perform mundane taskings that take them away from training; they're placed in charge of quarters, staff duty, red cycle tasking, white cycle tasking, funeral taskings, etc. The soldiers are the worker bees and the glue of an organization. The unit looks exceptional if the soldiers are great, and the leaders are good. Watching a unit that is well disciplined, well trained, and works as a team is inspiring; ultimately, leaders from outside entities can be left speechless and leave inspired after seeing an outstanding unit. Several nights earlier, soldiers from One Bravo were sitting around a fire and talking about going home. Going home seemed like such a foreign concept in the deployment. Then they started discussing how Vietnam veterans arrived home, and the American people disrespected them. The topic was brought up, "When we get home, it's doubtful that we'll ever forget this place. Hopefully, the people back home will learn the story of Stout, Durham, Pitman, Castro, Stansbery, King, and Weaver." During the deployment, the Top Guns had helped to save good men and contributed to killing bad ones. They'd seen good men die and sang to dying men during their final moments. They wept for soldiers they knew well and mourned those they hardly knew. During the fighting season, they were called to help tie tourniquets to what was once an arm or a leg and helped patch up holes in men, hoping to save their lives. Bullets had flown within inches of their heads. They'd stepped on IEDs and, by the grace of God, walked away. They'd had mortar rounds land close enough they should've been hit, and rocket-propelled grenades not hurt a soul within their kill radius. As the fighting season slowed to a crawl, the Top Guns began seeing the tides change. Their sacrifices for each other and the mission were coming to fruition. The question lingering in the minds of the "Sons of the Arghandab" was, what happens now the leaves have fallen, and the enemy is in observation mode?

CHAPTER 13

The Men Hidden Beneath the Rocks

Courage is not the absence of fear, but the ability to act despite it.

GENERAL DAVID PETRAEUS

The Arghandab is a luscious and vibrant area in the spring and summer, and with this lusciousness comes the bounty of fruit, marijuana, poppy, and other harvests the valley survives on. Once fall arrives, it's like the valley dies. It's not a slow descent into the depths of darkness, however—it's more alive today and dead tomorrow. The warfighters of the Top Guns were experiencing this drastic change for the first time. It was an odd feeling to wake up and not hear the typical sound of gunfire or the occasional rocket-propelled grenade (RPG) whistling through the air. The men at Combat Outpost (COP) Tynes had become accustomed to patrolling through Jelawur and Druia daily. They had become accustomed to entering the orchards and anticipating contact or getting spun up to assist with a QRF (quick-reaction force) element for COP Stout or COP Nolen. As of late, that hadn't been the case; things were quiet, almost eerie. One Bravo had pushed out a typical night patrol in Jelawur to observe any life patterns. During the patrol, Staff Sergeant Fontenot had pushed his men out to maximize dispersion; there was little to no life to be found, the new routine.

While Jelawur was the most populated village for the Top Guns, it saw minimal action. Most of the fighting came from inside the orchards, not from inside the village. COP Tynes had received a notification from COP Terra Nova that a high-value target was suspected of being inside Jelawur. Cell phone triangulation gave a general vicinity of the compound, but it wasn't a definitive area. After being in Jelawur for a few hours, Fontenot told his guys they would call it a night and head home. The patrol moved back across the open area under the cover of moonlight. The sky was clear and provided lots of illumination for the men to move under their night-vision goggles (NVG). By this point in the deployment, walking under their NVGs was second nature. As the patrol neared COP Tynes, they called up that they were returning to the post. Sergeant Junkin and Specialist Branch were in the command post (CP). They radioed up to the battalion that the patrol was back.

Fontenot and Junkin had been buddies since their days in Iraq, and not much had changed. Before deployment, they would go kayaking with their wives and enjoy life. Junkin was expecting his first daughter, and he was an excited, expecting dad, as most dads are. Fontenot, coming off the patrol, always had an abundance of energy because he was always anticipating the worst-case scenario. After their debriefing, with everyone released, Fontenot retreated to the CP to hang out with Junkin. It had become standard practice that, after night patrols, they would hang out and talk about life back home, talk about their spouses, and talk about Junkin's daughter. What wasn't typical about their time together was that it was generally spent with the two war fighters looking for what to buy for Junkin's little girl. Maybe it would be expected of some, but it's not what is considered normal in a war zone. Branch monitored the raid camera as the two men chatted and looked for kids' clothes together. As Branch panned to the north of Route Mariners, he spotted four men busy burying what appeared to be an improvised explosive device (IED) in the road.

"Hey, Chief, I think these assholes are digging an IED in the road."

"Sure, as fuck looks like it," agreed Fontenot. "Zoom in as close as possible to see what they are doing."

Branch zoomed in with the eye in the sky, getting as close as possible, and could see they were digging in the road. Junkin went looking for First Sergeant Baca to see what he would want the men to do. Baca arrived at the CP to look at the raid camera. He verified the men were digging in the road.

"Fontenot, get your men together and go fucking get those assholes."

Fontenot immediately ran to the north side of COP Tynes, where the vehicles and tents were located. He told everyone they were spinning up QRF. All the guys had just come off a lackluster patrol, so they were down for a bit of excitement.

Fontenot jumped in an MRAP (mine-resistant, ambush-protected) with Specialist Bibb as his driver; 2nd Lieutenant Pantaleo was the truck commander of his MATV (mine-resistant, ambush-protected all-terrain vehicle) with Corporal Parker, and "Smoke" Sturgeon, the new platoon sergeant, was in the other MATV. The men loaded up in the trucks with a fury. Sergeant Cox, Specialists Cooper, Dulaney, Cheatham, Miller, and

Staff Sergeant Beaudrie and the whole team were there and ready to roll. As they quickly called up their green report, they immediately left the COP heading north. Fontenot and Bibb were in the lead truck; Bibb was driving like a man on a mission. As they cleared the compound directly west of COP Tynes, they hit a graveyard that had open graves; the MRAP bounced around like a pinball machine; no one inside the MRAP knew if there were bodies inside the graves or not, all they knew was they were chasing after some guys digging in the road.

Pantaleo radioed to Fontenot, "One One, One Six, you guys alright up there? I see a lot of bouncing going on?"

"One Six, One One, we're good. Let's go," Fontenot replied.

As the convoy quickly approached the four men, the men began firing at the convoy with AK-47s; but identified their AKs were no match for the three gun trucks. Two jumped on a motorcycle and began speeding across the northern desert of Jelawur toward the mountains; the other two headed toward Jelawur. The men of One Bravo knew that if the fighters on the bike made it to the mountains, they wouldn't find them. They picked up the pace and began closing the distance, but; with the dust coming from the chase, it was hard to determine precisely where they had gone or if they were baiting them into an IED field.

Fontenot radioed to Pantaleo, "Hey, do you see these assholes?"

"No, not yet."

At that moment, Pantaleo and Parker's MATV launched off a cliff and landed on the motorcycle the men had been riding.

Pantaleo radioed Sturgeon and Fontenot. "One Seven, One One, One Six. We just crushed their motorcycle. No one was on it, but we just rode over it."

As the men continued their pursuit, Pantaleo radioed, "FOB Jelawur, this is Bulls One Six sparkle, the last known location of the fighters."

Much to their amazement, the sparkle landed in front of their convoy.

Fontenot radioed again. "FOB Jelawur, this is Bulls One One, sparkle, the last known location of the fighters."

Once again, they sparkled right in front of the convoy. At that point, Pantaleo halted the convoy, and Pantaleo and Fontenot dismounted to attempt to find the two men who had left their motorcycle. Once they were on foot, Pantaleo called back again for the ISR (intelligence, surveillance, and reconnaissance) platform to sparkle the location. The white light came out of the sky and told Pantaleo and Fontenot they were right on top of them. Pantaleo, now blinded by the beam, flipped up his NVGs.

"Fonty, go white light."

They continued to struggle to locate the fighters that had skirted north. They got online and slowly moved toward the base of the mountain. Pantaleo identified a dirty brown scarf under a pile of rocks.

"Fonty, dude, they're right fucking there."

At that moment, it was like a scene from *COPS*; Pantaleo and Fontenot started yelling at the men. "Delta Rasha, Delta Rasha, MOTHERFUCKERS!"

They were then rushed to apprehend them. The guys in the vehicles had begun dismounting and were assisting with dragging the two men out the side of the rocky hill where they had covered themselves with dirt and rocks. Parker, as well as several other soldiers, took extra care in placing them face down on the Afghan ground to zip cuff and then load them up to return them to the IED site.

There was still unfinished business for the One Bravo men. There was the business of attempting to find the other two guys who shot into Jelawur on the other motorcycle. The convoy headed back to the north side of the village and positioned themselves where Sturgeon's truck could pull security. This would ensure that if someone attempted to run from the village, they could apprehend them. Using the raid camera, Branch and Junkin walked the convoy onto the compound they suspected the guys had gone into. Pantaleo, Fontenot, Creighton, and Parker lined up at the compound's door. It was very early in the morning, so they knew the chances of someone answering the door would be next to none. The compound had a steel door; luckily, it wasn't secure. They pounded on the door and quickly entered with their SureFire lights on, scanning in all directions. The compound was massive; when they entered, the first thing they could see was the pillars of the entryway of the building. They rushed inside, and the team split, Fontenot and Pantaleo going one way and Parker and Creighton going the other. As one team cleared part of the compound, the other team pulled security; and they quickly cleared both sides.

The men were now four hours into this new adventure of chasing the men who had placed the IED. They were raiding this compound in the middle of the night, and the only intel they had was where the suspects were thought to have gone. Fontenot and Pantaleo ventured into the left side of the compound, and when Fontenot pulled back the sheet in the doorway, he revealed a room where several people were lying on the floor covered up.

"Hey, sir, we have several people under a sheet here."

"Take it off of them."

Fontenot ripped the sheet off them, revealing an old lady in her underwear and several scared kids.

Feeling bad for them, Fontenot said, "I'm sorry," and threw the sheet back over them, to which the old lady replied something in Pashto that was probably not very friendly. The rest of the guys continued going from room to room. Parker and Creighton came out of one of the rooms with two fighting-age males. Just before leaving the compound, Fontenot asked, "Did anyone clear the 'shit shack'?"

No one had. Creighton and Fontenot cleared it on their way out of the building and, lo and behold, there was the high value target the battalion had picked up cell traffic on.

"Hey, wake the fuck up," Creighton said.

"I don't think he speaks English, buddy," said Fontenot.

"Yes, he does. They all do."

"You're right, buddy, they all do. Fuckers."

The man was asleep and unsuspecting. Fontenot and Creighton zip-cuffed him and he was taken into custody.

At this point, the patrol had successfully apprehended several high-value targets. The problem was they still hadn't found the two suspects who left the IED site on the motorcycle. Junkin was on the radio with Top Guns main; he was attempting to get any information on the suspects or to see if the battalion could pick up traffic from their interpreters monitoring the enemy net. Luckily for the patrol, the battalion radioed that the suspects had entered a compound close to where they were. The guys once again took their team and breached the door; the first thing they saw when they entered the compound was the motorcycle. They employed the same clearing technique as before, quickly finding the two men asleep in separate rooms. When they brought them into the center of the compound, the men attempted to tell the story that they had been sleeping all night. The problem was that their motorcycle's engine was still hot. It didn't take long before the interpreters got them to break. They eventually admitted they were part of the team placing the IED and were taken into custody. One Bravo had started the evening with a lackluster patrol. It was now at a point where, after two compounds raided and a motorcycle chase through the desert, they had five high-value targets, had confiscated multiple AK-47s and five RPGs, and were finally completed for the night. Or so they thought.

Using extra caution, they positioned the gun trucks approximately two hundred fifty meters from where Junkin identified the four men were digging. It was now 3:00 am, and Pantaleo and Fontenot began walking two of the men over to where they had been digging.

"Ask them what they were doing digging in the road?" said Pantaleo to Mike, the interpreter.

"We were preparing for a picnic the next day."

Fontenot, starting to get tired and cranky, said, "Mike, tell him he's full of shit!"

"Do you want me to tell him that, sir?"

"Hell yeah!"

"Sir, Sergeant Fontenot says he thinks you're full of shit."

Pantaleo and Fontenot continued marching the two men closer and closer to the site as Junkin walked them on with the raid camera. It was becoming more evident that the two men were getting nervous as their pace was deteriorating drastically. As they got within about 25 meters of the IED, Pantaleo said, "Now you walk in front."

"No."

"Why not?"

The detainees were, at this point, visibly distraught. Fontenot told Mike, "Tell them to show us where the IED is." The men pointed directly in front of them.

Fontenot said, "No, that's not good enough. It would be best if you showed it to us. You are going to walk us right to it."

The men walked them to within about five meters in front of the IED and stopped. They pointed at the wires sticking out of the dust-covered ground where they had left in haste. One Bravo was not prepared for what they uncovered: 75 pounds of homemade explosives (HME) attached to a battery pack. With a Jersey swagger in his step Pantaleo, grinning from ear to ear, retreated to the other detainees in the back of the truck and advised them of what they had just found. The fighters began tearing up, possibly knowing they were caught red-handed and wouldn't see their families soon. The unfortunate part of the whole ordeal was that these men may have just been innocent farmers who the Taliban threatened. They may have been told harm would come to their families if they didn't do what they were told.

One Bravo had Bulls Main contact EOD (explosive ordnance disposal) to blow the IED, but it didn't look as if they could come anytime soon. Pantaleo decided that, due to the length of time, the platoon would leave two trucks at the site to pull security, and the other truck would take the detainees to Terra Nova. At first light, they would then escort EOD back to ground zero. Doing things this way would mean dropping off the detainees quickly. Then they could escort the convoy with EOD and the LEP (law enforcement professional). When the sun crested over the mountains of Afghanistan, the men from One Bravo got their first glimpse of the day's sunrise. The sun's orange glow gave way to the first resemblance of warmth they had felt in several hours. In the distance, the soldiers could hear the roar of engines and knew the cavalry was on its way. Their brothers were coming with EOD so their wait in the cold was nearing an end. The Arghandab had gone from one extreme to another in a very short period. It was blistering hot one second, and now it was freezing at night.

Once EOD was on the ground, many caches were discovered. One Bravo uncovered two pressure plates, six 82-millimeter mortars rigged to blow, a DFFC (directionally focused fragmentation charge), four battery packs, command wires, and additional mortars cached where the patrol was initially engaged at and where the men were seen digging in the road. They were hidden inside a culvert for quick access. Although it was a massive success that the men were able to capture the detainees and uncover the IEDs and caches, the idea that the two jugs of HME were enough to destroy an MRAP was concerning. What made it more concerning was that it was meticulously planned so first responders would initiate a pressure plate, and the DFFC, about ten feet away and attached to a command wire, would hit the first responders or EOD. It was some of the most violent and well-thought-out IEDs the men had seen set in place and was once again a reminder that life in the Arghandab was never safe. The soldiers collected all the evidence they needed, and Bibb ensured the detainees were in the HIIDE (handheld interagency identity detection equipment) system. Ultimately, it was seen as a good day.

CHAPTER 14

Strong Point Stansbery

> Never, never be afraid to do what's right especially if the well-being of a person or animal is at stake. Society's punishments are small compared to the ones we inflict on our soul when we look the other way.
>
> MARTIN LUTHER KING JR.

Another month down, and what seemed like an eternity to go until the end of the deployment. During the early months, things seemed to happen at hyperspeed. When you're getting shot at or trying to tend to someone else who's getting shot at, time doesn't seem like much of a concern. The Top Guns had finally reached November, and although the heat had subsided, there were still uneasy roads ahead. The new target of the battalion was now the Shuyens. The Shuyens were the farthest eastern villages in the Arghandab, even farther east than Babur. They would extend the battalion much farther than anyone ever dreamed of upon their arrival, especially after Specialist Moon was killed attempting to go into Babur. Now, in November, it was going to be a reality; a scary reality for the men understanding the amount of Taliban fighters held up in these villages, having been displaced from Tarok Kolache, Khosrow Solfa, and Lower Babur. Still it was a push that, regardless of whether the men believed it was worth the risk, was going to happen.

The battalion was once again on the eve of another major operation. The next day, the dreaded push into the Shuyens would begin. Some within Bravo Battery hoped to uncover caches; others remembered the horrors Sergeant Durham and Specialist Castro met. The Taliban undoubtedly knew the battery was coming, so it could go one of a million ways. The best-case scenario was that, since the Taliban had gotten the shit kicked out of them over the past few months, they would be less likely to want to pick a fight in the Shuyens, or they wouldn't be there at all. The intelligence gathered was that the Taliban were recruiting in Pakistan. If this were the case, they would not be around, and the process would be slow, deliberate, and precise, with minimal resistance. On the flip side, the worst-case scenario was that since they knew the battery was coming, they would be prepared, anticipate the arrival, and ambush early with complex ambushes utilizing heavy resistance, large improvised explosive devices (IED), sniper fire, and everything else they could bring to the fight. The reality of the operation was that the battery was expected to meet minimal resistance; it was expected that, once the enemy fighters saw overwhelming American and Afghan forces coming their way, they would stand down rather than fight.

As the Bravo elements began clearing through the Shuyens, it wasn't long before IEDs and caches were uncovered. It was the honey hole of the Arghandab. It was like Bravo Battery had just picked the winning lottery ticket at the 7-Eleven after finding it lying next to the gas pump. Shuyen-e Olya was the first to be cleared as it was the nearest to Babur.

During this enormous operation that cleared three villages 39 IEDs were discovered. That included those that were buried and those found but not yet connected. Ultimately, all 39 were located with no American or Afghan casualties.

One Bravo was in the process of clearing a compound in Shuyen-e Vosta. As they entered, two men shot out to the back of the compound; they were able to catch them. Their Afghan interpreter, Nabil, began speaking to one of the men.

"Why are you running from the soldiers?"

"I was running because I was afraid because I am of fighting age and did not want to get shot."

Nabil relayed this to 2nd Lieutenant Pantaleo and Staff Sergeant Fontenot; the latter, not buying it, told Nabil to keep probing for more details. Fontenot informed the Afghan and American soldiers to keep looking around. The Afghan National Army (ANA) men told Pantaleo and Fontenot they had found something outside in the courtyard. The Americans left the man with Nabil to see what was found. The ANA soldiers started breaking the base of the wall to the exterior wall of the compound. It was becoming apparent the man had weapons buried inside the exterior walls.

"Holy shit, man, fucking keep going, man," said Fontenot.

"I need to call this shit up," said Pantaleo. "Bulls Main, this is Bulls One Six. We found a cache."

"Bulls One Six, this is Bulls Main. We acknowledge. Just stand by until we get further guidance."

"Stand by? What the fuck? "Keep digging," Fontenot directed.

The ANA soldiers kept right on digging. After about half an hour, the ANA and several of the Americans had uncovered seven AK-47s, four PKM machine guns, hundreds of belts of 7.62-millimeter rounds, a Russian scope used to spy on the American soldiers, multiple grenades, several mortar rounds, IED-making materials, and long rifles.

"Bulls Main, Bulls One Six."

"Bulls One Six, this is Bulls Main."

"Bulls Main, Bulls One Six. We're gonna need EOD to bring several bars of C4 when they come over!"

"Bulls One Six, Bulls Main. Acknowledge all, and we will pass the message to them."

It wasn't long until the explosives ordnance disposal (EOD) team arrived on the scene; when they showed up at the compound, they had two blocks of C4 ready for the cache. They went inside, but when they saw the amount of stuff that had been uncovered, they realized they needed two additional blocks of C4. Much to the surprise of One Bravo, they were excited to see what would happen to this mountain of explosives. Everyone left the compound, and the EOD noncommissioned officer in charge called, "FIRE IN THE HOLE, FIRE IN THE HOLE, FIRE IN THE HOLE!"

The entire wall near the explosion erupted. The blast was so fierce that the wall the men had taken cover behind was hit so hard it was blown to pieces.

During the clearing operation, the battery set up two strong points. Strong Point Castro was established in Shuyen-e Olya in an enormous compound used as a homemade explosives factory and a Taliban hospital. The compound could comfortably house the whole battery, providing the men plenty of standoff from enemy fighters. The Afghan soldiers would also be postured with the Americans and would have their wing of the compound in which they would be responsible for providing overwatch. One Bravo and Two Bravo would rotate patrolling out of Castro; the other strong point, temporarily known as Durham, would be in another compound in Shuyen-e Vosta. This structure was previously used as a Taliban stronghold for an IED emplacement cell. Three Bravo and Four Bravo would patrol out of it. Most patrols since arriving in the Shuyens had been lackluster, however. The Taliban had either left or didn't have the manpower to do anything, or they were waiting for the fighting season to roll back around. From conducting key leader engagements, One Bravo got a feel for the malik of the Khosrows; it was painfully apparent he was working with the Taliban. Unfortunately, there wasn't much that could be done about that yet. Pantaleo had a bad feeling about him from their encounters and would have liked nothing more than to be rid of him, but he knew that wouldn't happen. Not yet, at least.

Pantaleo had gone through hell and back during the deployment, he'd been through firefights, stepped on IEDs, been on significant operations, helped save lives, and watched young men die, all as a 2nd lieutenant. His time had finally come to be promoted to 1st lieutenant; he had "grown up," as the NCOs in his platoon had so graciously put it. He was no longer a "butter bar." He was now a "real boy," as Fontenot would lovingly call him.

He thought to himself as he lay silent in the dark beside his men in the middle of the Shuyens. "How ironic it is that I've finally got promoted, and yet I still get to sleep in the dirt with my boys. Today is a good day to be a Bastard!"

As the morning sun came up and they were getting ready for their first patrol, the ANA treated them to a breakfast feast like they were yet to enjoy in the Arghandab. They had cooked small lamb strips and naan over an open fire for the soldiers to enjoy with olive oil. This was a welcome change from their usual "Jimmy Dean" (meal ration usually consisting of commercially available items, like a deli-style sandwich, etc.) for breakfast.

The men from Bravo Battery had been going nonstop for four weeks and were all beginning to lose touch with reality. Rest had become a thing of the past. The only thing that had mattered thus far throughout the deployment was the mission. Soldiers were a tool used to accomplish that mission. Their welfare was an afterthought; their mental well-being was rarely a consideration, or at least not yet. While this mission had been one of the better-planned ones, it had been one that had seen fragmentary order after fragmentary order change its trajectory, which led the battery into a shitstorm and constantly kept the leaders on the ground guessing what was going to come next; they figured if they were wondering, the enemy must be guessing as well. While patrolling through the Shuyens had been productive; the plan was to shut down Strong Point Castro and move into the pomegranate orchards in Lower Babur. The new plan was to clear down to Lower Babur, also known as Khosrow Solfa, and once the platoon was in the ruins inside Lower Babur, the next step was to set up another strong point.

No major operation happens without a precursor operation, or at least none within this current deployment. Earlier, during Operation *Eagle Claw*, also known as Operation *Bakersfield II*, an ODA (Operational Detachment-Alpha) team and an Afghan Commando unit attempted to clear into Lower Babur on October 6, 2010, but made it only halfway through the village. They then called it quits because they found so many IEDs that they ran out of demolition. They ultimately pulled back and carpet-bombed the shit out of it after realizing the entire town was much like Tarok Kolache, an IED factory filled with house-born IEDs. Since then, it had been quiet, but it was still suspected to be filled with IEDs and caches in the pomegranate orchards.

Lower Babur has been a Taliban stronghold ever since the movement came to prominence. One Bravo taking this critical piece of real estate meant that, in the subsequent fighting season, the Taliban would not be able to use it as a safe area or line of communication. The mission given to One Bravo was to clear down to Lower Babur through about six hundred meters of pomegranate orchards and set up a strong point in the middle of what was left of the ruins of the village. The men from One Bravo would be coming straight from Castro after being there for seven days, moving into their new home for the time being.

Just before One Bravo stepped off for Lower Babur, they got word they would lose one of their staple leaders from the beginning of the deployment. Corporal Miller would be staying at Combat Outpost (COP) Babur and going to Two Bravo; in return, One Bravo would be getting Sergeant Harold. This move was an enormous surprise to everyone, including the platoon's leadership. First Sergeant Baca made the move while he was at COP Babur. Harold had internal issues with his platoon at COP Babur, so he moved to One Bravo. The timing of the move couldn't have come at a more inopportune time, but when you're in the Arghandab, there aren't many good times. The platoon split into two squads to move to Lower Babur. They were going to need to be slow and methodical. Most of the men carried a tremendous amount of gear on their backs; the others carried gear that had been taken into the Shuyens by vehicle. As they began the move, they crossed over the first canal, always a point of contention for the soldiers. They crossed the well-constructed concrete bridge which appeared sound, unlike others that gave them reason to be concerned. As the patrol headed down the path and began its descent toward Lower Babur, they were greeted by several Afghan soldiers also on patrol. While it was nothing to be super excited about, it was nice to see a friendly face as these were the same ANA soldiers who had cooked them breakfast.

As One Bravo walked into Lower Babur and got their first glimpse of their new area of responsibility, the men knew they had nothing. Not nothing, but absolutely nothing. No water, no food, no shelter, nothing. In the entire area, there was only one standing structure. It was the remnants of an old mud structure that had been partially destroyed but was still usable. "Smoke" Sturgeon, the new One Bravo platoon sergeant, told Specialist Erickson to go up to the top of the building to set up the M240B machine gun as elevated cover. The remainder of the soldiers began conducting a perimeter sweep to clear the area. This would occupy the next several hours. During this time, Two Bravo would also be in the orchards assisting with the clearing effort; meanwhile, Creighton, Parker, Bibb, Dulaney, and Little filled sandbags. These were being carried up to the rooftop to fortify the gun position and to build a secondary position for the Afghan soldiers to utilize to have cover and concealment. The Seabees had finally arrived but weren't going to be able to begin working until the following day. Due to this, the One Bravo leadership employed the loader as a tower and threw sandbags on top of it for another machine-gun position. It had become apparent to all the men from One Bravo that they had just established the next COP Nolen. To the south, there were pomegranate orchards everywhere; to the west, there were pomegranate orchards everywhere; to the east, there were pomegranate orchards and marijuana fields; and to the north was a canal and marijuana fields, and an open area for a clear field of fire. What was exceptionally concerning about this location was that the strong point would be a hell of a place to be when the fighting season returned. There was zero standoff from enemy fighters. The battery was postured to endure the possibility the next fighting season could be even worse due to this new location.

As the sun set on the men of the Bastards, they prepared for their first night, utterly detached from the rest of the battery. They had little to nothing in the way of communication. They were using an ASIP (Advanced System Improvement Program) radio to check in with Babur hourly as that was the only COP they could reach. The reality of the situation was as if a shitstorm had hit them; their saving grace had to come in the form of COP Babur. Specialist Tebaldi could still reach *Longknife*, but other than that, the Bastards were on their own. Fontenot volunteered to pull the first sergeant-of-the-guard shift because he couldn't sleep anyway. Not sleeping was becoming a way of life for him; he often found himself awake in the middle of the night after patrols, in their makeshift gym, working out under the stars alone. He found peace in the solitude of being under the stars with nothing but his thoughts and his music. Fontenot found a few twigs and made a small fire on the backside of the loader between the building so it would be obscured. He walked around aimlessly, wondering if he would run into an enemy fighter or step on something he didn't want to find. He decided to go up on the rooftop to check on his guys pulling guard on the M240B and the Afghan soldier pulling guard.

As Fontenot walked up the crude staircase to the second level where the Bastards were sleeping, and the two gun crews were pulling security, he smelled the pungent aroma of marijuana. It was no secret the Afghan soldiers liked to partake in occasional marijuana. The American leadership always discouraged it when pulling guard and patrolling, especially when they were the only ones on duty. Fontenot saw a burning ember in the Afghan gun pit built for their PKM.

"Put out the hashish!"

"No, hashish is good," the Afghan soldier replied.

"Look, man, put out the hashish."

"No, hashish is good."

"Look, motherfucker, I'm not going to tell you again. The next time, I'm going to throw you off the roof. Now put out the fucking hashish!"

"No, hashishhhhhh …" Before he had the chance to finish the sentence, Fontenot grabbed him from the pit and pulled him to the side of the building as if he was about to hang his ass off the side of the building. An Afghan lieutenant asked Nabil, "What's going on?"

"Your soldier continues to smoke hashish after Staff Sergeant Fontenot repeatedly asked him to stop."

"Please apologize to Staff Sergeant Fontenot for me. I will handle him."

After that, the Afghan soldier was replaced for the evening with another soldier who didn't smoke hashish, and no one ended up getting thrown off the building.

The following day, the soldiers were up bright and early, working to attempt to make something out of their new strong point. It was now being called Strong Point Babur; the Bastards hated that name. Hearing Strong Point Babur being called up over the radio was like a thorn in their side.

While the soldiers worked, they could hear the roar of an engine coming down the dirt road that ran from COP Babur down to the strong point. The Ranger pulled up and out walked an Afghan soldier who drew a great deal of respect from the ANA men.

The Afghan lieutenant called for Nabil, who came and greeted the gentleman with great respect. They exchanged several words in Pashto, and then Nabil called Fontenot over.

Nabil said, "Staff Sergeant Fontenot, this is Major Salom. He fought with the Mujahideen against the Russians and is quite a legend. He would like to know what happened last night."

"I told your man to stop smoking hashish, and he told me, 'No, hashish good.' That happened three times, and after three times, I was going to toss him from the roof. That's what happened."

"Tell Staff Sergeant Fontenot I will take care of him!"

"Bring him to me!" Salom ordered the lieutenant.

The Afghan lieutenant had the soldier brought to Salom, who told him something in Pashto, backhanded him three times, then threw him in the back of the Ranger pick-up. "We will take care of him from here," he said to Nabil. The Americans never saw the soldier again.

With the ever-changing environment in the Arghandab, leaders learned to be flexible and versatile. They learned that dealing with the ANA leaders, especially leaders such as Salom, would yield exceptional results and hopefully pay dividends one day for their country. As the soldiers kept working meticulously, Fontenot located a shelter that was still intact. It wasn't anything special; it had one door and a small window. Fontenot decided it was the perfect size hut for a platoon leadership building, so he worked on it. He cleaned it after about four hours of shoveling dirt and bombing debris. Much to his chagrin, however, about an hour after he and Pantaleo called it home, the Seabees told them they would bulldoze the entire area. So much for that new home.

Sergeant Jackson was on the radio, and someone said, "I'm tired of hearing Strong Point Babur. It would be best if you said Strong Point Stansbery." Jackson, being Jackson, looked back and, with a smile, the platoon knew he would take that challenge.

"COP Babur, this is Strong Point Stansbery."

"Strong Point Babur, this is COP Babur. We read you, Lima Charlie."

"COP Babur, this is Strong Point Stansbery. Radio Check, over."

"Strong Point Babur, this is COP Babur. We read you, Lima Charlie."

"COP Babur, this is Strong Point Stansbery. Radio check, over."

At that point, Bulls Six came over the radio, furious, and said, "Strong Point Babur, you're not Strong Point Stansbery; you're Strong Point Babur until Top Gun Six says otherwise. ACKNOWLEDGE!"

"COP Babur, this is Strong Point Stansbery. Acknowledge all."

"Bulls One Six, this is Bulls Six," Captain Day wanted to speak to Pantaleo.

"Bulls Six, Bulls One Six."

"Bulls One Six, Bulls Six, you will make [code name] Jackson give a follow-on class on proper radio etiquette following that little stunt he just pulled."

"Bulls Six, Bulls One Six. Acknowledge all."

Shortly after that radio transmission, "Smoke" Sturgeon told Jackson he would give everyone a class on radio etiquette. Jackson was a staple of the

Bastards. He had been with the platoon since the beginning. He'd had a rough start during the initial infill with the Two Charlie men during the last patrol and went down as a heat casualty. He was always one to find controversy and, once again, had found it. He put together a short class in which he provided a block of instruction on how to conduct yourself while utilizing a radio in the Army, and he met the intent of what the battery commander wanted. Shortly after the class was completed, word came down that Strong Point Babur was no longer a thing, and Strong Point Stansbery was born.

Pantaleo received word he was to do a mission where he would take a squad out on a quick patrol that would do a cordon and block so the Afghan National Civil Order Police (ANCOP) could detain some Taliban in Jelawur and confiscate some of their supplies. The mission was supposed to be a quick turn-and-burn mission, but as most missions go, this one was now three hours in, and Pantaleo was being rerouted to COP Terra Nova. The target they were looking for was now in Druia, so they moved the cordon and block there. However, on the flip side, the good news was that, because they were at COP Terra Nova, they were getting to knock out promotions for Creighton from sergeant to staff sergeant and Tebaldi from specialist to sergeant. There was no better way for the One Bravo soldiers to keep moving forward during the deployment than to promote a few of the original Bastards. Unbeknown to the rest of the convoy with Pantaleo, a life-altering occurrence was happening. As Pantaleo geared up to leave Terra Nova, he reported he was not being allowed to leave due to a disagreement over Sergeant First Class Tatro's noncommissioned officer evaluation report (NCOER). The platoon was forced to go without him. For the first time in the deployment, the platoon was without its platoon leader because he decided to stand his ground about his rating of Tatro's NCOER. Pantaleo gave Tatro the rating he believed he deserved, but those above him disagreed, especially the command sergeant major. Pantaleo was forced to justify his rating and ultimately stood against the battalion elite, defiant to have his voice heard. He was told it wasn't a hill worth dying on, but to Pantaleo, it was the principle, and doing the right thing was a hill worth dying on. After several days of digging his heels in, he was eventually allowed to return to Stansbery to rejoin the platoon.

Back to building Strong Point Stansbery and beginning to patrol the new area of operation to learn the new terrain. The pomegranate orchards are intricate in their box structures; the trees weave in and out like slipknots. Going out into the orchards and patrolling from the strong point allowed the leadership to understand better how to build up a defense to protect the soldiers from avenues of attack. Three Bravo was coming into relieve One Bravo, and it appeared there would be a rotation between COP Tynes and Stansbery. Thankfully, the Hesco barriers were in place, and Arctic tents were coming. Three Bravo continued fortifying the position through position improvements, ultimately vastly improving the strong point. The towers eventually came to have MATV (mine-resistant, ambush-protected all-terrain vehicle) windows, providing bulletproof protection for the machine gunners. The Hescos were filled quickly by the Seabees, and an MWR (morale, welfare, and recreation) facility was promptly built. The ANA soldiers eventually built an outdoor kitchen to cook lamb, rice, naan, and other Afghan dishes. Although Strong Point Stansbery was strategically almost as bad as COP Nolen, during the time the Bulls occupied it, the Taliban were never able to mount any successful attacks on it.

CHAPTER 15

Strong Point Weaver

> Some had families waiting; for others, their only family would be the men they bled beside.
>
> BARRY PEPPER

After Operation *Bakersfield II* concluded and the bombs had officially stopped dropping, the ground was strewn with craters. There were massive holes from where 2,000-pound bombs were dropped on compounds containing explosives. Secondary explosions, which were potentially impressive displays of power, had left a violent imprint upon the Earth, and although the blast may not have been seen, the impression was left. The explosions had left craters up to ten feet deep. What was the point of going so far? What was the justification behind all of this? Ultimately, the Top Guns would have to pay $10,000 for each destroyed pomegranate tree because the trees were a portion of the farmers' harvest. It would take years for these trees to regenerate and produce fruit again. When the operation began, it was a component of Operation *Dragon Strike*, a more extensive operation the brigade carried out. Operation *Bakersfield II* was what the men would call the Top Guns' portion. Operation orders no doubt stated otherwise.

One Hotel's mission was to get to Khosrow Olya to establish a blocking position, allowing the sappers to infiltrate Tarok Kolache from the south, with One Bravo, by going west. History demonstrates how extraordinarily successful that effort was. Despite the numerous bombs dropped from the night sky, over thirty IEDs were discovered. Thus, there was some excitement. Strong Point Weaver had its share of difficulties, like any other facility near the operation. Despite being positioned in a perfect strategic position, the strong point was unquestionably in one of the worst conceivable locations from a safety viewpoint. For years, the Taliban had made extensive use of this crossing point to transport their wounded and smuggle weapons and drugs.

That would be methodically terminated in a heartbeat by Strong Point Weaver. The officers, soldiers, and noncommissioned officers of One Hotel would have an uphill climb to get the villagers of Khosrow Olya and those displaced from Tarok Kolache on their side.

The intersection closest to the south of the Arghandab River was where Strong Point Weaver was established. For those inside its walls, this was a problem. It was close to the orchards, like Strong Point Stansbery and COP Nolen, where Tarok Kolache had been, much to the contention of the Taliban and some villagers. During the original inception of the strong point; and its establishment, One Hotel stayed several days in fighting positions dug into the side of bomb craters. Everyone expected the enemy fighters to hold out in the same fashion as they had during the initial assault into Bakersfield. Still, they only resisted sporadically with probing fire and the ever-present, always expected, rocket-propelled grenade (RPG) that flew by randomly. Like any other erection of an Army base, the strong point's establishment was unpleasant and sluggish. The supply route down to the Tarok Kolache intersection was difficult, if not impossible, to reach with an LMTV (light medium tactical vehicle), "Flat Rack" (self-loading/unloading cargo truck), or MATV (mine-resistant, ambush-protected all-terrain vehicle), and the soldiers didn't have much to work with. Three-to-five-day rotations were the original intention. The process would repeat often, with platoons leaving from COP Stout and switching out at Strong Point Weaver. The men of One Hotel were determined to make the strong point their permanent residence after leading many rotations and learning it would bear 1st Lieutenant Weaver's name. One Hotel requested to stay at Weaver for the duration of the deployment because they weren't satisfied with the overall output and the production of the strong point. It was nothing more than a patrol base surrounded by Hescos; for it to be something they could call home they would need to put in quite a bit more work. They used MRAPs (mine-resistant, ambush-protected) in place of towers. Several times, enemy fighters fired randomly aimed RPGs at them with zero effect. A few small-weapons battles attempted to lure them in, but nothing so compelling that One Hotel was drawn out of the strong point's fortifications. At most, the engagements amounted to little more than poking the embers to start a fire. They were the fleeting efforts of dying men.

One Hotel consisted of 11 to 15 personnel during the initial infill of their new home. That was about average for a platoon at that time. There wasn't a single platoon in the Arghandab with manpower that was much more significant than that. The Afghan National Army (ANA) was augmenting each battery; perhaps that's how, in the end, they could all continue the struggle without becoming combat-ineffective. It was nothing new to the soldiers because they had been patrolling in the fields, furrows, and orchards at COP Stout for months. They were acclimated to their surroundings, and it was just another day in the "Dab."

Throughout their stay at Strong Point Weaver, One Hotel would experience a significant disparity in personnel. They had no other platoons available to split the workload for patrolling, force protection, taskings, or quick-reaction force (QRF). During their stay at COP Stout, they enjoyed having Two Hotel with them, sharing the load. They persuaded the authorities to provide them with access to a mortar tube. They knew the fundamental idea of using a mortar tube because they were artillerymen, and 1st Lieutenant Kinsel's experience allowed him to teach them the finer points. Strong Point Weaver would occasionally drop 60-millimeter mortars or provide illumination as the men worked to improve their craft while the patrols were in the field.

Kinsel and Sergeant First Class Lyon would go up to COP Stout every week to brief the battery command team on what the next week's patrols looked like. During the brief, any last-minute decisions would be made and discussed to prevent One Hotel from making the unnecessary trip back to Stout for another explanation of their patrol schedule. As a pressure relief to Havoc Battery Four, Havoc stood up with an abundance of infantrymen who were late arrivals from Fort Campbell. They wouldn't be going to stay at Strong Point Weaver, but they would be remaining to supplement Two Hotel at COP Stout. One Hotel had gotten a standard patrol cycle moving at Strong Point Weaver and, as they were conducting the patrols, moved further east into Khosrow Olya to check on patterns of life. Considering all the recent happenings, the patterns of life had returned to normal. With the Americans' assistance, the villagers could get their mosque up and were back having religious services and conducting study sessions. From all outward perspectives, things appeared to be on the up and up, the best soldiers can hope for.

It was an ordinary night; nothing stood out in the men's minds that would indicate something was about to happen. They sent a patrol to Khosrow Olya, something they had done so many times that the village leader gave Kinsel his Pashto name. As the patrol was navigating through the village, they received radio traffic informing them two individuals on a motorcycle were heading their way from Babur and were armed with RPGs. Specialist Ester was the new 13 Fox or joint fire support specialist who had replaced Private First Class Walters as Kinsel's radio-telephone operator. Kinsel heard the news over the net. For the first time, he realized that if they got into a significant firefight, it could be catastrophic. They were typically down to 10 men in the platoon on a good day. He was curious how long it would take QRF to reach them from COP Stout if something happened; or how long it would take for them to get a medevac to come to help them should they take a casualty because they would either need a jungle penetrator or have to take the casualty to the river. He factored in mid-tour leave. During rest and recovery, only six or seven American soldiers were present, with the rest of the patrols supplemented by ANA soldiers.

Strong Point Weaver's soldiers accepted their fate and made the best of a difficult circumstance because there didn't seem to be enough manpower in the Arghandab. Experiencing a lack of appreciation and disregard was among their issues. Strong Point Weaver was often so far away that it was easy to miss. Other combat outposts were more accessible, but Stansbery and Weaver were in remote, isolated areas. In the center of no-man's-land lay One Bravo and One Hotel. One Hotel was a fixed unit stationed at Weaver for an undetermined period, and One Bravo rotated with Three Bravo at Stansbery. One Hotel set up an OE254, which was able to intercept Taliban transmissions. They utilized it with their interpreter to intercept and translate what enemy fighters were planning and relay the information to the battalion. This information coming from the farthest southern strong point was valuable.

Kinsel was sitting alone at Weaver, reminiscing how much had happened in such a short period. It seemed like he had just arrived yesterday, and they were conducting some of their initial patrols out of COP Stout. He chuckled as he remembered one of his favorite moments with Lyon. They had been assigned to Building 10, previously known as Building 666. As they went to clear it, they realized they were being shot at from holes in walls, the same holes One Bravo and so many others had been shot at from. They decided to try to breach through the rooftop. Kinsel was on one side, and Lyon was on the other side of the ridged roof; they started linking up at the high points and sliding down the wall. Lyon uncovered a lamp cord, and both men discovered they were sitting on wires. Then they found they were sitting on top of mortar rounds, and the pressure plate was under Lyon's feet, but he wasn't tall enough to reach it because he hadn't slid far enough down the wall to do so.

"I've never been so happy that someone was short all my life," Kinsel chuckled at the memory.

In another instance, Kinsel was getting ready to step off with a small kill team and would be going out with several Afghan soldiers. This was a common occurrence, especially at this point. Kinsel's mom was part of the Blue Star Mothers of America, so she would lovingly send him care packages that often included things like tuna, tabasco, crackers, chips, etc. On this specific occasion, as Kinsel was getting ready to step off for the patrol, he received a care package from the Blue Star Moms. His only request was that his men leave him one bag of chips to eat with his tuna. Typically, he would never make this request. He would eat his tuna without chips, but on this occasion, he wanted his bag. The patrol was executed without incident, and upon returning to Strong Point Weaver, Kinsel found that all the chips had been eaten. He was hurt; he was crushed. Of all the times he had provided sustenance to his guys, this was the first time he had ever requested even as much as a bag of chips, and this was how he was being repaid.

Staff Sergeant Casey said, "Oh my God, sir, it's a bag of chips. You're an officer. You can afford a store of these things."

"Casey, that's not the point."

"Sir, that's exactly the point."

"Look, man, I don't want to get into an argument with you about this. It's not worth it."

"Here, sir, have the chips."

Casey walked over to him as Kinsel sat down to eat his chips. He was sweaty and tired from his patrol, wanting to enjoy his tuna and chips. Casey looked him dead in the eyes; and crushed his bag of chips without warning! He immediately followed that up by flexing like the Incredible Hulk and saying, "Now what?"

Kinsel could only laugh. This was so out of character for Casey that it was genuinely hilarious. Everyone around at the time couldn't help but laugh at Kinsel's expense. The fact that Casey was so much smaller and acted like the Incredible Hulk made the event memorable.

CHAPTER 16

Infrared Chem Lights and IEDs

> They found combat to be horror, destruction, and death and hated it. Anything was better than the blood and carnage, the grime and filth, the impossible demands on the body, anything that is, except letting down their buddies.
>
> STEPHEN AMBROSE

Each deployment has two extremely dangerous phases: the first and last 90 days. Part of the issue of these two phases stems from the fact that complacency, a soldier's worst enemy, builds. The Top Guns could see the end coming, the finish line was in sight.

A small kill team (SKT) from One Hotel was assembling to patrol Takia village. The mission was to locate, identify, and capture an improvised explosive device (IED) developer known to be in the area. The patrol would consist of 1st Lieutenant Kinsel, Staff Sergeant Casey, his team leader Terrazas, "Doc" Lindemuth, and their new forward observer, Specialist Ester. The patrol departed at roughly 9:00 pm on March 9, 2011, heading south toward the Arghandab River. The open area next to the river could have provided plenty of IED territory for enemy fighters with the right tactics. However, the location was unstable due to its proximity to the river; if an enemy fighter planted an IED there, it would have to be placed in the hopes an American soldier would initiate it soon after. If the river rose slightly, the creeks woven into the land's fabric would also increase, ruining enemy fighters' opportunities to cause chaos.

Under the Afghan sky, the members of One Hotel embarked on another adventure in the Arghandab. Adventures had more substance now as the men would soon return to Fort Campbell, Kentucky. As the Alpha team took over point with Terrazas in the lead, everything appeared to be going smoothly. The crew had grown closer since 1st Lieutenant Weaver's death in September. Kinsel had made a substantial contribution to the platoon. They ensured they had infrared chem lights to illuminate the cleared path before stepping off and checked all the other specifics like weapons, night-vision goggles, and ammunition. They knew where they were going might have several questionable locations, so they wanted to ensure their safety. Terrazas was identified as one of the Arghandab's most sought-after team leaders. His leaders praised his performance and his ability as a non-infantryman. Kinsel had complete faith in his talents and constantly trusted him with route planning and navigation through the orchards. He had witnessed on multiple occasions how he would take charge during a firefight or a medevac to ensure success.

The patrol proceeded into an area with a network of smaller canals leading directly into the Arghandab River. The villagers had been using the raised path to get from one side of the river to the other. Enemy fighters didn't need to put an IED in this area because the river would rise and wash it away, wasting their time and resources. Not to mention that American forces had rarely patrolled the area.

As the patrol neared the river, moonlight reflected off the water. The reflection was inspiring in a way that made some of the soldiers take notice and the Afghan soldiers appreciate their homeland. The Alpha team cleared up and across the riverbed, heading south toward Takia, advancing farther up the next clearance area, with the Bravo team on track to clear shortly after. Due to limited manpower, Casey was assigned to the Alpha team, while Kinsel was assigned to Bravo with his radio-telephone operator (RTO), Elder. When the Alpha team cleared the path, they planned to drop a chem light to identify it. However, when Casey went to position the chem light, he had used up all the ones he had, so he decided to take a knee and wait for Kinsel, as he had done a thousand times before.

Several weeks before their patrol, the men were unaware that another unit had gone into Takia and caused havoc, inflicting casualties and taking over compounds. They occupied Takia for several days. During this time, they had several different engagements with enemy fighters. During these engagements, multiple enemy fighters from Takia had been killed. When the unit left, they exited by heading north toward the river, where they were picked up by helicopters and lifted to safety. Several weeks later, One Hotel found themselves in the same area without prior knowledge of earlier encounters. Casey, wanting to wait for his platoon leader to ensure he got across with no issues, took a knee and instantly felt a jolt of pressure through his body.

BOOM!

Casey was sent flying through the air, coherent the entire time. He felt like everything was in slow motion. "There's no fucking way this is happening right now, not a shot!"

Then his body encountered the ground once again, and he landed in the crater of the IED that had just erupted under him.

"IED, IED, IED!"

Terrazas was aghast as to how he could have missed the IED. He was using the Vallon mine detector, and he was careful. Casey was one of his role models, and he wouldn't let him go out like this. He ran to help him.

"Terrazas, stay the fuck over there, there's probably another one. Stay the fuck out of the danger area. Walton, you and Hagan help pull security. Elder, you need to call up the nine-line for LT."

"Doc" Lindemuth had gotten his bell rung as well and was hit by shrapnel. He got up and got over to Casey.

"Casey, I got you now. Just try and relax."

Kinsel was also on the side of the blast as Casey knelt on the pressure plate. Shrapnel had hit him, and he was knocked unconscious. When he came to, he knew his first action needed to be to get his nine-line started for Casey.

"Havoc Main, Havoc One Six … BREAK, BREAK, BREAK, nine-line follows. Let's go, Doc, get the damn tourniquet on his leg!"

"Sir, I'm trying. There's not much to grab onto, so I cannot emplace the tourniquet."

Casey's right leg had been amputated mid-thigh, he had suffered a traumatic shock to his body from the blast, and the impact of hitting the ground hadn't done him any favors. He had been peppered with shrapnel, especially in his left arm, and that was going to require immediate attention. His left leg was also damaged but looked much better than the right. Reality started to set in for Casey; he grabbed Kinsel's belt as he started slipping into shock. The men were working to help him under the crimson glow of their red-lens headlamps, which slowed the process down.

"Sir, don't let me die in this fucking field. Let me die in the hospital, but not in this field."

"You're not going to die, Casey. Just relax, I got you. Doc, give him some morphine, damn it! And we still need to get that tourniquet on his fucking leg!"

Remembering his training back in the rear, Kinsel took his knee and pressed on the inside of Casey's nub to help get a tourniquet on his leg. He heard a pop; it was Casey's hip, which had popped out of the socket.

"Damn it, man, Casey just can't catch a break!" he thought.

Casey screamed out in pain, "FUCK!"

They finally applied the tourniquet to his leg, which was a success. Casey was still positioned in the crater that had nearly claimed his life, and he was now battling the elements and time. "Doc" Lindemuth worked as quickly as possible to wrap what was left of the leg, but he had so many other injuries this would be a painful process. Kinsel was extra vigilant with the lessons learned from Specialist Bixler's injuries.

"Doc, be sure to check his ass to make sure he isn't sliced open." Lindemuth replied, "I got it, sir. Relax."

"LT, don't let me die in this fucking field."

"Casey, relax, man, I got you."

Casey was now battling exhaustion, low blood pressure, and shock. He looked down and saw how high his amputation was.

"LT, am I okay? Is everything still in place?"

Kinsel paused for a second under his red lens. He investigated whether Casey had been injured in a way that would have taken away his prized jewels,

"Yeah, you're good, man."

"You hesitated! You're fucking lying to me. Damn it, LT, don't fucking lie to me!"

By this point, the adrenaline had worn off, and the morphine was drowning the pain. Rotors could be heard in the distance as the helicopters were approaching over the mountains in the night sky. Kinsel told everyone to ensure they were set for the medevac. Casey said, "LT, take my watch and give it to Reed. He'll know what it means."

The Black Hawk hovered over the spider web of canals inside the Arghandab River while the One Hotel men carried Casey to the medevac site. Casey was slipping away due to the morphine. When he got on the Black Hawk, he took a deep breath to attempt to center himself for whatever was to come next when, out of nowhere, the flight medic slapped him.

"Stay with me, man."

"Don't fucking slap me. I've got enough shit going on already. I'm just trying to catch my breath."

With that, the Black Hawks lifted off into the darkness of the Arghandab sky. The men standing in the river watched as one of their leaders was carried off toward a canvas of emptiness and a future of uncertainty. They knew they were close to home but not close enough to consider safety even for a second.

With the medevac on its way to Kandahar and the quick-reaction force (QRF) firmly on the ground, the men were tasked with finding Casey's sensitive items and anything else they could locate. Mainly, and understandably, they found pieces of stuff. Both the SKT and the QRF continued to walk ground zero for the remainder of the night, finding parts of Casey's leg, his weapon, and his gear until they were exhausted. Four Hotel was tasked with overwatch to ensure no enemy fighters had an opportunity to come in during the night and place additional IEDs; once relieved, One Hotel made the dreaded walk back to Strong Point Weaver. When they returned to the strong point, and everyone had a chance to get out of their gear, Kinsel addressed the team. He wanted to ensure they knew it was no one person's fault and, if anything, he would accept the blame. He was furious inside, however; Casey had gotten hit, and he knew how impactful the man was to the platoon, and they would need to reconsider and figure out what to do next. Some soldiers reminisced how Casey had an uncanny ability to read paths, walls, or the terrain. Ninety percent of the time, he would be right.

"I always felt that he was just like Lieutenant Weaver. I thought he was indestructible. I swear I cleared that path. I don't know what happened," said Terrazas.

Kinsel looked across the faces of his guys, and he could sense they had the mindset of "He was better than us, and if he was hit, then we are fucked." A few guys lost control of their temper and thought, "Let's just go Lord of the Flies." In the end, the adrenaline subsided, and they returned to Earth. They had lost a fantastic leader essential to their squad and platoon. They were saddened, mourning, and angry. Ultimately, they knew they needed to do right by him.

The men received a follow-up call from Kandahar about Casey's condition. While they sat and listened attentively, they were relieved and horrified. Amid the turmoil, the men failed to notice that Casey had homemade explosive (HME) chemical burns running up his back between his plate and skin. Despite his amputation and need for many surgeries, he remained stable. Due to their proximity to the explosion and the fact they were both struck by shrapnel, Kinsel and Lindemuth underwent the concussion protocol the battalion could administer. It was concluded both men would require further evaluation at Kandahar Airfield (KAF), where they both assessed positively. The night could not have gone much worse for One Hotel: they had lost Lindemuth and Kinsel for an unspecified amount of time and now lost Casey permanently. Lyon did his best to rally his troops and let them know they still had lots of fighting left but the end was near. Stay vigilant, persist, and, more importantly, do your job. "Everybody Fights, Nobody Quits."

Back at Combat Outpost (COP) Tynes, Staff Sergeant Fontenot was on as sergeant of the guard. He was in the command post with Sergeants Junkin and Estep. He overheard the battle roster number being called over the net and was instantly furious. He had Junkin reach over to Havoc and confirm with Sergeant McKissock who had been hit. Fontenot was enraged when she said it was Casey. However, the good news was that he was stable.

"How the fuck did this happen? We are so close to going home."

"Fonty, I know, man. Just calm down," Estep replied.

Fontenot, being so enraged, couldn't speak with anyone. He walked around the landing zone in front of COP Tynes for what appeared to be hours. The next day, One Bravo went out on a patrol into Jelawur. During this patrol, Fontenot was determined to get answers for Casey, knowing that if anyone would know, it would be the village elder.

"Where are the IEDs? My buddy lost his leg last night, so where are the IEDs?"

"No IEDs."

"I'm going to ask you again, where the fuck are the IEDs?"

"No IEDs."

"Everyone faces out and pulls security," Fontenot told his guys.

"Fonty, what are you doing?" 1st Lieutenant Aldaya asked.

"Sir, pull fucking security."

"Where are the IEDs?" he asked the elder again.

"No IEDs."

Fontenot gave him extra encouragement, befitting something you might see in WWE wrestling. He then pulled out a map and asked again, "Where are the IEDs?"

The elder started pointing to the areas on the map where he knew IEDs were. Conveniently, one of the IEDs was where Casey had taken his knee.

A follow-on patrol was moving out early the next day. They headed to ground zero to explore the area and search for Casey's leg and any other recoverable items. The next patrol included Lyon, Staff Sergeant Reed, Private First Class Deatherage, and "Doc" Fontenot. The patrol was also going to be supplemented by Afghan soldiers. Despite the previous night's horrors, the men awoke to a gorgeous day. The air was inviting, a change from the relentless, aggressive temperature. After returning from Kandahar, Kinsel and Lindemuth were confined to the command post, where they sat nervously by the radios.

As the patrol headed north to the Arghandab River, they believed there was almost no chance enemy fighters could have infiltrated the perimeter to plant IEDs. It was well known that Four Hotel had been monitoring the area all night, and they were comprised of infantry soldiers, so they no doubt remained vigilant. Staff Sergeant Trueblood led his explosive ordnance disposal (EOD) team, accompanied by Captain Motto (Havoc 6). As the men descended onto the site where Casey had hit the IED the night prior, 1st Lieutenant Dieter of Four Hotel found Casey's foot. Once they had secured it, they bravely continued moving forward. The patrol advanced towards the upper corner of the field, where the dam had a steep slope. That was where Casey had hit the IED. The EOD team was perpendicular to where the Havoc soldiers were by this time. Motto was on the radio with the RTO from One Hotel when the fury of the Gods erupted.

BOOM!

The soldiers from One Hotel were on QRF and were already moving toward ground zero when they heard the explosion.

"Guys, we need to pick it up. Someone just set off another fucking IED," Lyon said.

Trueblood stepped on a pressure-plate IED with two 82-millimeter mortars and HME buried beneath it. The EOD medic started chest compressions on Trueblood as he was already in terrible shape. Motto placed a tourniquet on his right leg; simultaneously, another soldier placed a tourniquet on his left leg. Trueblood had lost both legs and both arms. Multiple soldiers were attempting to put tourniquets on Trueblood's extremities, but he was declining rapidly. Two other EOD soldiers were also peppered by shrapnel.

"Havoc Main, this is Havoc Nine, BREAK, BREAK, BREAK, nine-line follows," 1st Lieutenant Tseng radioed.

After receiving tourniquets on every extremity, Trueblood was placed on a litter to be prepared to move toward the river for medevac.

QRF arrived, and as soon as they were on the ground, Lyon and "Doc" Fontenot moved over to help Trueblood.

Upon clearing the tree line to the field where the Arghandab webbing began, Private First Class Deatherage looked across the landscape and recalled thinking, "If this place weren't so deadly, people would like it here." It was early morning in Afghanistan; it was not blistering hot, and dew was still on the ground. The river glistened like something out of a *National Geographic* magazine. Upon arrival, there was nothing out of the ordinary initially. No enemy was in sight, and there was no shooting going on. It was almost peaceful, except for the humming of those working to save the casualty. They had gone down to assist in the unsecured area north of the river. Unbeknown to the soldiers, somehow, in the middle of the night, enemy fighters had come in and seeded the fields south of Takia with IEDs. The One Hotel men and the QRF element tirelessly searched the field the previous night and did not encounter any additional IEDs after the one Casey hit. When EOD arrived, it was not long before one of the new IEDs made its presence felt.

Trueblood had been a staple with One Hotel. While patrolling the orchards and fields over the past few months, he helped them discover multiple hidden caches. He was often with them when they had a win against enemy fighters. During a search and recovery patrol, Trueblood had uncovered a cache with mortar rounds still in their original packaging. They wore the markings of a superpower country that was supporting terror. What was more horrifying to the men was that they had been sent to the Arghandab recently, according to the markings. Trueblood's body now lay in a massive crater, his face covered with blood, his body a mangled mess. It looked like something out of a horror movie to those not tending to him. It was clear that the IED Trueblood initiated had been comparable to the one Bixler hit.

"Has anyone given him morphine yet?" Fontenot asked.

"We weren't given morphine, so no, Doc," one of the EOD soldiers replied.

Their efforts were falling short. While working on Trueblood, it became apparent the EOD soldiers hit by shrapnel required immediate attention.

There was a raised footpath that divided the spider-webbing canals of the Arghandab. Deatherage had the 240B and noticed a well-worn spot that seemed perfect for a machine-gun pit. He thought it was likely safe because the locals used it often. Due to this, he suspected there was next to no danger. He maneuvered to his machine-gun position, passing three trees, a bush, and three more trees. When he initially moved to the position, he stepped over the bush, not wanting to get caught up in it.

Lyon started yelling at Deatherage. "Deatherage, we're in a minefield. Get the fuck out of here."

As Deatherage tried walking out of the minefield carefully, he retraced his steps with focus and tenacity. When he approached the random bush on the path, the ground gave way, and he slid toward the bush.

BOOM!

"IED, IED, IED!"

Deatherage went flying. He was coherent and knew precisely where he was throughout the event. He understood that nothing good would come when he hit the ground. Deatherage was on his back when his body encountered the ground. He looked down and saw that his right foot was severed; it was dangling by a piece of muscle. His tibia and fibula were exposed, displaying the ivory white of his bones. He had already lost a tremendous amount of blood. He could feel his blood pressure dropping rapidly and remembered to conduct self-aid. His clock on the golden hour had officially begun.

"Fuck, that leg isn't in good shape." He looked toward his left leg. "Shit, my leg looks like a Nike swish."

All the bones in his leg had been broken or shattered. As he lay on the ground, he once again thought, "Maybe if I can move my legs, it's not as bad as it looks, and they are still there."

As he wiggled his broken legs, he could hear the bones crunching, and he felt like he was going to be okay. He knew he was going to lose his foot but figured surgeons could salvage his leg.

"Hey, I think I'm okay. My legs are just fucked up, get me some tourniquets," he yelled. "Sergeant Reed, I need your help. Can you throw me tourniquets to put on my legs?"

Reed couldn't get to him due to Deatherage being in a crater in an IED belt laid out across ground zero.

The belt consisted of four rows of IEDs, with three in each row, making navigating the field dangerous and impossible.

"Deatherage, you're in an IED field," said Reed. "I can't get to you. Remember, use your tourniquets, and we'll get to you as soon as possible."

When Deatherage detonated the IED, Specialist Pangus was nearby and had also been struck by shrapnel. Despite his ailments, he contributed to the QRF. Knowing Deatherage was now an amputee, and his golden hour was running out, "Doc" Fontenot ran over to him to provide aid. Once he arrived, things escalated quickly.

"I'm fucked, aren't I, Doc?"

"You're going to be okay. I got you now. I'll give you some morphine, and we'll get a medevac on site as quickly as possible."

Fontenot began placing tourniquets on his legs as high as he could get them. As he was conducting his assessment of Deatherage, he thought to himself, "Deatherage, you're one lucky motherfucker compared to Trueblood and Bixler."

Deatherage had shrapnel throughout his body, his arms, and his hands. It was going to be a long road to recovery. The One Hotel and EOD men could hear the medevac coming in. When the Black Hawks arrived, the flight crew needed to understand the severity of the situation.

"Look, we just hit another IED. Can you get both to KAF?"

"Load them up. We'll take care of them," the flight medic replied.

Given the circumstances, Deatherage was extraordinarily fortunate. The medevac could carry Trueblood and him to Kandahar. The men of Four Hotel and EOD watched the Black Hawks take off once more, a little more mournful than before.

With each passing day and soldier lost, the men asked, "Why are we some of the only squads still patrolling non-stop in the orchards?"

Captain Motto escorted the Top Gun 6 personal security detail team to ground zero. By the time they arrived, the medevac had already departed. Lieutenant Colonel Flynn had lots of questions regarding what happened over the past 32 hours and how the enemy fighters could have possibly laced the area with IEDs when it was being overwatched.

Kinsel and Lindemuth were now back with their men.

Kinsel said, "We have a job to do, and we'll continue to do our job until we get on a plane home. Stay focused, stay vigilant. We will be okay."

CHAPTER 17

Living in the Grape Furrows Watching the Leaves Turn

> Our very survival depends on our ability to stay awake, adjust to new ideas, remain vigilant, and face the challenge of change.
>
> MARTIN LUTHER KING JR.

The Top Guns accomplished the impossible when it seemed they were headed for a collision course with a suicidal train. Now, the farmers were returning to their fields, the orchards were blossoming, and marijuana and poppy were growing abundantly. The leaves on the vines and the trees again turned a vibrant green. This signified a few critical things. First, the fighting season was rushing in like rapids in overflowing streams. Second, the Top Guns had received marching orders to return to the United States. The 10th Mountain Division would replace the Top Guns, and the leaders on the ground had already begun capturing everything they could to pass on to the incoming unit. Headquarters and Headquarters Battery (HHB), Alpha, and Bravo were all still gainfully employed in the orchards and furrows. Over the winter, the soldiers made a monumental impact by uncovering several large caches.

Just north of Combat Outpost (COP) Stout was a pomegranate orchard; grape furrows were just west of it. Two Hotel was tasked with pushing a patrol toward the fields to see what they could locate. Ironically enough, the men had been in the Arghandab River Valley for almost a year. While they had unearthed several caches, there was nothing significant yet that would be a game changer.

One of the original Havoc soldiers pulled from the killing fields was Specialist Ritsema. He was the fortunate soldier who had been told to put his eye protection back on just before Specialist Stansbery set off the improvised explosive device (IED). Ritsema returned to the Arghandab to finish the remainder of the deployment with his fellow Havoc soldiers. Two Hotel planned their patrol and determined that, since One Hotel covered south of Stout, they would head north and northwest toward Jelawur. This would bring them into the orchards and the grape furrows, both of which were generally uneventful patrols. It was a beautiful spring day in the Arghandab. The weather was inviting, and it was slightly overcast. The soldiers enjoyed patrolling in 80° Fahrenheit temperatures, a tremendous improvement from what they walked into at the start of the deployment and what 10th Mountain would fall into. Ritsema was responsible for having the Vallon mine detector in his hands on this patrol. As he walked through a set of grape furrows, a yellow homemade explosives (HME) jug with a white lamp cord attached to it caught his attention.

Sergeant First Class Tivao and Sergeant Naquin came over to see what had been uncovered. It was clear it was HME. The positive side was that the jug wasn't attached to anything, so why was it there? Was it something they were going to set up as a trip wire? Or was it a cache they used for quick refills when one of their own was set off? Ritsema took his digging tool and carefully dug around the jug to see if there was anything else. Much to everyone's amazement, there was a significant amount. Ritsema began pulling on the white lamp cord, which led to another jug of HME. After one was uncovered, the men checked for another, then another, and another until they officially knew they had uncovered a massive Taliban HME area. The soldiers from Two Hotel got busy uncovering one of the most significant caches in the Arghandab. There were HME jugs, pressure plates, and lamp cords all buried in the bottom of the grape furrows. The soldiers from the 82nd, the 101st, and many before them had walked right by these furrows and never thought of them. This slight misstep by the Taliban had now given the Top Guns fuel to uncover even more. Interpreters began picking up ICOM traffic.

"They've found some of the jugs buried in the grape field. What do you want us to do?" asked an enemy fighter.

"They will stop before it gets out of control. Just sit by and wait to see what happens," said his commander.

The call from Havoc went across the Top Guns' net, stating they had uncovered a monumental cache south of Jelawur. That was all the battalion command team needed to hear. Three Bravo was currently on rotation as Strong Point Stansbery, so it was determined One Hotel and their new platoon leader, 1st Lieutenant Aldaya, would head off into the grape furrows to see what, if anything, they could uncover as well. The soldiers from Bravo Battery went to the grape furrow west of Jelawur, located between COP Nolen and COP Stout.

Specialist Bibb was the Vallon operator for One Bravo and checked the furrows to see if anything was out of sorts. What was intriguing about the whole thing was the HME jugs and lamp cord alone would've never set off the Vallon. The battery pack on a pressure plate may have set it off. Still, nothing was attached to them because these were just explosives enemy fighters had been stashing throughout the winter in preparation for the fighting season. As One Bravo began their clearing operations in their grape furrows, it didn't take long before Bibb got a hit on the Vallon. He started digging in the furrow and uncovered several mortar rounds. The more the men continued to dig, the more the Taliban truth became evident. It slowly and painstakingly became apparent the Taliban had been stashing weapons and homemade explosives under their noses.

One Bravo was patrolling in Lower Babur much like they were in south Jelawur; it was the same team of Bastards, and they were doing their due diligence to attempt to uncover something that would break the Arghandab wide open. As the men patrolled with their Afghan National Army (ANA) counterparts, an ANA soldier got Nabil's attention.

"They have something buried here. It's something big."

"How do you know that? There's nothing there?"

"Do you see that marker in the tree? That's a significant marker; they only place those when there's something important nearby."

"Okay, let's see what we can find. Sergeant Fontenot, the ANA, said there's a significant item buried around here that we should be looking for."

The One Bravo Bastards went on the hunt to see what they could uncover. With the foliage growing back, it was easy to see how enemy fighters could bury items. As the patrol moved southwest from Strong Point Stansbery, the platoon got a hit with the Vallon unlike before. They began digging with their tools, being extra vigilant not to set off an IED. As they dug, they came across a blue jug. This was no ordinary blue jug. This was a plastic 55-gallon drum that had been buried and made watertight. There were AK-47s, mortar rounds, HME jugs, pressure plates, and belts of 7.62-millimeter ammunition buried in this one jug. It was hard for the men even to fathom how many of these were buried throughout the orchards. One Bravo unearthed the jug and called up EOD to have it blown in place. This was a significant find, and if the Top Guns could continue to uncover these types of caches, it would be disastrous for enemy fighters in their fighting season campaign.

Two Hotel had uncovered so much HME that they had to get battalion approval to blow it in place.

BOOM!

The explosion was so enormous it shook the walls that lined Route Phillies, and the pomegranate trees shook as if they were fixing to be uprooted. "This is a real explosion, fuck you, Hollywood," "Doc" Fontenot said. Some of the men were pelted by falling dirt and shrapnel. "Owww, fuck, shit!"

The Two Bravo men called up EOD; ultimately, their findings would be consolidated with what HHB was finding in their field. The soldiers went row by row, slowly and deliberately destroying the grape furrows. Ironically, any ordinary farmer would've come out to complain that the batteries were destroying his fields; however, no one complained. It was like the Top Guns were giving the farms back. They were once again gaining the rights to their land.

Three Bravo were still busy patrolling in the orchards outside Strong Point Stansbery and the villages surrounding COP Tynes. With fighting season just getting started, IEDs were beginning to find their way back into the patrol cycle. On March 21, 2011, during one of their patrols south of Druia, they were headed toward the Arghandab River, toward a barrier leading them into the open area before the river. During their descent, Sergeant Huber initiated the IED. Huber, one of the infantry team leaders attached to the Bulls, and Private First Class Cheng were both hit by shrapnel, and Cheng was found in a tree, but, considering the previous IEDs, they were both fortunate. Neither soldier suffered violent injuries like their predecessors. The men were treated and sent to Kandahar for further evaluation.

The destruction of the grape furrows continued as more and more items were found buried. Still, little to no word of complaint was spoken. Was it because the fields were owned and operated by Taliban fighters who had stolen the ground from the villagers? Two Hotel and One Bravo were now tasked with a 24-hour operation throughout the deployment. When they weren't on their

12-hour rotations, they were responsible for force protection, quick-reaction force, and the soon-to-be relief in place with 10th Mountain.

Grape furrow after grape furrow, the walls were knocked down. Soldiers in the fields with sledgehammers smashed the mud walls that had stood between them and success over the past year. With each wall that came down, more explosives were found, more ammunition, and more pressure plates. The soldiers looked through most of the remnants of what had been found, primarily American trash. The Taliban had been using their waste against them. When the Top Guns first got into the Arghandab, One Bravo went to Terra Nova on a convoy. While at Terra Nova, kids were rummaging through burn pits and trash piles, pulling out different items. No one considered anything unusual about this but, looking back, those were the same items utilized to make the IEDs. The kids acted as spotters for when the American patrols would leave their COPs. They would also acquire the items necessary to end the lives of some of the soldiers.

Fontenot was in one of the villager's fields when a man approached him. "Mister, I have this knife and would like to trade it with you."

"Sir, I only have this knife, and it's been by my side the entire time we've been here."

"But, mister, this is a good knife."

"I don't doubt that your knife is a good knife but look at the blade on my knife."

Fontenot took out his knife and put the blade on his hand so the Afghan villager could see the difference. One Bravo had patrolled in Jelawur for the better part of a year, and the villagers had gotten accustomed to when units would switch out. The villagers, possibly anticipating the 101st would be leaving soon, wanted a keepsake or a weapon from them.

"But, sir, I have nothing from you or your men. May we trade knives?"

"Yes, we can trade."

"Sir, you know your knife is better than his, right?" said Nabil, the interpreter.

"I know, Nabil. I know I'll never see this man again, so maybe this knife will protect his family."

HHB and Bravo took this as an opportunity to go on a treasure hunt. Staying busy provided the Havoc soldiers with the chance to combat complacency. The soldiers were smashing grape furrows left and right. It almost felt like an act of defiance against the Taliban. The more they could find, the more it felt like a win for the battalion. After being in the fields for several days, no more furrows were left to destroy. Both batteries had been going non-stop for 24 hours a day and constantly uncovering weapons stored in the fields. The Taliban had been using this as a spot to hide their guns and equipment all along. When they used an HME jug, it was easy to replace it by simply taking some water and patching up the mud hole in the wall where everything was hidden. The heat would dry the patch and make it look like everything else within a few hours.

The soldiers from 10th Mountain had officially begun arriving in the Arghandab. Fontenot was introduced to the squad leader who would be taking his place, and he welcomed him with open arms. He brought him into his little makeshift room inside the mosque and explained the deployment's high and low points. Fontenot explained what they had learned over the last year and had a map of the AO (area of operation) hanging in his room with pins that marked catastrophic IEDs, IEDs they had found with no injuries, and buried caches that were uncovered. He explained the different routes they had used to attempt to give the new squad leader the most up-to-date information possible. The squad leader from 10th Mountain looked at him like he was crazy.

"Look, I appreciate all your effort and information. However, we aren't going to go looking for IEDs with our feet."

"Neither did we, but we found them in the orchards."

"We aren't planning on entering the orchards. We will shut down all these additional places you set up."

Fontenot felt deflated. An internal fire had just been reignited. The Top Guns had worked so hard over the past year to ensure they had taken ground from the Taliban. The ground was vital because it prevented enemy fighters from having freedom of movement to do whatever they wanted. Now, according to this young man, it would be for nothing. The platoon leadership was being summoned to the command post.

Captain Day said, "Look, we're about to head home but have a job. We must ensure these guys get a good handoff and continue putting security on the fields we just destroyed."

"So, we're going to go nonstop to the finish line. We will stay in the fields 24 hours a day while at the same time conducting a relief in place?" Fontenot asked.

"That's the plan."

"Yeah, Roger!"

"Smoke" Tivao, Ritsema, Sergeant Naquin, and "Doc" Fontenot were all in the furrows, pulling their shift of guarding the destroyed grape furrows. Staff Sergeant Fontenot and Cheatham started discussing how close they were to going home. Seeing familiar faces from other batteries was always pleasant, no matter the circumstances. The soldiers shared a few harrowing stories, and the Bravo boys returned to their field. It was at that point that Fontenot decided they were too close to going home to risk having any of his guys getting fucked up.

"Team Leaders, come to me. We need to chat."

"What's up, Chief?" Cheatham and Sergeant Cox asked.

"Here's the deal, we are entirely too close to going home to get anyone fucked up at this point. So, I will position the guys when we come into these fields. Pending us getting into a firefight, they will stay exactly where I put them. They won't even move to take a piss. Do I make myself clear?"

"Clear, Chief."

As night fell on the men of One Bravo, they enjoyed the air in the Arghandab. It was hard not to drift off and think about being back home with family. It was hard not to imagine better times. For Fontenot, he thought about how great it would be to get home to his wife and start their life again. Right about that time, an ANA soldier came running over to where Fontenot.

"Mister, mister, Taliban!"

"Not a fucking chance," Fontenot said.

"Sergeant Fontenot, follow us. He will show you," said Nabil.

The ANA soldier, Nabil, and Fontenot moved toward the middle of the field. There was another field they hadn't yet gone into. As they peered through an opening in the field, they could see a figure with a weapon jumping from grape row to grape row.

"Taliban!" the ANA soldier said.

Fontenot replied, "Fuck him, shoot his ass."

Several One Bravo soldiers approached the wall to engage the fighter passing in the field next to them.

"Chief, do you want to chase after him?" Cox asked.

"Hell no, for him to walk us in on an IED. Look, we will stick to the plan, no one fucking moves unless I tell them to. We are all going home one way or another."

CHAPTER 18

Graveyards Filled with Broken Dreams

> Those who have long enjoyed such privileges as we enjoy forget in time that men have died to win them.
>
> FRANKLIN D. ROOSEVELT

1st Lieutenant Todd Weaver

When speaking with soldiers, it is expected to hear them say, "Some of the best ideas are the ones that never came to fruition because they are buried in graveyards." These remarks could not be more accurate when considering the Top Guns. These soldiers were predisposed to greatness.

Todd Weaver was bound for success; he was well-versed in numerous cultures and was compassionate while remaining steadfast in his determination to imprint what he considered was the right path on each of his subordinates. In his short life, Weaver lived in Budapest, Hungary, but this was just the beginning of a lifetime of travel across five continents. He later lived in Lagos, Nigeria; Sofia, Bulgaria; St. Petersburg, Russia; Mosul, Iraq; and Kandahar, Afghanistan. His life was cut short when he had the world in his hands.

Todd's inherent attributes of humor, fellowship, leadership, athletics, and scholarship were evident at a very early age. The youngest of four children, he learned patience and humility. He constantly sought guidance from his brothers and sisters while showing respect and love. However, his mischievous and comical nature may have been his best attribute, as it was the one thing that made him unique and may have made him a daddy in the end. Chaplain Tietje said, "He demonstrated incredible strengths in leadership, fellowship, and dedication that all he came in contact with admired."

Private First Class Brandon King

Brandon King was the first casualty the 1-320th Field Artillery suffered in the Arghandab. Upon hearing of his passing, Fontenot recalls a great deal of sadness in not having known him better. One thing is painfully apparent when speaking with his friends and his mom, Carolyn—Brandon was a young man on a mission. Regardless of whether he remained in the Army or chose to step away, he had goals, and he wanted to live up to those lofty goals. Brandon was artistic which in the artillery is a unique trait. Many artillery soldiers are known for their destructive nature as they are professionals at destroying objects but Brandon was a word expert and had the ability to create magic with a pen. He also had great admiration and unconditional love for his friends. It was glaringly apparent Brandon was a pivotal member of his family and was observed as being a loving son, brother, uncle, grandson, friend, and cousin. Brandon was known to be a card shark and loved a good game of spades; and partaking in video games. He was a true gamer. As often as soldiers engage in a game of cards, it's easy to expect that Brandon was in on more than one. His love for games and his love for his friends was awe-inspiring. Upon completing his service in the Army, he had set his academic goal to attend Full Sail University to learn how to code and create video games and get into programming. He also loved playing basketball, relaxing with his family, and watching movies. As a young man, he dedicated his life to his religious beliefs and serving the Lord. His mom Carolyn stated that one of the things that has helped their family over the years is knowing that although he is dearly missed, Brandon is with their Savior. That brings the family peace, but they still miss him every day. She was aware COP Babur should've become known as COP King, and had mixed emotions about that, but was proud to know the battalion named their conference room "the King Conference Room." "While it hurts to know some Army leaders disrespected him, I am thankful they beautifully honored him."

Brandon was born on September 22, 1986, in Key West, Florida, and attended public schools in Bellevue and Kent, Washington. He was killed on July 14, 2010. Brandon had untapped potential and could have positively impacted his community and had a significant impact on our nation's youth in a meaningful way, both with his art and his gaming. The King family is incredibly proud of Brandon as they believe he died fighting for a cause he believed in and for the freedom of others. The family has honored him and his memory by establishing a scholarship fund at the Tallahassee Community College. Education was essential to Brandon and is crucial to his family. They encourage others to pursue their educational goals in Brandon's name by assisting them financially.

Carolyn said, "It is never too late to pursue your educational goals and create a healthy and prosperous family unit." Over the past several years, the Brandon M. King Scholarship has raised $30,000 and has had the opportunity to award three scholarships in Brandon's name. Some recipients have been the first in their families to attend college, which speaks volumes about the importance of the scholarship. The family continues to be humbled year after year that people continue to donate to deserving students and help them receive the scholarship. It is still active and helps motivated members of Brandon's community to meet their educational goals. Anyone wishing to contribute to the Brandon M. King Memorial scholarship fund can visit the college's website, www.tcc.fl.edu/foundation, and select the "donate now" button.

Regardless of which side of the war line you stand on, chances are you've known someone impacted. All who were killed had dreams, and their families had dreams for them as well. Whether those dreams were to have a family or raise a child who would become a doctor or an engineer, there was a dream that was interrupted all the same. The wars we fight fill graveyards with broken dreams.

Nabil

Often in the middle of evening patrols, when night would fall upon the orchards, and it was dead calm, there was nothing better to do but listen and admire as the orchards came alive with the sounds of the Arghandab. Looking up at the sky, one could wonder if the constellation was built while sitting in Afghanistan, as there couldn't have been any other place on Earth where one could see the stars so effortlessly. Why is it that something that appeared so serene and peaceful could change as soon as you took one step? The reason was that evil men sit behind closed doors and make sure it is this way. Ironically even in a place where horrific acts are conducted by peaceful men for the benefit of those who sit safely behind those closed doors there are those who join in a brotherhood simply through the chaos of battle.

Fontenot and Nabil had bonded over the year spent together in the Arghandab. Patrol after patrol and mile after mile they shared stories of family members, stories of life back in America and life in Afghanistan, and both dreamed of what life would look like after the war in Afghanistan would finally be over. With the horrific evacuation of Afghanistan, it's easy to speculate for many soldiers what had become of their interpreters. Nabil was one of the interpreters at COP Tynes that was loyal throughout the year and ensured that the leaders of Bravo Battery were able to easily communicate with the villagers, imams and anyone else they may encounter. One of the many nights that Fontenot and Nabil sat in the furrows behind Jelawur, they talked about their plans and what they wanted for their families upon the conclusion of the war. Nabil knew Fontenot was married at the time and had a son; he wished for a similar existence for his family. He hoped that one day, his service would be recognized as noble and that the American leaders would send him to America so he could raise his family safely away from the atrocities that are commonplace in Afghanistan.

Prior to the withdrawal Nabil reached out for letters of recommendation for his service to help bring him to the United States once his service to American forces was complete. LTC Flynn, SSG Fontenot and others wrote him letters of recommendations and these letters were enough to ensure that he would be brought to America to live his life safely with his family. Nabil now lives his life with his family in the southern part of the United States and he has been blessed with two sons and two daughters and is enjoying his life in the land of the free. He was blessed to not be faced with the hardship that some of the interpreters faced during the withdrawal from Afghanistan and has since built a successful life for his family.

Sergeant Kyle B. Stout, one of 1.3 million

The Arghandab has claimed the lives of many young men. After the terror attacks on September 11, 2001 the lives of many young men were altered forever on the battlefields in Afghanistan and Iraq. Graveyards were enriched with dreams in a way they hadn't been since the Vietnam War. The global war on terror may have just as well been known as World War III. This decade-long war reportedly consumed 1.3 million souls from up to 20 different nations. Maybe the loss of those souls strikes a nerve with those behind closed doors, or maybe it's just because that was the same projected number of losses of life in Vietnam between American and North Vietnamese soldiers. Or maybe it's just public opinion that truly matters. When taking into consideration that public opinion plays an enormous factor in wars across the globe, America may have been influenced to end the war in Afghanistan only once the death toll reached that 1.3 million number.

Kyle Stout was only one of that 1.3 million but was an exceptional leader in his own right. He had a bright career ahead of him, and there's no telling what path he would've ultimately taken had he lived. Guessing based on current trends would lead one to believe he may have become a warrant officer, commissioned or may either be a First Sergeant or Command Sergeant Major. Stout was a good leader who genuinely cared about his soldiers and about the organization's success; these two things combined are a few of the things that lead Fontenot to say that he may have been led to the "dark side" of commissioning. During his short time in the Army Stout had the opportunity to accomplish things that some young soldiers will never do. He deployed to Iraq in support of Operation *Iraqi Freedom*, during that time he had the opportunity to go to Qatar where he went swimming, which most of us will never do. He competed and won soldier and NCO of the Month and Quarter boards at the battalion and brigade levels and was often recognized for his outstanding performance with his howitzer.

What's troubling is when thinking of how Stout and most of these 1.3 million men and women's lives were cut short, is how their families' lives were altered forever. Families do receive a life insurance policy (that is substantial) but it is thrown at the family to stop the bleeding; it dulls the pain and lessens the blow of their loss, but the reality is still there. No more laughter, no more birthdays, anniversaries, or anything else for that matter. For the 1.3 million souls whose lives were cut short, both American and Afghan, those were lives that could have done something special. There's no doubt that if SGT Kyle B. Stout were still around today, he would've made it to the rank of Command Sergeant Major or would've done something special with his life. His nephew later enlisted in the Army and followed in his footsteps. Having a family member follow in a soldier's footsteps is a testament to the type of example that the soldier set during their life. Now many years later, friends of Stout still celebrate his life and visit his resting place; he has a bridge named after him in his hometown and his legacy follows him as his brothers and sisters have not let his name, or his memory, die with his body.

Another Afghan Graveyard

During a patrol in north Jelawur, Fontenot was given the task to set in his security for a key leader engagement. Setting in the American soldiers was easy; it was as simple as positioning them alongside an avenue of approach, a grape furrow, or something along those lines. The Afghan National Army, however, was a little more challenging. On one of the patrols that incorporated the ANA, Fontenot recalled telling Nabil to tell the ANA soldiers to move to the north side of Jelawur facing toward the mountains. Shortly after, Fontenot was moving about conducting inspections to ensure everyone understood their sectors, had water, and was generally okay. As he got to the north side of the compounds, an ANA soldier was sitting in a graveyard. He was positioned behind two stone structures and several flags on what appeared to be bamboo staffs. The tombs were nothing more than mounds of stones raised vertically from the ground with ornamentation that looked as if someone had visited them at some point, possibly just on the day of their internment. Fontenot couldn't help but think, "I wonder if that young man knows someone under those stones?"

We often fail to comprehend during periods of intense bouts of violence in war that our enemies are impacted much in the same ways we are. Fontenot often finds himself sitting under the stars wondering how the children of 2010 are doing now in 2024/25. Those children who were running around them at age 4 or 5 are now about twenty years old. They may have been impacted by losing a brother, a father, or an uncle. Their homes may have been destroyed, raided or they may have had to endure seeing friends turned into a blood mist. When Fontenot saw the Afghan soldier sitting in front of the graveyard back in 2010, he thought that it was a profound picture back then. He still believes that it's a profound picture now and that's why it was included as part of the cover of the book. Looking across the landscape of the world today and seeing how the global war on terror has played out even after 24 years, a war by a different name is still a war. The world still rages on as terror still moves from country to country. As troops move from America to Syria back to Iraq, to Ukraine and to Korea the world is still a very unstable place. During 2010–11 the soldiers of the Top Guns watched as the graveyards slowly filled with the bodies of dead Afghan fighters. They attempted to fight against a relentless force that refused to withdraw and paid the price. As we lost our beloved brothers and sisters, ultimately in the end so did they. Someone's brother, sister, dad or mother was put in a grave attempting to stop the war machine in Afghanistan. Fontenot recalls one soldier stating "I wish somebody had pictures of the cemeteries from when we got there, to our fighting season and then right before we left. So, our people could see we were arranging interviews for the enemy." No one wins in war. Soldiers fight for those to their left and to their right and are willing to sacrifice life, limb, and eyesight for their brothers. Though ultimately what they saw during their year in Afghanistan was the rise of several more Afghan graveyards.

Revenge for a Slaying

When Bravo Battery settled in at Combat Outpost (COP) Tynes, an enemy fighter was seen speeding through Druia on a motorcycle with an AK-47 strapped to his back. Tower Two notified the sergeant of the guard. Specialist Hernandez was Three Bravo's assigned marksmen, he had proven that he was an outstanding shot. On more than one occasion he had been called to take a shot on a stationary target, but this target would prove to be a little more difficult. The man on the motorcycle was moving from east to west across a wide-open area at a high rate of speed so it gave Hernandez minimal time. Hernandez sprinted to Tower One to see if he could get off a shot at the man. As the man cleared the Afghan National Police compound just to the west of COP Tynes and was headed into Jelawur, he came across a clearing. Hernandez saw his opportunity. With a single shot, he sealed the man's fate.

CRACK!

The man went down; Hernandez hit him dead on. QRF (quick-reaction force) was dispatched to secure the body, but as was typical, by the time they arrived, the Taliban had taken it and vanished, but the bike remained, smeared in blood. It was retrieved and brought back to COP Tynes. It looked like the bullet had passed through the man's torso, killing him instantly, and then went right down into the gas tank. The next day, Fontenot was on patrol in Jelawur when a man with blazing red hair, which generally indicated he was a Taliban member, approached him. He informed Fontenot that his brother had been killed the day before. Much to Fontenot's amazement the man had zero regard for the fact that his brother was dead, his main focus was whether there would be any compensation for his family for the slaying of his brother. Fontenot advised the man that, due to his brother carrying an AK-47, he would get no reparations as he was considered an enemy fighter, and that's why he was engaged. In speaking to the brother, Fontenot was informed that, in Afghan culture, it is their responsibility to get revenge for the slaying of their family member. As the two men discussed the man's passing, Fontenot and Nabil got a more concrete belief that he was Taliban, but there was nothing tangible to prove it. They withdrew from Jelawur without incident despite being encircled by both locals and, no doubt, enemy fighters.

"Nabil, you know we'll see him again in the fields, right?"

"I know, sir, he is a Taliban fighter."

Many men have gone to the grave for what they believe. Their honor was intact, and they had not lost any favor in the eyes of their God, but what they had lost was the breath in their lungs, the blood in their veins, and the dreams of tomorrow that joined their bones in their graves. Afghanistan was one of the places that fits the mold for this statement. They were all fighting for what they believed—be that freedom, each other, or the Afghan way of life; they were all there fighting twenty-four hours a day. There were many men and women who sacrificed the breath in their lungs and the blood in their veins for the advancement of their nation's political agenda.

Specialist Christopher Moon

The stale desert air of Arizona will slowly steal your breath away, much like draining air from a balloon. Your energy will be depleted until you die or learn to live harmoniously with the environment. Mother Nature is undefeated; striving to fight her will result in a tired and weathered corpse. The soldiers who walked into the Arghandab couldn't have known what they were getting into, and that's something the adversary always had on their side. Christopher Moon, who was from the Navajo Nation, understood the harshness of the area better than most. How can we coexist with it instead of fighting against it? He hoped to return to the United States, finish college, and pursue his baseball career. His influence was felt in the Navajo Nation and his community before he enlisted in the Army, as a standout star athlete in Arizona. Moon had the opportunity to be the athlete who made a difference in the world. He might have been the star of ESPN's coverage of Veterans Day, playing in a major league game while children wore his jersey. His ceiling as a driven, well-spoken young man was as high as the heavens where he now resides. He runs free in the desert or soars among his Navajo tribe's ancestors. It is now well known that his time here on the rock we call Earth was cut short, and so were his dreams.

Moon was the 12th Navajo Nation soldier killed during the war on terror since 9/11. He was a star baseball player for his high school of Tucson High Magnet and was named the Southern Arizona baseball player of the year in 2006. He was guaranteed a spot to be a starter at the University of Arizona, and he was also sought after by the Atlanta Braves for the opportunity to play professional baseball. Moon gave up everything to serve his country. Moon is Kinyaa'áanii (Towering House Clan), born for Bilagáana. His maternal grandfather is Táchii'nii (Red Running into Water Clan) and his paternal grandfather is Bilagáana. The Navajo Nation was so impacted by his passing that Navajo President Joe Shirley Jr. ordered that flags be flown at half-staff in his honor. Of the 42 platoon members from the Two Charlie, 508th PIR that were assigned to patrol the grape fields, and pomegranate orchards around Tynes, six were killed in action, and 14 were wounded in action. That is a casualty rate of nearly fifty percent.

When Moon was hit, it was a sobering reality of how quickly things can go bad in the Arghandab River Valley. Moon had a discipline level that was unparalleled, and as a sniper, his shot was unbelievable. July 13, 2025, marked the 15th anniversary of his passing. He decided to serve for a greater cause and his country owes it to his family, and his tribe to never forget him.

"Doc" Fontenot

One challenge faced by many soldiers returning from combat zones is the significant stress they endure in the face of adversity. One such soldier is "Doc" Fontenot; he was subjected to more casualties at his young age than anyone should be. Considering the challenges he overcame and the lives he saved, it's reminiscent of Eugene "Doc" Roe of Easy Company, 506th Parachute Infantry Regiment, 101st Airborne Division. He is known for his incredible story, portrayed in *Band of Brothers*. "Doc" Roe, a young man, witnessed daily casualties during World War II, which later led to combat fatigue, identified as post-traumatic stress. "Doc" Fontenot, like "Doc" Roe, was from Louisiana.

These men saw the dreams of so many soldiers disappear from their eyes as they slipped into eternal sleep. They would fight until it just wasn't feasible to fight any longer to save someone's life. Fontenot was one of the youngest soldiers in the Strike Brigade to be awarded the Bronze Star with valor during Afghanistan. At one point during the deployment, there was a team of therapists that came to the Arghandab to evaluate the state of the men due to the casualties suffered. When they spoke to "Doc" Fontenot, it was determined that he needed to be pulled from the line. Imagine being instructed to leave your family after witnessing several souls pass from your hands. Fontenot was later taken to Forward Operating Base (FOB) Jelawur. After only a few days of hearing bombs exploding in the orchards, and daily gunfire, he knew his place was with his troops, not sitting at Jelawur. One Bravo had a patrol go to FOB Jelawur to pick up mail. The men were busy "acquiring," which is a polite way of saying stealing, anything they could when they got there. "Doc" saw a familiar, friendly face in Staff Sergeant Fontenot and fired his shot to try and get a ride back to COP Stout.

"Hey, Big Sergeant, can I talk to you for a second."

"Of course."

"Doc" Fontenot understood that what he asked would be entirely against the rules. Since both men were from Louisiana, he decided to start the conversation with an icebreaker.

"Big Sergeant, do you know where I can get some boudin around this place?"

"No, Doc, my man, but if you find some, let me know. Now, what's on your mind?"

"They pulled me from my guys and sent me here. I cannot stay here. I need to be with my guys. Can you get me back to Stout?"

"Hurry up and load your gear."

"Give me five minutes."

"Doc" took off to his tent and grabbed his gear. He threw it in the back of Fontenot's vehicle, jumped in, and Fontenot closed the hatch. The men began their movement across the north Arghandab desert toward COP Stout. As they approached COP Stout, Fontenot said, "Doc, we're doing a quick turn and burn to get you back with your guys, so get ready to grab your stuff. My .50-caliber gunner will cover you until you get back inside after we lower the ramp."

Within seconds, "Doc" was back inside COP Stout with his brothers after they flawlessly performed the drop. This is only one of many similar stories. Soldiers are reluctant to leave their brothers' sides because they consider themselves their keepers. They are the barrier that keeps their dreams out of graveyards. Doc Fontenot returned to COP Stout and ultimately played a part in saving several more soldiers during the duration of the deployment. Upon returning to the United States, Doc walked away from the military and found peace in the sky. He now spends an endless amount of time jumping from planes, enjoying the freedom the sky gives, and hiking and enjoying nature without the fear of having the ground erupting below his feet.

"Smoke" Tatro

When the original order came down that the Top Guns would be heading to Afghanistan for an infantry mission, "Smoke" Tatro said he wasn't on board with that decision. He stated he was an artilleryman and would be there in a second if his men needed him. Tatro was easily one of the most compassionate leaders who attempted to go above and beyond to do what was right based on doctrine. Leaders often find themselves in unusual situations where the same doctrine that governs them is the same doctrine that can bring them down. Tatro was there when the patrol inside "the Devil's Playground" occurred. He was there with water for Fontenot to give him life and to pour on his crotch because he was severely overheated. Despite the overwhelming backlash Tatro endured during his short time as part of the Bastards, he always remained a beacon of hope for the men. He would have his wife send care packages with "apple juice," always a pick-me-up for his soldiers, especially after a mission that went south.

Tatro's country accent and drive to improve the lives of the men at COP Tynes were apparent as he took over as the FOB mayor. He handled all the FOO money as the field ordering officer, allowing them to purchase two shower trailers and a water blivet to help the men stay clean despite the conditions. Tatro was also a pivotal member in ensuring the front and back areas of COP Tynes were improved significantly. By the time he departed the Bastards, he had set in motion a front and rear landing zone for medevacs. These would prove critical later in the deployment, even after he moved on.

Upon his exit from the Bastards, Fontenot and Pantaleo were informed they needed to change the platoon's name.

"Why should we change the name of our platoon? This is who we are."

Lieutenant Colonel Flynn replied, "Because the name has a negative connotation, it would be better if it were changed."

Little did Flynn know, but Fontenot was the one who had named the platoon, and he had based it on the lineage of the 101st.

"Sir, we aren't changing the name. Much like the 'Battered Bastards of Bastogne,' we continue to overcome insurmountable odds. For this reason, we will not be changing the name because this is who we are, and it's our war cry."

Shortly after, the men from One Bravo went down to Lower Babur as the lone element to get everything set up. Upon their first evening at the strong point, one of the soldiers set fire to the top of the building to keep it warm. The smoke had stained the side of the building, and with that, the sign "The Bastards" was etched on the side of Strong Point Stansbery. Despite whether he finished his career the way he wanted to or not, "Smoke" Tatro made a monumental impact on his soldiers.

Tatro was no longer in the platoon when the platoon maneuvered down into the orchards of Babur. They were now being led by their new platoon sergeant "Smoke" Sturgeon and Pantaleo. "Smoke" Sturgeon proved to be a very knowledgeable leader who had come from 3-320th and had the patience to deal with some of the NCOs in the platoon who were "hot headed." He had years of experience both in and out of combat, which would prove pivotal during the remainder of the deployment. Little did he know that shortly after arriving at Strong Point Stansbery that he would be leading the platoon alone due to Pantaleo being pulled away. Pantaleo was pulled away until the controversial situation with Tatro's NCOER was finally resolved and then he was returned to the platoon. However, during their darkest hour, Tatro and Sturgeon proved to be the Smokes the Bastards needed and ultimately prevented them from losing their dreams to the graveyards; they were always mentors and leaders to the soldiers of One Bravo despite losing the platoon based on "disloyal statements." Smoke Tatro was always considered their beloved "Smoke."

The Real Casualties of War

The Army's conveyor belt never stops moving. "Count the brave, count the true, who have fought to victory." Only 1 percent of American citizens serve in the armed forces. Not everyone will take a stand and defend the fundamental values we cherish. Those who perished paid the ultimate price, as did their loved ones. They are the ones who are left to carry on the dreams of the departed.

When Atlas was two years old, the Top Guns left for the Arghandab. While families spent their last moments together, Sergeant Durham followed Atlas outside the battery footprint. He had no idea at two years old that something that would change his life was about to happen. All he needed at that point was his father's attention. After 14 years, at the time of writing, Atlas has developed into a kind, ambitious young man. He still yearns to feel a connection to his father's memory, dreams of hearing him laugh, talk, or tell a story fill his heart. Even though Atlas still has his father's appearance and speech pattern, he has begun to follow his own path and generate his own dreams.

Kiley was nine months old when her father got on his flight to the Arghandab. She's put in great work to become an outstanding artist, and she didn't want her journey to end with the story of the young girl from 1st Lieutenant Weaver's tale.

The casualties of our nation's wars are the children who are left behind. The victims of faceless wars come from many different countries, including America, Russia, Ukraine, Afghanistan, Pakistan, and Iraq, just to name a few. The echoes of voices no longer here remain long after the wreckage of life has finished, and the screaming has stopped. Every soldier signs a blank check for one reason or another. Regardless of the reason why they joined, they still served. Some people participate for citizenship, college, or other reasons, but the result is the same: they have served their nation. When President Obama ordered 30,000 additional troops to be sent to Afghanistan in 2010, during the height of the surge, the American people responded with tremendous support, enlisting 74,577 soldiers. It's difficult to say how many of those soldiers who joined sustained traumatic brain injuries, amputations, shrapnel wounds, or other injuries.

The fight in the Arghandab River Valley will continue to be a war fought against the "Ghosts of the Arghandab." This battle tragically continues to haunt individuals who patrolled in "the Devil's Playground" and produces stress for family members of Gold Star Families. Sixty-five souls from the Strike Brigade made the ultimate sacrifice for our country, and thousands, if not millions, of hopes were buried beside them in graveyards already filled with broken dreams.

CHAPTER 19

The Final Mission

> You can outrun the enemy, but you can never outrun the war.
>
> JOSEPH J. FONTENOT

As soldiers, we are infamous for the saying "Never leave a fallen comrade." Fourteen years after the war had ended in Afghanistan for the Top Guns, for many, it still raged on. I know this because I was one of them. It's hard to acknowledge the internal demons and struggles carried forward from the Arghandab. Looking at my brothers and sisters in arms, outwardly they appear to have it all together. Some have achieved and retired as command sergeant major, colonel, or a wide array of other ranks. Some have continued to be productive and have had thriving careers after the Army. The Top Guns can even boast that one of their own has achieved the rank of brigadier general. All these things make it hard to step back and be humble but, sometimes, that's the only thing we have left. In August 2024, the screams, the pain, the depression, and the anger all became too much. I needed and wanted it all to come to an end. I wanted it to end sooner rather than later; as a soldier, I was trained to make it end violently and abruptly. I chose my destruction method, and while it wouldn't be violent, it would be abrupt.

I was methodical in making my stops along my route home. I visited my spouse to say I loved her despite our flaws. I secured a four-day from my chain of command, and the only stipulation was that I stop to tell my counterpart that I would be enjoying the next few days off. I stopped quickly at our battery and could barely hold it together during our conversation. After our brief but impactful discussion, I said my goodbyes to Nate and exited. On my way out the door, I didn't feel the need to show my pain to anyone, so I donned my sunglasses, put on my ballcap, and on my way home I went, but not before I made one last stop to pick up the charges for a few fire missions.

I arrived home and, within seconds, my mind had decided to delay no longer.
ENEMY IN THE OPEN!
FIRE MISSION!
TWO ROUNDS!
CHARGE 4! SHELL HE, FUZE PD
PERMISSION TO PRIME! PRIME!
PERMISSION TO HOOK UP!
HOOK UP! STAND BY! FIRE!

The first fire missions were executed perfectly, and the plan was proceeding as anticipated. There were very few things in my life I had done up to this point without forward thinking, including making sure the story of the Top Guns saw the light of day. I sent one final text message to the responsible party, who I had confidence would complete the mission, Mr. John Naquin. I told him to ensure the book was published; he assured me I would be here to see it through. I told him I might be leaving for a little while, so I just needed him to ensure things were being handled. Being a great buddy, he said, of course, and just asked for me to include him in emails to the publisher.

Once complete, I was on to the next portion of my chaotic banter. I screamed at my mirror to stop the pain but, almost mocking me, it refused to answer and stared back in disgust. There was a growing sense of numbing in my lips and a dizzy feeling that came across my body as I swayed and slammed from wall to wall. I looked at myself in the mirror and thought, "Maybe this is how the noise stops." I wiped my face and saw the Oklahoma dust smear across my cheeks, much like I had seen it do in the Afghan desert when I shed tears for Kyle, Pat, A. J., Chris, Todd, Michael, and the many others who were injured or the kids we'd seen turned into mist. I felt like the walls in my home were quickly closing in on me, and I knew I had succeeded in my desire to find peace. I walked into the kitchen with foggy eyes from my tears, grabbed an old Gerber, and chose a serrated blade in my dissolution as a backup in case my "fire missions" missed their target. I was tired of being revictimized by my mind, television, social media, and society. I wanted it to go away. I tried to stop the anger and the pain that was holding me confined inside my own body like a prisoner. The tears rolled down my face as I stood in my kitchen looking at the memorials of my mom and sister and considering the pain my son, my dad, my spouse, and my friends would feel, but I was going to do the one thing a soldier is trained to do. I was going to kill this pain. The numbness in my face, along with the tears in my eyes, made it so I was able to have complete tunnel vision on what I wanted, and that was to stop the buzzing, stop the noise, stop the screaming, and turn off my mind.

I was ready for my next fire mission as I readied my charge, primer, and round for the second and final mission. I saw a car pull up to my home. A gentle giant named Scott G., who resembles a sasquatch, approached. I was almost in disbelief that he was there, and then my fatal flaw emerged. Scott was a retired first sergeant. My commander Nate spoke with Scott and told him about how I had left work. Scott and I have had many conversations because we share mutual friends, and we've endured some of the same traumas, so he rushed to my home to check on my well-being. I honestly don't remember what was said after that point. The one thing that I do remember, however, is the ending of the conversation.

"Top, if I leave, will you be okay?"

"Yes."

Because of that conversation and my respect for Mr. G., I didn't want the last thing I said to him to be a lie. Because of that question, I lay on my couch with my pit bulls and, as they laid their heads on my lap, I said, "Well, ladies, END OF MISSION!" and fell asleep. Later, I received a call from my commander, Captain Hill, telling me I was meeting with my battalion commander, Lieutenant Colonel Dermody, my command sergeant major, CSM Turner, and the behavioral health team in the morning. There, I was told, "We need you to consider attending Mission Resiliency."

I arrived at Mission Resiliency at about midnight on August 13. Scott and Captain Hill were my chosen escorts. The ride there was approximately six hours. During the ride, I took in as much of the scenery as possible, not knowing what to expect when I got there. I had a few text messages but, for the most part, I didn't tell many people where I was going. One person who had been steadfast in their persistence in going to Mission Resiliency was Andrew Bragg. Andrew and I met in the Arghandab, as anyone who has read this far knows, and he has been pivotal in ensuring the story of the Top Guns in the Arghandab sees the light of day. He's also been pivotal in ensuring that "the Valley does not claim more lives." Andrew called during my trip and said just to be patient, learn as much as possible, and be open to whatever training they were teaching because, when I leave, I could use it to teach others who are struggling.

Once I got all my information taken, I was taken to my room at about 3:00 am. My new roommate, Marshall, was sound asleep, so I wasn't allowed to shower, not to wake him. I expressed my displeasure about having a roommate, which didn't help the cause. I would walk around in my filth for more than 24 hours; it wouldn't be the first time. I was woken up at 6:00 am by this sweet little lady for vitals. I followed the herd, slowly marching toward the front desk.

I'm standing in this line. The guy beside me says, "You must be the new guy. Welcome to the Tribe." I received my vitals and, shortly after that, was introduced to everyone in the Tribe. There was Andy from Tennessee; he was a captain and had been drinking since he had gotten off the plane to get to Mission. Shayne, "the Showman," was a sniper. Graham, who was consistently referred to as "the Graham show," was also a sniper. The "Chief" of the group was Tommy, a Force Recon Marine. Jasen was from the Coast Guard. Ricky was leaving soon but was a warrant officer with the Criminal Investigation Division. Then there was Zach, Delo, Justin, and Evan, who were in the Army, and Simon and Carlos who were retired. Everyone had their trauma addressed while they were there.

One of Mission Resiliency's biggest and most-talked-about treatments was sharing in "the War Room." Inside the War Room, one designated soldier was able to speak about a trauma that had been identified and discussed with their therapist. This trauma was carefully addressed, identified, journaled, logged, and readdressed over several sessions. This method is known as prolonged-exposure (PE) therapy.

When I began my therapy session with my therapist, Deb, we started recording my sessions. My sticking point boiled down to Sergeant Durham's and A. J.'s deaths, as well as all the events that followed that day, but we couldn't address all those events. We had to narrow it down. I'll be the first to admit I'm kind of a pain in the ass when it comes to the Army, my experiences, and treatment. I don't want to budge when it comes to speaking about my experiences, and if there's one word I hate more than any other in the English language, it's "hero."

Initially, Deb started me off on PE therapy. She had me listening to the event over and over, journaling about it, and being exposed to the word "hero" and all the things that pissed me off about August 28, 2010; there I was in Mission and what date rolls along but August 28, 2024. I woke up that morning, and my blood pressure was already through the roof; by 6:00 am, I was so enraged I felt like I was going to explode. The day's first lesson for us was psych education; needless to say, it struck a nerve in me. I went off like a stick of dynamite. That got back to Deb; I'm sure the instructor went and advised her that I didn't react well. I didn't believe the PE was working for me, and I felt like Deb thought I was bullshitting the treatment. I reached back to my treatment team in Oklahoma and advised them I didn't know what was going on. Something needed to change.

Deb and I sat down for our next session, and I could tell she needed to explore a new treatment for me. We had been working with cognitive processing therapy for about a week because we got off to a late start, which put us behind the eight ball. Now, we were going to be shifting gears. I was scheduled to present my story in the War Room the next day, so she said to continue moving forward with that. She wanted me to try a new mindfulness therapy that would help me to be more grounded. She gave me an approximate seven-minute recording and said, "I want you to listen to this. Don't do anything else. Just focus on the recording and journal after." I will be transparent and say I went into the recording hopeful but pessimistic. After the recording, I truly felt like I had an awakening. How could I have had an awakening in seven minutes? I went to my room with Marshall and we sat and talked as we often did. We spoke about my concerns for the War Room and I wrote a journal entry for the first time.

The following day, I awoke with the understanding I would present my story about my experience in the Arghandab to a group of veterans who may or may not understand my experience. One of the guys I never expected to become friends with was a Marine named Zach. He was abrasive, worked at Fort Leavenworth, and was a prick, but he's exactly like me, and that's why I get along with him. He and his "celly," Matt, were perfect for each other, much like Marshall and me. They complemented each other perfectly. Both were sarcastic as hell and when one would say something borderline offensive, the other would say something almost polite enough that you would let the other guy's comment slide.

I shared my story in the War Room and, after I was done, Zach said something along the lines of, "Joe, I'm not sure that you should feel bad about the story, man. It almost seems like you should feel like a 'hero' for getting the guys out of the blown-up truck." Matt followed that up, saying, "It must be hard knowing that your friend died. You were once in his position." Typical yin and yang, like usual. After the War Room was done, Zach came to hug me, and I said, "So that you know, I hate the word 'hero.'" He said, "Oh shit, man, I didn't know that!" From that point on, he would make it a point to say comments like, "I'm grateful we have a hero among us. It's great to have heroes in the room," or other smartass remarks like that.

After that, I continued to get better, receiving mindfulness therapy and working on art therapy. While at Mission Resiliency, I learned about moral injury, which I had never heard of before. Moral injury is an injury to an individual's moral conscience and values. This can often result from perceived transgression by themselves or others. While we were in the Arghandab, this happened more times than I care to admit, not only to myself but to my brothers and sisters. I witnessed leaders' careers ruined; I watched lives altered, and bodies changed forever. Moral injuries are when people feel profound guilt, shame, moral disorientation, and societal alienation based on events that have taken place or things they've witnessed. I think specifically about good friends like Sergeant Junkin, who wasn't supposed to deploy but did. He spent the entire deployment handling a responsibility that needed to be dealt with at COP Tynes but, in the end, he received no end-of-tour award. I think of leaders like First Sergeants Banister, Brown, and Hartlaub, who were artillery leaders and were miraculously replaced during a combat deployment in front of their soldiers with infantry first sergeants. I think of young men who deserved valorous awards, and those overlooked entirely or were combined with end-of-tour awards because leaders felt that, because of their rank, they couldn't justify them getting a valorous award, such as "Gunny" Torres of Bravo Battery and several other Bravo Battery soldiers. These are all perfect examples of moral injuries.

For the better part of 15 years, I've resisted being diagnosed with post-traumatic stress disorder. I didn't want that label; I didn't want to be "broken," and I didn't want people to feel as though they had to walk on eggshells around me because of what I may or may not have witnessed or lived through. Now I realize that not only do I suffer from post-traumatic stress, I suffer from moral injury and survivor guilt.

The most significant part of my subconscious mind that was constantly screaming in my ear was the part that reminded me that, before that deployment, incremental changes were made that resulted in monumental results. One soldier who I had the utmost respect for was Sergeant Kyle Stout. We grew up together as privates. I watched as he attempted, poorly, to mature through life while enjoying each day to the fullest. I saw him succeed as a noncommissioned officer (NCO) and section chief and earn the respect of his peers and subordinates as an artilleryman. Kyle was a family friend and even knew my spouse before I was introduced to her. We competed against each other at the Soldier and NCO of the Month boards, and I watched him go up to win the Soldier of the Quarter board while we were in Iraq. Then, I was promoted to staff sergeant. I was asked if I wanted to go to HHB

(Headquarters and Headquarters Battery) to take a squad or if I wanted to take over Stout's section. Of course, I wanted my section. The section was already stacked; it had Sergeant Junkin as the gunner, Specialist Bibb, Parker, and Little, and Privates First Class Cooper and Santoro. Little did I know how the story would end. When I heard that Kyle was killed, the first person that came to mind was Casey, his best friend. The following person was in my platoon: Sergeant Creighton. To take my mind off my pain, I went straight to Creighton and focused my energy on him, taking care of his suffering. I continued to do that for the next 14 years until the relentless volume of my mind screaming eventually cornered me and refused to let me go until I confronted it. Unfortunately, not only did I have one issue to encounter, but I also had another.

Being gifted with injury prone knees has been the gift that keeps on giving. When I initially arrived at Fort Campbell from South Korea, I came with a torn anterior cruciate ligament (ACL). At that time, Staff Sergeant Torres chose not to have me in his section because, according to him, "I was broken." Torres chose another private by the name of Rutter. I had my first ACL surgery in October 2007, which was the month the 1-320th deployed to Abu Ghraib, Iraq, in 2007. I ended up fast-forwarding my physical therapy and was on the first plane smoking toward Iraq in February. Looking back, I realize that probably wasn't my finest decision-making moment. Later in the deployment, I tore my ACL again; that required ACL surgery number two. I did finish the deployment with a torn ACL, though, all while still patrolling, still with my guys.

Being in the 101st Airborne, one thing was inevitable: if the nation is in a time of war, the 101st is going to be deploying. I was nearing five months post-op and had been in the training room recovering. I had a get-together for a UFC fight, and in typical fashion, Stout and Parker were enjoying their liquor too much like soldiers often do.

Parker entered the living room.

"Hey, Fontenot, do you know much about fighting?"

"Yeah, man, I know enough. Why?"

"I bet you do, you paper pusher."

"That will be the last time you say something stupid like that. You won't come into my fucking house and disrespect me, do you fucking understand?"

The house went eerily silent.

"Shit, Petey, I didn't think you were gonna say it," Stout said.

Five months later, I spoke to my platoon sergeant, Sergeant First Class Hafner, and said I was ready to return to the line. The only place for me to move back to on the line would be in place of Sergeant Durham. Once the switch was made SGT Durham would move over to 4th Platoon with Sergeant First Class Hafner and I would take his place. That move would prove to be a fatal move that we didn't understand at the time. Looking back neither of us had any way of knowing how it would end come August 2010, or we may have both chosen otherwise.

As fate would have it, Parker would also move over to become my team leader for the deployment to Afghanistan. So, from that smart-mouthed little punk in my living room he became a young man that I entrusted with my life each and every day that we stepped outside the wire. A young man that I grew to love like my own son. I'm sure some that have read up to here are wondering how things got so twisted. Well, the way things ended were catastrophic in many ways. When I sit alone in my little corner of the world, and I look over the mountains that resemble Afghanistan in Oklahoma, I can't help but reflect and feel guilt about the swap that took place between SGT Durham and I as well as the one that took place between SGT Stout and me. There are many other soldiers in similar situations whose brothers- or sisters-in-arms have lost their lives, and they suffer from survivor guilt. The reality of the situation is that I had no way to control the intangibles of that scenario. I look back, and have carried survivor guilt, moral injury, and post-traumatic stress with me since we left the Arghandab. And sadly, I almost let the valley win.

Going to Mission Resiliency wasn't what I wanted to do but, in the end, it was what I needed to do. My life may have been saved because of that opportunity. At the end of the day at Mission Resiliency, we're asked what we're grateful for. I usually have a smartass comment for my buddy Zach, something along the lines of, "And last but certainly not least, I'm thankful for Zach carrying ..." however, this time, I'll say I'm thankful for the opportunity to bring the story of the Top Guns in the Arghandab to like-minded people in the hopes that this story can close open wounds for some and bring pride to our brothers and sisters because now they will know that, no matter what the world tells them, we have done our part to ensure the next generation remains free and has a next Rendezvous with Destiny.

A soldier screams at a mirror with pain in his heart and tears in his eyes

Tell me how to shut out the noise, the soldier cries

The mirror, being heartless, remains defiant in its silence

Much like the battles he's seen with unclean eyes

The walls rush around him as he fights to silence the noise and vocalize his goodbyes

The soldier cradles an old rusty knife, serrated and unclean

Prepared to do the unthinkable because he remains traumatized from the unspeakable things he's seen

Stop the war that replays as he's re-victimized again and again

Stop the anger designed to undermine his mind

Stop the pain holding him confined like a prisoner

He screams to feel something real

He cries to silence their screams before he goes insane

He does the one thing a soldier is trained to do

He killed the pain

CHAPTER 20

Eulogies, Uniforms, and Sad Stories

> Walking alone in life is not the difficult part; coming back alone after walking hundreds of miles with others is.
>
> FARAAZ KAZI

> The people you choose to surround yourself with will ultimately surround you, so choose your friends carefully.
>
> JOSEPH J. FONTENOT

The men from Two Charlie had a mantra: "The Valley Always Wins." The soldiers from the 1-320th Field Artillery arrived in the Arghandab River Valley in June 2010. An abundance of time has passed since the eventful day when the Top Guns landed in Kandahar. During the deployment, they lost several stellar soldiers such as Private First Class King, Sergeant Stout, Specialist Stansbery, Master Sergeant (Ret.) Pittman, Sergeant Durham, Specialist Castro, First Lieutenant Weaver, and Staff Sergeant Trueblood. These losses have stayed with the leaders and soldiers of the Top Guns since 2010 and 2011. The men returned to Fort Campbell, Kentucky, to a hero's welcome for overcoming unbelievable odds.

Unfortunately, the war wasn't over for everyone. Staff Sergeant Ryan McCorkhill was an energetic young man looking forward to spending time out of the Army with his son. He signed a declaration statement saying he was leaving the service. Unfortunately, McCorkhill was one of the men of Babur and had been on multiple combat tours with the Top Guns. He suffered from demons he faced before, during, and after the deployment. On May 22, 2011, McCorkhill was found unresponsive.

Sergeant Justin Junkin was the tactical operations center noncommissioned officer in charge at COP Tynes and an amazing young man. He had a wife, a newborn daughter, and a fantastic life ahead of him. As he finished leaving the Army, he said goodbye to the men of Bravo Battery. Fontenot told him,

"I'll see you soon, bro. Let's get together and go kayaking." Junkin replied, "We will do something, Fonty. Stay angry, Big Angry." Junkin then left and went home. As he sat and watched videos of his brothers who had died in the Arghandab, the immense weight of his burden sat on his shoulders. Junkin suffered from survivor guilt and succumbed to his war on September 23, 2011. Private First Class Michael Lovely would take his life shortly after Junkin. Lovely battled through a tumultuous relationship and internal demons that he decided were too strong to overcome. He had asked several friends for help, but it fell on deaf ears. On October 30, 2011, Lovely became the third member of the Bulls in a short period to succumb to his battle.

The soldiers of the Top Guns had now suffered through one of the hardest deployments in the history of the Strike Brigade, and now they were home struggling through loss that was only gaining steam. Sergeant Brandon Tiller, one of the "Boys of Babur," had lived through some of the horrors of the Arghandab and had battles of his own. When he returned home, he struggled with internal demons that eventually caught up to him; he was killed in an automobile accident on August 20, 2013.

Sergeant Tyler Girardello from Alpha Battery had seen some of the most intense fighting in the Arghandab at COP Nolen. We will never know if this was a factor in his final decision, but, ultimately, Girardello succumbed on November 11, 2019.

Sergeant Donald Jackson was part of One Bravo and was known for being one of the cleanest in the platoon; perhaps he should've been a medic rather than an artilleryman. It wasn't uncommon to see him taking baby wipes to clean the floor in his room at COP Tynes. Jackson was on the infamous last patrol with Two Charlie. He lost the battle with his demons on February 3, 2019.

Major John Dabrowski, formerly of the Bravo Bulls Three Bravo "Boys of Babur" element, was haunted by something no one knows. He was known among the "Boys of Babur" for his humor and being upbeat within the Babur family, and he always lifted the spirits of his men. He succumbed to his battle on July 20, 2021.

Specialist Darius Dozier was from Greenville, Texas. He was a forward observer with Three Bravo and was known for his exceptional morale. He had an uncanny way of uplifting his brothers in his platoon during the roughest times of the deployment. Dozier lost his life in a freak motorcycle accident on October 19, 2019.

Specialist Leroy Hernandez from Three Bravo had his life cut short by COVID-19 on August 26, 2021, hand in hand with his father they lay in a hospital together battling for their lives. Both of them passed while holding onto each other. It was hard to recall a time when Hernandez didn't have a smile on his face.

First Sergeant Thomas Banister, the beloved original first sergeant who led the Bulls into the Arghandab River Valley, despite being loved by many, succumbed to his battle on February 23, 2022.

Mr. David Smith was a civilian contractor who served with the Top Guns at COP Terra Nova; he was a 20-year veteran of the Baton Rouge, Louisiana police force and had the displeasure of dealing with many Afghan detainees at the battalion level as the law-enforcement professional. He was a tremendous asset. He lost his battle on February 19, 2022.

No one left the Arghandab unscathed. Some brought war home and fought it alone. The Arghandab River Valley is a place that grabs your soul and refuses to let go. Maybe it's the spirit of past fighters, or perhaps it's just the actual Valley of Death. When you're born into the world of the valley, you can check out, but you can never leave. The Top Guns have left their keys at the front desk of Hotel "DAB." This is one time the valley will NOT win.

As the Top Guns returned home, they slowly moved on with life: "Doc" Stegehuis is now Doctor Stegehuis; Staff Sergeant Peltier is now First Sergeant Peltier; Sergeant First Class Krabbenhoft retired as a command sergeant major; as did Sergeant First Class Sturgeon; Sergeant First Class Tivao was promoted to command sergeant major; Staff Sergeant Fontenot won *Army Times* Soldier of the Year in 2015 and retired as a first sergeant; 1st Lieutenant Pantaleo was promoted to captain, then left the service after a successful career; Corporal Parker was promoted to staff sergeant and was eventually medically retired; Cheatham was promoted to sergeant and later left the Army and went on to work for Veterans Affairs; Staff Sergeant Zavalla worked for Veterans Affairs; Major Raymond was promoted to brigadier general; Lieutenant Colonel Flynn was promoted to colonel and then retired; and the list goes on and on.

The Top Guns also enjoyed their share of successes but suffered from setbacks. In 2014, Private First Class Mendiola was sentenced to 20 years after he was convicted of manslaughter. Mendiola was one of the first to try and help Private First Class King after he was shot and had volunteered to pull his guard in the tower in blood-soaked boots until the sun came up.

Specialist Santoro was sentenced to a total of 30 years after he was convicted of negligent homicide and criminal endangerment. Santoro had been on the ground with Top Gun 6's personal security detail team all around the Arghandab and had been with One Bravo in some of the most violent parts of the deployment.

The bottom line is that the Top Guns and Strike Brigade may not have left the Arghandab without any scars, but they did win. More importantly, America's most unwanted children, the soldiers of the 1-320th Battalion, had overcome insurmountable odds. However, winning does come at a cost, and the Top Guns still pay that cost daily. You can never unsee what you've seen, but the wounds fade in time and eventually blend with the skin. A few stand above the others when thinking of things that were said during the deployment and how monumental they were. Sometimes, people say things out of anger and frustration; instead of having a positive impact, they have a negative one. One statement made early on was, "As soon as we aren't here to save your ass, you're fucking dead!" The men on that patrol could've folded like a deck of cards but instead stood up and demanded more of themselves.